Meaningful Texts

Corpus and Discourse

Series Editors: Wolfgang Teubert, University of Birmingham, and Michaela Mahlberg, Liverpool Hope University College.

Corpus linguistics provides the methodology to extract meaning from texts. Taking as its starting point the fact that language is not a mirror of reality but lets us share what we know, believe and think about reality, it focuses on language as a social phenomenon, and makes visible the attitudes and beliefs expressed by the members of a discourse community.

Consisting of both spoken and written language, discourse always has historical, social, functional, and regional dimensions. Discourse can be monolingual or multilingual, interconnected by translations. Discourse is where language and social studies meet.

The *Corpus and Discourse* series consists of two strands. The first, *Research in Corpus and Discourse*, features innovative contributions to various aspects of corpus linguistics and a wide range of applications, from language technology via the teaching of a second language to a history of mentalities. The second strand, *Studies in Corpus and Discourse*, will be comprised of key texts bridging the gap between social studies and linguistics. Although equally academically rigorous, this strand will be aimed at a wider audience of academics and postgraduate students working in both disciplines.

Published and forthcoming titles in the series:

Studies in Corpus and Discourse
English Collocation Studies: The OSTI Report
John Sinclair, Susan Jones and Robert Daley
Edited by Ramesh Krishnamurthy, including a new interview with John Sinclair conducted by Wolfgang Teubert

Research in Corpus and Discourse
Meaningful Texts: The Extraction of Semantic Information from Monolingual and Multilingual Corpora
Edited by Geoff Barnbrook, Pernilla Danielsson and Michaela Mahlberg

Meaningful Texts

The Extraction of Semantic Information from Monolingual and Multilingual Corpora

Edited by Geoff Barnbrook, Pernilla Danielsson and Michaela Mahlberg

continuum
LONDON • NEW YORK

Continuum
The Tower Building
11 York Road
London SE1 7NX

15 East 26th Street
New York
NY 10010

First published 2005

www.continuumbooks.com

British Library Cataloguing-in-Publication Data
A catalogue record for this book is available from the British Library.

ISBN: 0-8264-7490-X (hardback)

Library of Congress Cataloguing-in-Publication Data
A catalogue record for this book is available from the Library of Congress

Typeset by RefineCatch Limited, Bungay, Suffolk
Printed and bound in Great Britain by
Cromwell Press Ltd, Trowbridge, Wilts

Contents

List of Contributors

Chang Baobao
Peking University

František Čermák
Charles University, Prague

Pernilla Danielsson
University of Birmingham

Lauren Delfs, Susanne Wolff and Martha Palmer
University of Pennsylvania, Philadelphia

Gaël Dias
Universidade da Beira Interior, Covilhã

Eva Martha Eckkrammer
University of Salzburg

Christiane Fellbaum
Princeton University

Sanja Fulgosi
University of Zagreb

Vojko Gorjanc
University of Ljubljana

Gregory Grefenstette
Clairvoyance Corporation, Pittsburgh, Pennsylvania

Silvia Hansen-Schirra
Saarland University, Saarbrücken

Riitta Jääskeläinen
University of Joensuu
Savonlinna School of Translation Studies

Primož Jakopin
Fran Ramovš Institute of Slovenian Language, Ljubljana

Régis Kawecki
Hong Kong Polytechnic University

Dorothy Kenny
Dublin City University

Ferenc Kiefer
Hungarian Academy of Sciences

Simon Krek
DZS Publishing House, Ljubljana

Cvetana Krstev
University of Belgrade

José Gabriel Pereira Lopes
Universidade Nova de Lisboa, Caparica

Sara Madeira
Universidade da Beira Interior, Covilhã

Rūta Marcinkevičienė
Vytautas Magnus University, Kaunas

Anna Mauranen
University of Tampere

Inguna Skadiņa
University of Latvia

Krešimir Šojat
University of Zagreb

Marko Stabej
University of Ljubljana

Dominic Stewart
School for Interpreters and Translators at Forlì,
University of Bologna

Marko Tadić
University of Zagreb

Wolfgang Teubert
University of Birmingham

Andrius Utka
Vytautas Magnus University, Kaunas

Špela Vintar
University of Ljubljana

Duško Vitas
University of Belgrade

Geoffrey Williams
Département Langues Etrangères Appliquées
U.F.R. Lettres et Sciences Humaines, Lorient

Xu Xunfeng
Hong Kong Polytechnic University

Introduction

Geoff Barnbrook, Pernilla Danielsson and Michaela Mahlberg

The concept of meaning and its exploration has always been of crucial importance to users of language: this is true for both linguists and non-linguists. The meaning of a text is often seen as a fundamental and pre-theoretical property. Despite this, the study of linguistics has often focused more upon the form than on the ways in which meaning is transmitted through texts. Meaning has so far proved too elusive a concept to be captured adequately by the various formal approaches developed. The title of this collection describes both the texts themselves and the approaches adopted for their exploration. Texts are essentially made up of complexes of dynamically linked meanings, which the following studies seek to extract or explore using the contextual information provided within the texts.

Many of the papers in the collection were originally presented at the 5th and 6th TELRI Seminars held in Ljubljana, Slovenia and Bansko, Bulgaria. Their variety and scope testify to the significance of the TELRI projects in creating not only Language Research Infrastructures but also stimulating work based on them.

We have divided the papers into two sections: those based on monolingual corpora and those addressing multilingual corpora. This is a categorization that initially focuses upon purely outward criteria but continues to represent the more recent developments of multilingual approaches in corpus linguistics. However, the two groupings will show that although the methods are different there are also many similarities in the results obtained.

For instance, we find that questions of lemmatization have to be discussed in both monolingual (cf. Utka) and multilingual environments (cf. Tadić, Fulgosi and Šojat). Similarly, noun collocations can raise interesting questions when examining a single language but new aspects may be discovered when comparing two or more languages (cf. Čermák as well as Marcinkevičienė).

The relationship between methodology and theory is an important characteristic of corpus linguistics. In Kenny's paper on translation studies, she presents an innovative approach by combining the use of both comparable and parallel corpora. The crucial relationship between the method and the purpose of a study becomes obvious when specific corpora – instead of a general-purpose corpus – form the point of departure (cf. Dias, Madeira and Pereira Lopes; Eckkrammer; Jakopin; Williams; Skadiņa).

In corpus linguistics computers play a major role. They help the researcher to gain insights into the language or languages under investigation. Computers can also perform tasks that aim to identify or link textual segments automatically (cf. Grefenstette; Baobao, Danielsson and Teubert; Skadiņa; Krstev and Vitas). They can provide tools which may be used in teaching (cf. Xunfeng and Kawecki) or which may be helpful to humans performing tasks, such as the translation of texts (cf. Jääskeläinen and Mauranen).

The creation of automatic systems for word sense disambiguation relies on 'training corpora'. These corpora involve a great amount of human work in the annotation. In their paper, Fellbaum *et al.* describe how these processes may give an insight into cognitive representations. Such results highlight the shortcomings of dictionaries. Other lexicographic problems are discussed in Krek, Gorjanc and Stabej and in Kiefer.

Corpus linguistic investigations can further shed light on social and cultural aspects of language (cf. both Teubert and Stewart) and these aspects can also be analysed in stylistic terms (cf. Vintar and Hansen-Schirra).

The topics covered show that the study of meaning may be approached from many different angles. These are linked by a common reliance on corpora. This collection of papers testifies both to the importance of corpus linguistics in modern linguistic studies and to the new emphasis on the use of corpus methods in the exploration of the meanings of which texts are composed.

Part One

Monolingual Corpora

1 Extracting concepts from dynamic legislative text collections

Gaël Dias, Sara Madeira and José Gabriel Pereira Lopes

Introduction

Selecting discriminating terms in order to represent the contents of texts is a critical problem for many applications in information retrieval. Ideally, the indexing terms should directly describe the concepts present in the documents. However, most of the Information Retrieval systems index documents are based on individual words that are not specific enough to evidence the contents of texts. As a consequence, evolutionary retrieval systems use multiword terms previously extracted from text collections to represent the contents of texts (Evans and Lefferts 1993). Indeed, multiword terms embody meaningful sequences of words that are less ambiguous than single words and approximate more accurately the contents of texts.

However, most multiword terms are not listed in lexical databases. Indeed, the creation, the maintenance and the upgrade of terminological data banks often require a great deal of manual effort that cannot cope with the ever-growing number of texts to analyse. Moreover, due to the constant dynamism of specialized languages, the set of multiword terms is opened and to be completed (Habert and Jacquemin 1993). As a consequence, there has been a growing interest in developing techniques for automatic term extraction. In the context of the PGR Project, funded by the Portuguese Ministry of Justice, we propose a new architecture for retrieving relevant documents in a dynamic legislative text collection (see Figure 1.1). It combines the SINO search engine (Quaresma *et al.* 1998) with the SENTA software designed for the automatic extraction of multiword lexemes (Dias *et al.* 1999). At this stage of the project, the set of multiword lexemes is manually checked and filtered out in order to insert useful indexing terms into the search engine thus producing a high quality retrieval process.

In this paper, we will focus on the SENTA module that has recently been added to the global architecture of our system. SENTA (Software for the Extraction of N-ary Textual Associations) has been devised around two main principles (Dias *et al.* 2000). Firstly, following *the rigidity principle*, we

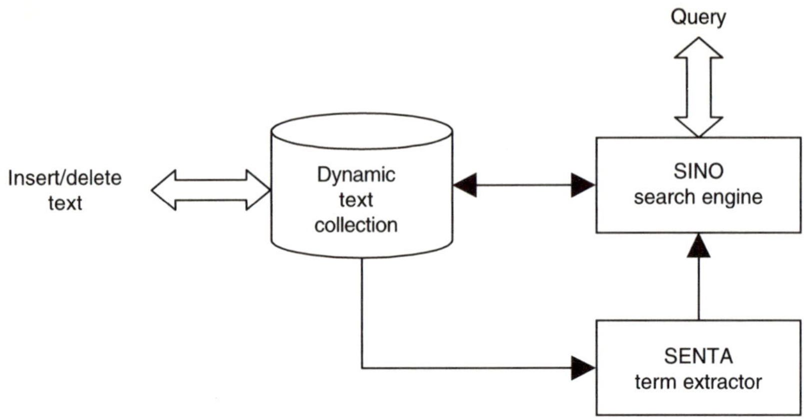

Figure 1.1 The global retrieval architecture

propose that the general information appearing in raw texts should be sufficient to extract meaningful multiword lexemes without applying domain-dependent or language-dependent heuristics. Secondly, following the *corpus integrity principle*, we propose that the input text corpus should not be modified at all (i.e. the text is neither lemmatized nor pruned with lists of stop words). So, SENTA retrieves from naturally occurring text, contiguous and non-contiguous multiword lexemes on the basis of two complementary techniques: the Mutual Expectation measure and the LocalMaxs algorithm (see below). One particularity of our architecture is to follow the changes in the text collection. Indeed, according to Manning and Schütze (1999), lexical regularities appear and disappear as language evolves. Thus, a particular lexical relation that may not be an expression at any given time *t*, may well form a multiword unit at time *t+1* and vice versa. So, whenever a new text is inserted or an old one deleted, SENTA is re-run over the collection. Thus, new expressions may be discovered and old ones may disappear.

Data preparation

The first step of our methodology performs the transformation of the input text into a set of n-grams (i.e. contiguous or non-contiguous sequences of n words). Indeed, a great deal of applied works in lexicography evidence that most of the lexical relations associate words separated by at most five other words and assess that multiword terms are specific lexical relations that share this property (Sinclair 1974). As a consequence, a multiword term can be defined in terms of structure as a specific word n-gram calculated in the immediate context of three words to the left-hand side and three words to the right-hand side of a pivot word. This situation is illustrated in Figure 1.2 for the pivot word *Lei* (*Law*) being given the input sentence (1).

(1) *O artigo 35 da* <u>*Lei*</u> *de Imprensa prevê esse precedimento em caso de burla agravada.*

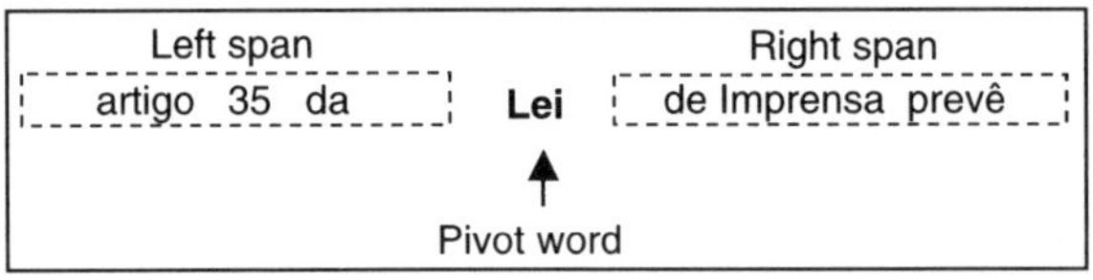

Figure 1.2 The context span

Indeed, *Lei de Imprensa* (*Press Law*) is a specific multiword term. By definition, a word n-gram is a vector of n words where each word is indexed by the signed distance that separates it from its associated pivot word. Consequently, an n-gram can be contiguous or non-contiguous depending on whether the words involved in the n-gram represent a continuous sequence of words in the corpus or not.

For instance, if we consider the sentence (1) as the current input text and '*Lei*' the pivot word, contiguous and non-contiguous word 3-grams are respectively illustrated in the following table.

Table 1.1 Sample word 3-grams calculated from the pivot word *Lei.*

u_1	$position_{12}$	u_2	$position_{13}$	u_3
Lei	+1	*de*	+2	*Imprensa*
Lei	−3	*artigo*	+3	*prevê*

Generically, an *n-gram* is a vector of *n* textual units where each textual unit is indexed by the signed distance that separates it from its associated pivot textual unit. By convention, the pivot textual unit is always the first element of the vector and its signed distance is equivalent to zero. We represent an n-gram by the following ordered vector $[p_{11}\ u_1\ p_{12}\ u_2\ p_{13}\ u_3 \ldots p_{1i}\ u_i \ldots p_{1n}\ u_n]$ where p_{11} is equal to zero and p_{1i} (for i=2 to n) denotes the signed distance that separates the textual unit u_i from the pivot unit u_1. For example, the two n-grams shown in Table 1.1 should be represented by the two following vectors: [0 *Lei* +1 *de* +2 *Imprensa*], [0 *Lei* −3 *artigo* +3 *prevê*].

Normalized expectation and mutual expectation

In order to evaluate the degree of cohesiveness existing between textual units, various mathematical models have been proposed in the literature. However, most of them only evaluate the degree of cohesiveness between two textual units and do not generalize for the case of n individual textual units (Church and Hanks 1990, Gale and Church 1991, Dunning 1993, Smadja 1993, Smadja 1996, Shimohata 1997). As a consequence, these mathematical models only allow the acquisition of binary associations and bootstrapping techniques have to be applied to acquire associations with more than two textual units. On the other hand, for the specific case of word associations, the proposed mathematical models tend to be oversensitive to frequent words. In order to overcome both problems, we introduce a new association measure called the Mutual Expectation (ME) that evaluates the degree of rigidity that links together all the textual units contained in an n-gram ($\forall n, n \geq 2$) based on the concept of Normalized Expectation (NE) (Dias *et al.* 1999).

Normalized Expectation

The basic idea of the Normalized Expectation is to evaluate the cost, in terms of cohesiveness, of the loss of one textual unit in an n-gram. So, the more cohesive a group of textual units is, that is the less it accepts the loss of one of its components, the higher its Normalized Expectation will be. In other words, we define the Normalized Expectation existing between *n* words as the average expectation of the occurrence of one word in a given position knowing the occurrence of the other *n-1* words also constrained by their positions. For example, the average expectation of the following *3*-gram [0 *Lei* +1 *de* +2 *Imprensa*] must take into account the expectation of *Imprensa* occurring after *Lei de*, but also the expectation of the preposition *de* linking together *Lei* and *Imprensa* and finally the expectation of *Lei* occurring before *de Imprensa*. This situation is graphically illustrated in Table 1.2 where one possible expectation corresponds to one respective row.

Table 1.2 Example of expectations to take into account in order to evaluate the NE

Expectation of the word to occur	Knowing the gapped 3-gram
Lei	[0 _____ +*1 de*+2 *Imprensa*]
De	[0 *Lei*+*1* _____ +2 *Imprensa*]
Imprensa	[0 *Lei*+*1 de*+2 _____]

The underlying concept of the Normalized Expectation is based on the conditional probability defined in Equation 1.

$$p(X=x \mid Y=y) = \frac{p(X=x, Y=y)}{p(Y=y)}$$

Equation 1 Conditional probability

The definition of the conditional probability can be applied in order to measure the expectation of the occurrence of one textual unit in a given position knowing the occurrence of the other *n-1* textual units also constrained by their positions. However, this definition does not accommodate the n-gram length factor. Naturally, an n-gram is associated to *n* possible conditional probabilities. It is clear that the conditional probability definition needs to be normalized in order to take into account all the conditional probabilities involved in an n-gram.

Let's take the n-gram $[p_{11}\ u_1\ p_{12}\ u_2\ p_{13}\ u_3 \ldots p_{1i}\ u_i \ldots p_{1n}\ u_n]$. It is convenient to consider an n-gram as the composition of *n* sub-(*n-1*)-grams, obtained by extracting one textual unit at a time from the n-gram. This can be thought of as giving rise to the occurrence of any of the *n* events illustrated in Table 1.3 where the underline denotes the missing textual unit from the n-gram.

Table 1.3 Sub-(*n–1*)-grams and missing words

Sub-(n–1)-gram	Missing word
$[p_{11}\ \_\_\ u_2\ p_{13}\ u_3 \ldots p_{1i}\ u_i \ldots p_{1n}\ u_n]$	u_1
$[p_{11}\ u_1\ p_{12}\ \_\_\ p_{13}\ u_3 \ldots p_{1i}\ u_i \ldots p_{1n}\ u_n]$	u_2
...	...
$[p_{11}\ u_1\ p_{12}\ u_2\ p_{13}\ u_3 \ldots p_{1(i-1)}\ u_{(i-1)}\ p_{1i}\ \_\_\ p_{1(i+1)}\ u_{(i+1)} \ldots p_{1n}\ u_n]$	u_i
	...
$[p_{11}\ u_1\ p_{12}\ u_2\ p_{13}\ u_3 \ldots p_{1i}\ u_i \ldots p_{1(n-1)}\ u_{(n-1)}\ p_{1n}\ \_\_]$	u_n

So, each event is associated with a respective conditional probability. One of the principal intentions of the normalization process is to capture in just one measure all the *n* conditional probabilities. One way to do it is to blueprint the general definition of the conditional probability and define an average event for its conditional part, that is an average event *Y=y*.

Indeed, only the *n* denominators of the *n* conditional probabilities vary and the *n* numerators remain unchanged from one probability to another. The Normalized Expectation, based on a normalization of the conditional probability, proposes an elegant solution to represent in a unique formula all the n conditional probabilities involved by an n-gram. For that purpose we introduce the concept of the Fair Point of Expectation (FPE). In order to perform a sharp normalization, the FPE is the arithmetic mean of the denominators of all the conditional probabilities. Theoretically, the Fair Point of Expectation is the arithmetic mean of the *n* joint probabilities of the (n–1)-grams contained in an n-gram and it is defined in Equation 2.

$$\mathrm{FPE}([p_{11}u_1p_{12}u_2 \ldots p_{1i}u_i \ldots p_{1n}u_n]) = \frac{1}{n}\left(p([p_{22}u_2 \ldots p_{2i}u_i \ldots p_{2n}u_n]) + \sum_{i=2}^{n} p\left(\left[p_{11}u_1 \ldots \hat{p}_{1i}\hat{u}_i \ldots p_{1n}u_n\right]\right)\right)$$

Equation 2 Fair Point of Expectation

In particular, the '∧' corresponds to a convention frequently used in Algebra that consists in writing a '∧' on the top of the omitted term of a given succession indexed from 2 to n. Thus, the normalization of the conditional probability is realized by the introduction of the FPE into the general definition of the conditional probability as defined in Equation 3.

$$NE([p_{11}u_1 \ldots p_{1i}u_i \ldots p_{1n}u_n]) = \frac{p([p_{11}\,u_1 \ldots p_{1i}u_i \ldots p_{1n}u_n])}{FPE([p_{11}\,u_1 \ldots p_{1i}\,u_i \ldots p_{1n}\,u_n])}$$

Equation 3 Normalized Expectation

For example, the Normalized Expectation of the *3*-gram [0 *Lei* +*1 de* +2 *Imprensa*] would be:

$$NE([0\ \textit{Lei}+1\ \textit{de}+2\ \textit{Imprensa}]) = \frac{p([0\ \textit{Lei}+1\ \textit{de}+2\ \textit{Imprensa}])}{1/3(p([0\ \textit{Lei}+1\ \textit{de}]) + p([0\ \textit{Lei}+2\ \textit{Imprensa}]) + p([0\ \text{de}+\textit{1}\ \textit{Imprensa}])+}$$

Mutual expectation

Justeson (1993) and Daille (1995) have shown in their studies that frequency is one of the most relevant statistics to identify multiword terms with specific syntactical patterns. The studies made by Frantzi and Ananiadou (1996) in the context of the extraction of interrupted collocations also indicate that the relative frequency is an important clue for the retrieval process. From this assumption, we deduce that between two word n-grams with the same Normalized Expectation, the most frequent word n-gram is more likely to be a relevant multiword unit. So, the Mutual Expectation between n words is defined in Equation 4 based on the Normalized Expectation and the relative frequency.

$$ME([p_{11}u_1 \ldots p_{1i}u_i \ldots p_{1n}u_n]) = p([p_{11}u_1 \ldots p_{1i}u_i \ldots p_{1n}u_n]) \times NE([p_{11}u_1 \ldots p_{1i}u_i \ldots p_{1n}u_n])$$

Equation 4 Mutual Expectation

Compared to the previously proposed mathematical models, the Mutual Expectation allows the evaluation of the degree of cohesiveness that links together all the textual units contained in an n-gram (i.e. $\forall n, n \geq 2$) as it accommodates the n-gram length factor.

Acquisition process

Most of the approaches have based their selection process on the definition of global frequency thresholds and/or on the evaluation of global association measure thresholds (Church and Hanks 1990, Smadja 1993, Daille 1995, Shimohata 1997, Feldman 1998). This is defined by the underlying concept that there exists a limit value of the association measure that allows us to decide whether a word n-gram is a pertinent word association or not. However, these thresholds are prone to error as they depend on experimentation. Furthermore, they highlight evident constraints of flexibility, as they need to be re-tuned when the type, the size, the domain and the language of the documents change (Habert *et al.* 1997). The LocalMaxs (Silva *et al.* 1999) proposes a more flexible and fine-tuned approach for the selection process as it concentrates on the identification of local maxima of association measure values. So, we may deduce that a word n-gram is a multiword term if its association measure value is higher than or equal to the association measure values of all its sub-groups of (n−1) words and if it is strictly higher than the association measure values of all its super-groups of (n+1) words. Let *assoc* be an association measure, W an n-gram, Ω_{n-1} the set of all the (n−1)-grams contained in W, Ω_{n+1} the set of all the (n+1)-grams containing W and *sizeof* a function that returns the number of words of a word n-gram. The LocalMaxs is defined as follows:

$$\forall x \in \Omega_{n-1}, \forall y \in \Omega_{n+1},$$

$$W \text{ is a multiword term if } \quad (sizeof(W)=2 \wedge assoc(W) > assoc(y)) \vee (sizeof(W) \neq 2 \wedge assoc(W) \geq assoc(x) \wedge assoc(W) > assoc(y))$$

Among others, the LocalMaxs shows two interesting properties. On the one hand, it allows the testing of various association measures that respect the first assumption described above (i.e. the more cohesive a sequence of words is, the higher its association measure value will be). On the other hand, the LocalMaxs allows the extraction of multiword terms obtained by composition. Indeed, as the algorithm retrieves pertinent units by analysing their immediate context, it may identify multiword terms that are composed of one or more other terms. For example, the LocalMaxs conjugated with the Mutual Expectation elects the multiword term *Presidente da República Jorge Sampaio* (*State President Jorge Sampaio*) built from the composition of the extracted terms *Presidente da República* (*State President*) and *Jorge Sampaio* (*Jorge Sampaio*). This situation is illustrated in Figure 1.3.

Indeed, roughly exemplifying, one can expect that there are many State Presidents inside the European Union. Therefore, the association measure value of *Presidente da República Jorge* (*State President Jorge*) should be lower than the one for *Presidente da República* (*State President*) as there are many possible words, other than *Jorge*, that may occur after *Presidente da República* (*State President*). Thus, the association measure of any super-group containing the unit *Presidente da República* (*State President*) should theoretically be lower than the association measure for *Presidente da República* (*State

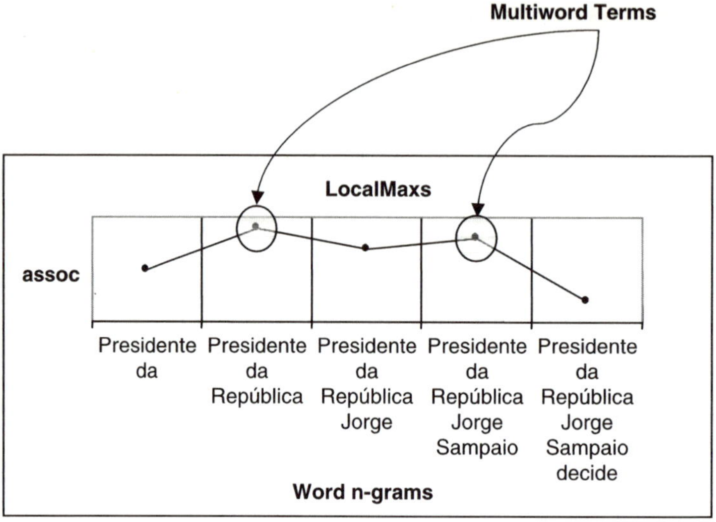

Figure 1.3 Election by composition

President). But, if the first name of the President is *Jorge*, the expectation for *Sampaio* to appear is very high and the association measure value of *Presidente da República Jorge Sampaio* (*State President Jorge Sampaio*) should then be higher than the association measure values of all its sub-groups and super-groups, as in the latter case no word can be expected to strengthen the overall unit *Presidente da República Jorge Sampaio* (*State President Jorge Sampaio*).

So, the LocalMaxs algorithm proposes a flexible and robust solution for the extraction of multiword term candidates as it avoids the definition of global frequency and/or association measure thresholds based on experimentation.

The web-based architecture of SENTA

The web-based implementation of SENTA has been realized at the Portuguese University of Beira Interior. The application allows any authorized user to insert new texts (via browser) into the text collection and consult the set of the extracted multiword lexemes for further validation (see Figure 1.4).

When submitting the request to the Web Server, the text is pre-processed and stored in the database. The three steps of SENTA are then run locally on the database server. Finally, the results are displayed (see Figure 1.5) in a table along with their frequency. The results show that relevant multiword terms are extracted: *normas legais* (legal norms), *Conselho Consultivo* (Consultive Council), *ex-administração ultramarina* (ultramarine ex-administration).

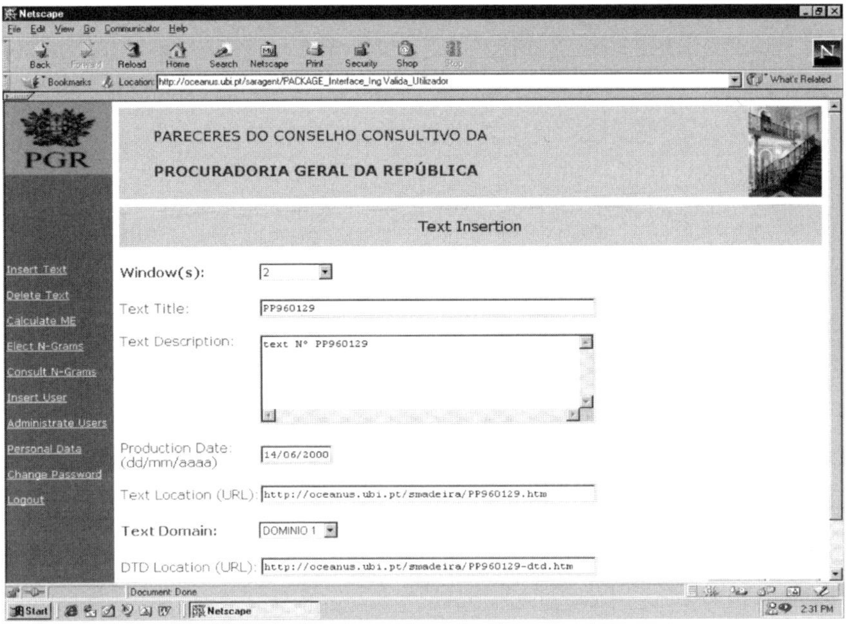

Figure 1.4 Text insertion

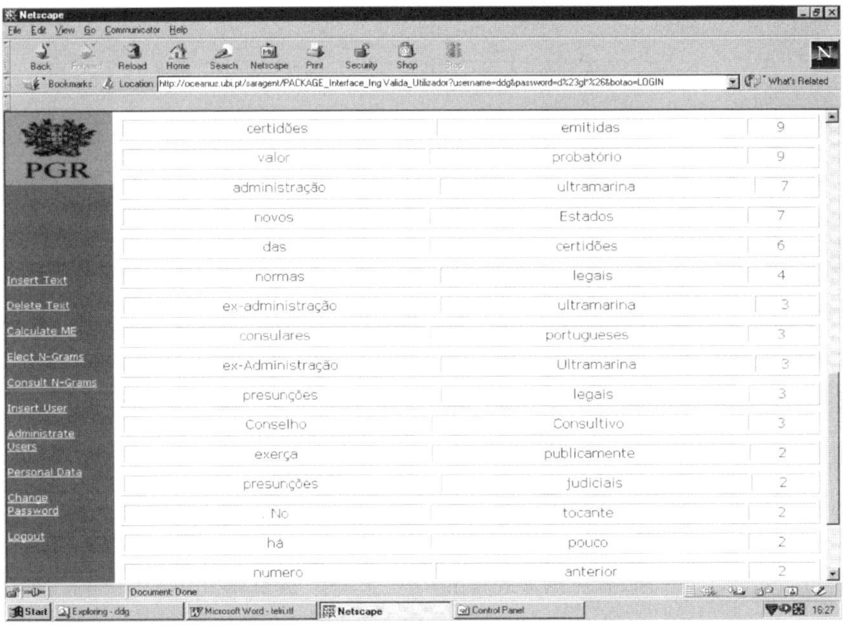

Figure 1.5 Consult page

From this interface, an expert in Law terminology can then easily select the relevant multiword terms to be integrated as indexing terms in the search engine SINO. This stage is still done manually but we are working on a fully automated version that would avoid human intervention and post-editing. So, the user is guided by SINO in his search for information by accessing a list of complex terms that embody fundamental concepts of the document collection. For example, if one is interested in getting information about crime, the system suggests a list of complex terms related to the query. Thus, the user is able to refine his search by selecting one of the terms in the list and thus access the most relevant documents. As illustrated in Figure 1.6, the user may choose one of the following phrases related to crime: *crime militar* (military crime) or *crime internacional* (international crime).

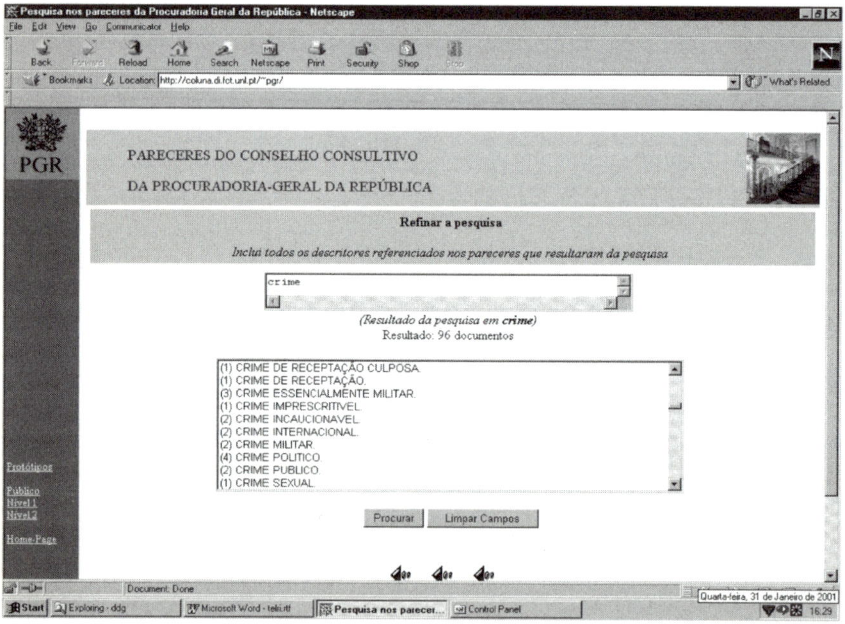

Figure 1.6 SINO search engine

Conclusion

In this paper, we have proposed a web-based integrated solution for enhanced information retrieval which combines the search engine SINO with the term extractor SENTA. This work is the result of the collaboration between two Portuguese Universities for the purpose of the 'PGR-Acesso Selectivo aos pareceres da Procuradoria Geral da República' project that is being funded by the Portuguese Ministry of Justice. Our fundamental goal is the automatic extraction of multiword lexemes (concepts) to improve information retrieval by introducing new indexing terms (a fundamental issue in information retrieval). We are actually planning to improve our Consult Interface by introducing a set of tools (concordancer, hypertext links and other association measures) to ease the decision-making of terminologists. The application can be accessed by the following URL:

http://oceanus.ubi.pt/saragent/package_interface.form_password.

References

Church, Ken W. and Hanks, Patrick (1990) 'Word Association Norms Mutual Information and Lexicography', *Computational Linguistics* 16(1): 23–9.

Daille, Béatrice (1995) 'Study and Implementation of Combined Techniques for Automatic Extraction of Terminology', *The balancing act combining symbolic and statistical approaches to language*, Cambridge, MA: MIT Press.

Dias, Gaël, Guilloré, Sylvie, Bassano, Jean-Claude and Pereira Lopes, J. Gabriel (2000) 'Combining Linguistics with Statistics for Multiword Term Extraction: A Fruitful Association?', *Recherche d'Informations Assistée par Ordinateur (RIAO'2000)*, Paris, France.

Dias, Gaël, Guilloré, Sylvie and Pereira Lopes, J. Gabriel (1999) 'Language Independent Automatic Acquisition of Rigid Multiword Units from Unrestricted Text Corpora', *Traitement Automatique des Langues Naturelles*, Institut d'Etudes Scientifiques, Cargèse, France.

Dunning, Ted (1993) 'Accurate Methods for the Statistics of Surprise and Coincidence', *Association for Computational Linguistics*, 19(1).

Evans, David A. and Lefferts, Robert G. (1993) 'Design and Evaluation of the CLARIT-TREC-2 System', *TREC93*: 137150.

Feldman, Ronen (1998) 'Text Mining at the Term Level', *PKDD'98*. Lecture Notes in AI 1510, Springer Verlag.

Frantzi, Katerina T. and Ananiadou, Sophia (1996) 'Retrieving Collocations by Co-occurrences and Word Order Constraint', *16th International Conference on Computational Linguistics (COLING'96)*: 41–6, Copenhagen.

Gale, William A. and Church, Ken W. (1991) 'Concordances for Parallel Texts', *Seventh Annual Conference of the UW Center for the New OED and Text Research, Using Corpora*. Oxford: Oxford University Press.

Habert, Benoît and Jacquemin, Christian (1993) 'Noms composés, termes, dénominations complexes: problématiques linguistiques et traitements automatiques', *Traitement Automatique des Langues*, 34(2). Association pour le Traitement Automatique des langues, France.

Habert, Benoît, Nazarenko, Adeline and Salem, André (1997) *Les linguistiques du Corpus*, Paris: Armand Colin.

Justeson, John (1993) 'Technical Terminology: Some Linguistic Properties and an Algorithm for Identification in Text', *IBM Research Report*, RC 18906 (82591) 5/18/93.

Manning, Christopher D. D. and Schütze, Hinrich (1999) *Foundations of Statistical Natural Language Processing*, Cambridge, MA: MIT Press.

Quaresma, Paulo, Pimenta Rodrigues, Irene and Pereira Lopes, J. Gabriel (1998) 'PGR Project: The Portuguese Attorney General Decisions on the Web', *The Law in the Information Society*, Instituto per la documentazione giuridica del CNR, ed. Costantino Ciampi and Elisabetta Marinai, Florence, Italy.

Shimohata, Sayori (1997) 'Retrieving Collocations by Co-occurrences and Word Order Constraints', ACL-EACL'97.476–81.

Silva, Joaquim, Dias, Gaël, Guilloré, Sylvie and Pereira Lopes, J. Gabriel (1999) 'Using LocalMaxs Algorithm for the Extraction of Contiguous and Non-contiguous Multiword Lexical Units', *9th Portuguese Conference in Artificial Intelligence*, Springer Verlag.

Sinclair, John (1974) 'English Lexical Collocations: A study in computational linguistics', Singapore, reprinted as chapter 2 of Foley, J. A. (ed.) (1996), J. M. Sinclair on *Lexis and Lexicography*, Uni Press.

Smadja, Frank (1993) 'Retrieving Collocations From Text: XTRACT', *Computational Linguistics* 19(1): 143–77.

Smadja, Frank (1996) 'Translating Collocations for Bilingual Lexicons: A Statistical Approach', *Association for Computational Linguistics* 22 (1).

2 A diachronic genre corpus: problems and findings from the DIALAYMED-Corpus (DIAchronic Multilingual Corpus of LAYman-oriented MEDical Texts)

Eva Martha Eckkrammer

Introduction – connecting text, discourse, genre, diachrony and corpora

Besides allowing powerful advances in lexicography and grammar, corpus linguistics has paved the way to gain further and better insight into discourse and its underlying genres. Hence, there is no doubt that the construction and analysis of electronic corpora increasingly gains ground in modern philology. However, current trends seem to point to preferences in corpus design which do not offer problem-solving devices in the study of discourse and genre. One of the ruling principles seems to be the dominant premise claiming 'big is beautiful' or even 'only big is relevant'. It relates to the fact that after powerful advances in technology as well as a fervent shift towards the digitization of knowledge in the last decade of the twentieth century large corpora seem to play a primary role in the field. If the effectiveness of large core corpora which embrace a representative degree of variation (diatopic, diachronic, diastratic, genre-specific, medium-specific, etc.) is undoubted in the context of lexicography and grammar, this might not hold for discourse and genre analysis and even less for contrastive textology.[1] According to Foucault's definition embedded in cultural studies, that we favour, the term discourse is applied to refer to communicational practices which are constructed to be consistent with specific culturally bound rules. It is crucial that these practices are distinctive from those which determine other discourses. Within a categorization of discourses, however, it seems necessary to distinguish between discourses induced thematically (e.g. political discourse), socially (e.g. academic discourse) or by the applied medium (e.g. cyberdiscourse). Even if the three categories intermingle considerably, the relevance of the dominant means of induction has to be accounted for in order to allow proper analysis of the discursive devices in question.

As a matter of fact, discourses represent extensive communicative usages with culturally bound conventional linguistic patterns that embrace a variety of genres. Therefore, in many respects the analysis of discourse is forced to remain on the qualitative surface of the text and, due to the heterogeneity of the involved texts, rarely admits a 'deep dive' into the macro- and micro-structure of the concerned genres. If we want to close up on the pragmatic framework as well as the discursive devices applied in the texts and include a comparative analysis of different speech communities it seems therefore, in our view, indispensable to focus on functionally clearly discernible patterns of communication: text genres (or shorter 'genres'). In this context we set off with the fact that genres (as much as the discourses they belong to) can only be understood from a diachronic perspective as they mirror social moves, achievements and change. By doing so we base our observations on a linguistically framed genre concept that is, in the first place, committed to the early German attempts deriving from typological approaches to texts. Hence, it refers to the conceptual framework of the term *Textsorte* (such as conveyed by Gülich and Raible 1972 or Sandig 1983), which is considered as equivalent to the English term genre. Hence, we basically apply the term genre to refer to different classes of texts within a hierarchically structured typology of texts characterized as much by text internal as text external or pragmatic linguistic features. Given the fact that complex and repeated speech acts determine the conventional discursive devices of a genre in a specific culture, this framework of genre can easily integrate the dynamic genre concept established by the Russian formalists and the Bakhtin circle, in the second place. If genre is regarded as a dynamic communicative event that is conventionalized to an extent that facilitates communicative processes within a society it relates to social practices, which are fundamental to the Australian and North American approaches to genre (cf. for instance Halliday 1978, Martin 1984, Halliday and Martin 1993, Bazerman 1988). Hence if, for the purpose of raising insightful linguistic questions, the social component of genre and the usual partners involved in the communicative process with their specific backgrounds are stressed, the Australian and American approaches are far from representing a contradiction with the previously developed concept of genre. Moreover, they shall be integrated in the third place in order to bridge useful attempts in text linguistics. The same accounts for Swales (1990) and further approaches to academic writing (particularly the cross-linguistic studies by Clyne 1993, etc.), which emphasize the social factors of the discourse community and their effects on genre conventions. Thus, if we additionally take the digital turn including the step from text to hypertext into account and foreground the current necessity to reconsider linguistically and/or extend our concept of text (cf. for instance the recent volume by Fix *et al.* 2002) a stringent definition of genre might be formulated as follows: a class of communicative occurrences in social interaction which share the same pragmatic features as well as the main body of (implicit and hierarchically structured) communicative purposes, accomplished by the means of discursive devices (textual patterns) which are recognized and (unconsciously) known by the participants of the (discourse) community they belong to.

With reference to corpus linguistics this implies that genre-specific diachronic (multilingual) corpora would allow us to answer particularly insightful questions with regard to contrastive textology. This is why our point of departure is genre specific and only on a second level discourse specific. Let us now briefly discuss the usefulness of specialized genre-corpora in Language for Special Purposes (LSP) and some design features of diachronic corpora which shall, then, lead us to an examination of a particular attempt in this context: the compilation of the DIALAYMED-corpus (see below).

Where the genesis and evolution of language and linguistic strategies applied in genres are concerned the construction of special diachronic genre corpora seems vital,[2] particularly in the context of Language for Special Purposes. Such corpora are certainly unable to compete with large reference or core corpora in terms of size (a criticism that the first attempt regarding diachrony, the Helsinki Corpus consisting of 1.5 million words, was confronted with on several occasions, even if it prepared the ground for similar projects, cf. Rissanen *et al.* 1993). But these corpora allow meaningful diachronic and contrastive approaches which can be fundamental to further psycholinguistic research (e.g. on the intelligibility and readability of instructional third category LSP texts according to the scheme established by Ischreyt 1965). Taavitsainen (1993) emphasizes the light genres are able to shed on diachronic issues, but also states that 'genre or period styles are often mentioned in the literature, but their development in a longer perspective still needs charting' (Taavitsainen 1993: 172). The reason why few attempts have been made so far to trace genre developments on a corpus linguistic base is apparent if we lay stress on the fact that generic shifts, genre clusters and changing genre conventions mirror long-term social changes. As a result, the evolution of genre(s) can only be approached as a dynamic process embedded in a changing socio-historic situation throughout various centuries. This of course implies not only a solid analysis of the underlying subject(s), but also a solid (functional) definition of the analysed genre and a 'relevant' number of carefully chosen items. The compilation of such a corpus cannot be based on generic labels, which substantially change through time, but are bound to a high degree of functional equivalence. Hence, it is not surprising that Taavitsainen (1993), who refers to experiences drawn from selected genres of the Middle English section of the *Diachronic and Dialectal Helsinki Corpus of English Texts* (=Helsinki Corpus), confirms that a solid functional approach which considers text as a product of interaction between a specific text-producer and an audience which disposes of 'precise knowledge of generic forms and expectations' (Taavitsainen 1993: 173) is crucial if genres are analysed diachronically. Her methodological pilot study examines stylistic features of different literary and non-literary genres of Middle English (for example religious treatises, biographies, biblical histories) in order to find out how fruitful generic approaches could be in terms of generic distinction. It does not, however, carry out a genuine diachronic focus since an approach which traces the observed features chronologically is not challenged.

The compilation of a diachronic corpus is certainly more demanding in terms of comparability and representativeness. Most corpora built of old texts are multipurpose corpora screening a certain period in the past (e.g. the CORDE corpus for Spanish, the TFA-database for French), but rarely permit us to follow an evolutionary path of a specific genre. They usually correspond to one synchronic cut in the past which can be compared to a more recent cut in order to examine language change. In any event, the problem of representativeness and sampling seem to play a crucial role in the construction of diachronic multipurpose corpora (i.e. the ARCHER Corpus). Firstly, because it is impossible to sample genuine orality for the early periods. Secondly, because it is difficult to choose representative registers and include sufficient variation (the textual cosmos of early stages is only vaguely known in many contexts). Thirdly, because of practical constraints. Old texts are not accessible in the same number and quality, and require transcription and special coding, etc. Yet again, a genre-specific corpus offers a solution for the first two matters given the fact that the *tertio comparationis*, hence the basic criteria of inclusion, continues to be linked to the dominant function of the text in society (given the restriction to a written genre with a wide geographical and chronological distribution). Still, it should be the research purpose that determines the corpus and not vice versa, since corpus linguistics basically provides effective methods (operating with increasingly complex paradigms) to pave the way for linguistic understanding.

Linguistic framework and corpus design – the DIALAYMED experience

The state of the art

Unsurprisingly, for non-English corpora specialization seems to be the rule not the exception to the rule, since activities by individuals or small groups of scientists can be very efficient in constructing an insightful special corpus, but will hardly succeed in building and annotating a large core corpus for a language (unless it is a dead language with few texts and utterances). The manifold approaches stem from different focus areas and comprise for example acquisition corpora (e.g. the Maria-corpus for Spanish), historic corpora (e.g. the French TFA-database), corpora restricted to a medium (e.g. newspaper corpora for various languages such as the negr@ corpus for German newspaper texts) or to a mode (spoken v written, e.g. the CORIS/CODIS project for written Italian or the corpus of spoken Israeli Hebrew). In any case, the non-English language communities, even if they are prestigious, still lag behind the advances of corpus linguistics with reference to English. As a result far-reaching comparative and contrastive approaches, which would be beneficial to all involved communities, are still out of reach (e.g. general questions to be answered in contrastive syntax, morphology or textology). For now there is little possibility of comparing results across corpora, neither within the same nor between different languages and certainly not in terms of language change. The DIALAYMED corpus, which we shall now focus on in detail, verges on this gap.

The DIALAYMED: premises and fundamentals

This multilingual corpus restricted to the medical self-counselling genre attempts to incorporate diachrony and contrastiveness, two issues which imply multiple problems in terms of representativeness (a lively discussion on this topic persists, cf. for example Biber 1993; Kennedy 1998). This limitation to a clearly defined genre, or to be more precise to a dynamic cluster of interconnected socially and functionally similar genres that are bound to a very specific communicative situation and subject, does not only permit advances in methodological matters, but also the drawing of subject-oriented conclusions; particularly if we keep the crucial claim of corpus linguistics in mind that 'the most important skill is not to be able to program a computer or even manipulate available software (. . .). Rather, it is to be able to ask insightful questions which address real issues and problems in theoretical, descriptive and applied language studies' (Kennedy 1998: 3). The DIALAYMED, which is currently compiled in Salzburg with support of the Austrian Science Fund (FWF), includes exclusively medical information texts dedicated to the layman (self-counselling texts) and aims at monitoring and describing them chronologically and comparatively.[3] The first part of the corpus, that we refer to in this paper, is restricted to a specific subject: selected infectious diseases (explicitly bubonic plague, smallpox, syphilis, cholera, tuberculosis, typhus and AIDS). The basic functions of the genre that is clearly tied to popularizing medical discourse are summed up by Al-Sharief (1996: 11) as follows:

- providing a scientific background of the illness or health problem in question
- preparing the reader/patient for the treatment by providing information about how normally the treatment will be carried out and what are the steps that the doctor will take
- persuading readers to stop unhealthy habits or at least to take steps that will make them less harmful
- giving *practical* advice that will help to prevent complications of the illness or will complement the treatment
- arguing against some misconceptions about the disease and/or its treatment (words like *myth(s), misunderstandings, misconceptions* are not infrequent in medical leaflets)

Interestingly enough, popularizing medical discourse has become a subject of growing interest over the past thirty years. On linguistic grounds this is fostered, on the one hand, by the more general interest in scientific and/or academic writing and, on the other hand, by an increasing discontent regarding face-to-face interaction between doctors and patients. Numerous publications, usually on the base of small non-electronic corpora, give evidence of this development (cf. Salager-Meyer 1989, Redder and Wiese 1994, etc.). However, little attention has been paid so far to genres of written medical discourse, particularly with regard to those disseminating knowledge to the layman.

The functional analysis, that we can only briefly sketch due to restrictions of space, comes to the conclusion that the functional dominance of the text (according to Jakobson 1960) is conative. The reader is informed and explicitly guided in his conduct to prevent sickness or in his behaviour in case of a particular infectious disease. Consequently, the frequent referential, emotive, phatic and metalinguistic text sequences are subordinated in order to guarantee the effectiveness of the message. Concerning the text type, we deal with more than one type since medical information texts are descriptive and argumentative, but may also contain narrative sequences.[4] If we expand the typological system with an instructive type (that relates to argumentation) the dominance in terms of type turns clearly instructive.

Before addressing details with regard to the compilation of the DIALAYMED corpus it is necessary to point out, in a few words, some basic linguistic questions that the analysis of the corpus shall answer. The aim of the study consists in providing substantial insight on the communicative patterns of the medical information text addressing a lay audience. Questions relate to quantitative as well as qualitative issues and include pragmatic input. To mention some of them explicitly 1. Which models/patterns does the genre relate to when it emerges (no text is created *ex nihilo*)? 2. How is the genre interconnected in a cluster of similar (sub)genres and how does this cluster evolve in time? 3. How is the text organized/structured (macrostructure, text volume, headings, paragraphs, etc.)? 4. Which macrothematic sequences can be considered as prototypical for the different speech communities – and how does content engineering differ in the textual and hypertextual samples of the genre? 5. Which discursive devices can be considered as conventional for the genre? 6. Which word classes and types of non-verbal information are dominant in the text and how is the pictorial and the verbal linked (i.e. according to the paradigms established by Kress and van Leeuwen 2001). 7. What kind of terminology (technical terms, acronyms, eponyms, abbreviations) and metalinguistic devices are typical for the genre? 8. Do features of scientific medical LSP persist (advance organizers, hedging) and are they related to intergeneric translation? 9. How does the sender address the reader (interactive profiles between specialist and layman) and which form of directivity is most frequently used in the different speech communities? etc.

More generally speaking, the study aspires to provide a systematic way of identifying particular structural, discursive, pragmatic and interactional features of hybrid LSP writing. The hybridity of the genre derives from two facts. On the one hand, the genre includes a variety of discursive devices that are conceptually oral (linguistic preferences deriving from the setting similar to the doctor–patient interview as e.g. implicit dialogues, anticipated questions). The structure and wording, on the other hand, might also stem from the first and second level medical LSP, in view of the fact that (implicit) intertextual influences (preferences of the authors) or intergeneric translation processes might favour certain patterns. Moreover, an important focus is placed on the interaction in the text, thus how information and instruction is communicated with regard to mood, reference and (multi)modality. To find out whether a specific device is prototypical for the genre in a specific linguistic community and/or period and to analyse existing variants (e.g. for implicit dialogues, direct instructions, creation of intimacy, etc.) the corpus is (manually) coded. All the questions mentioned previously shall be addressed from a contrastive and diachronic angle to trace the genesis and evolution of the genre and to find out which elements of intertextuality play an important role and how the genre is clustered. Finally, questions concerning intelligibility can be raised. Such as, to what extent does the text miss the target and fail to transmit the message? Do intergeneric influences (intertextual borrowing) from academic style (syntax, terminology, structure, discursive devices) interfere with the new role of the text?

The wide range of questions to be raised in order to paint a complete picture of the genre does not only demand the construction of a consistent and representative corpus, but also requires the reflective examination of the socio-linguistic and pragmatic framework. Moreover, it turns out that some textual elements need diligent annotation or are not very suitable for annotation at all. A hybrid approach connecting the traditional and electronic mode of analysis will be necessary to reach the goal. This fact perfectly complies with the image of modern corpus linguistics as conveyed by Kennedy (1998: 2ff):

> It should be made clear, however, that corpus linguistics is not a mindless process of automatic language description. Linguists use corpora to answer questions and solve problems. Some of the most revealing insights on language and language use have come from a blend of manual and computer analysis.

The corpus comprises six languages (Spanish, French, Italian, Portuguese, German, English) and is divided into seven periods (Late Middle Ages, Renaissance, seventeenth-century, eighteenth-century, nineteenth-century, twentieth-century texts, twentieth- and twenty-first-century hypertexts). The minimum size for the first subject area (infectious diseases) is 150,000 words per language and period (a minimum of five sample texts and a maximum size of 250,000 words) which brings us to a total of 1,050,000 to 1,750,000 words per language and a total corpus of 6.3 to 10.5 million words (currently the first million with a focus on Spanish and Portuguese is completed and is undergoing annotation).

Generalizing the insights from the linguistic communities focused on so far, the medical information text emerged due to social necessity in the Late Middle Ages, but more specifically as a reaction to major pest epidemics in the fourteenth century. The generic designation(s) and the genre itself perform fundamental changes in the following centuries. A split into a variety of subgenres and an increasing clustering of interconnected genres belonging to popularizing medical discourse is obvious (e. g. the medical treatise, house-book, information folder, medical leaflet, flyer, self-counselling text). Furthermore, one has to be aware of the dissimilar role printed texts played in the early periods due to the gradual development of typographic culture. Only few people possessed reading skills in those days, which led to a differing pragmatic situation for the text. A mediator was necessary to divulge the information and the real event of information and instruction might pass from the written to the oral mode. However, it would not be the right strategy to exclude the early samples from the analysis due to pragmatic differences if we aim at understanding the genesis and evolution of a genre.

The intercultural approach

'Communication can take place only and exclusively via some shared culture. This characteristic of communication is present in the relationship between author and message as well as in the relationship of audience and message' (Ulijn and Gobits 1989: 216). Textual products undoubtedly require a social and semiotic framework. With regards to Peircean semiotics this means that the community does not only share the same language, but the construction of the same interpretant. Hence we have to extend the distinction of Reiss (1977) between linguistic community (*Sprachgemeinschaft*) and communicative community (*Kommunikationsgemeinschaft*) to an interpretational community (Saville-Troike 1989).[5] If the *tertio comparationis* on text linguistic grounds remains the purpose or function (with regard to functional hierarchies in texts cf. Dressler and Eckkrammer 2001), intercultural differences and similarities can be extracted. These shall, as we hope, allow conclusions on the cultural boundaries of illness, because according to Stolberg (1996) the awareness of the bodily routines as well as symptoms of disease such as pain are perceived in different ways in different cultures. Hence, the explanations and instructions given in the medical information leaflet reflect these culturally-bound syndromes as much as language-specific preferences in discourse that we find in other genres (see our studies concerning obituaries, job ads, dating ads or cooking recipes, cf. Eckkrammer 1996, Eckkrammer *et al.* 1999, Eckkrammer and Eder 2000).

Finally, it has to be mentioned that the DIALAYMED is designed as a dynamic corpus which is open to other speech communities and which could be expanded with regard to specific periods, diatopic differences, or account for more medical topics (e.g. heart diseases, allergies). The option for a genre corpus (parallel text corpus in terms of contrastive textology, cf. Arntz 1990, see note 2) implies, as we have previously stated, a very clear-cut genre concept and definition as well as functional equivalence (to the possible extent) which guarantees a high degree of cross-cultural comparability. According to basic methodology of contrastive textology the levels of comparison start with the individual language in order subsequently to compare intralingual results interlingually. The same accounts for the axis of the medium or channel since the analysis never mixes text-determining media-environments (e.g. text – hypertext, written – spoken). Only after scrutinizing prototypes for each medium are the results contrasted (for details cf. Eckkrammer and Eder 2000 and previous studies with regard to genre development and blending in virtual environments, for instance Crowston and Williams 1997).

Problematic issues

Let us now turn to some crucial problems that currently challenge the compilation and annotation of the DIALAYMED. In the first place, the inclusion of the early texts causes problems, because if they are edited at all they frequently apply differing transcription systems. Therefore well-thought-out homogenization procedures are required. The multilingual feature of the corpus additionally signifies that the different systems used for different languages and editions have to be reduced to one (per language) or eliminated. If our interest were to be purely historical and subject-oriented an elimination could be favoured. Within the context of proper philological work, however, it is impossible to neglect these peculiarities of the language(s). This means that the system applied by most edited texts is chosen (e.g. BOOST for old Spanish texts) and applied in the case of individual transcriptions or imported data from electronic libraries (which represent an ideal but rare source). On practical grounds even good folio-wise transcriptions trigger problems with regard to concordancing as words are often scattered down into several elements. As we could see from several test analyses stringent decisions are required in order to apply the same tool to all periodical subdivisions of the corpus and the schemes and categories applied to the texts (so far TATOE, TACT, ATLAS.ti and NUD*IST were used). In any case time-consuming manual preprocessing and annotation seem indispensable.

A second crucial problem is the inclusion of hypertexts (see also Eckkrammer 2002 for methodological basics). Coding is required to attribute consistent value to nodes, links and non-verbal components. The non-linear structure of hypertexts has to be dissolved in order to integrate them into the corpus, but at the same time proper coding has to allow the reconstruction of the non-linear text construct (so far the typological model proposed by Storrer 1999 seems most applicable). Another problem arises due to the unlimited nature of non-linear hypertextual structures. To process a hypertext in a corpus we have to know where it begins and where it ends, hence the dynamic property has to be handled and the imported file can only represent a static picture of the hypertext and pay attention to modularization and linkage. Even if this approach does not allow us to integrate all aspects of hypertextual features, the medium-specific dimensions can be captured to a certain extent.

A third major problem subsists with regard to the inclusion of interconnected visual information into the corpus, particularly strongly blended forms of inter-semiotic layering. However, most of the digital text tokens collected so far seem to rely on the pure text level and use visual information primarily for illustrative purposes. Hence they do not challenge more than traditional print products in this respect. However, we expect that fused and synchretic blending will gain popularity in the near future.

Conclusion

We have observed the necessity to expand our concept of text and genre to an integrative socially, pragmatically and semiotically grounded approach that also accounts for cognitive aspects of communication if it is to meet the needs of contrastive textological research, particularly if based on insightful corpus compilation and analysis. Even if a universal taxonomy of genre is still lacking it seems crucial that a diligently constructed cluster of a specific genre within its diachronic context (including all subgenres and the social constraints involved) should pave the way for solid results.[6] The applied side of this plea becomes obvious if we aim at proceeding from the information society to a knowledge society. In a knowledge society the claim that texts have to be user-friendly, in other words readable, intelligible, usable (also from an interactive viewpoint), becomes more and more fervent. However, if we want to render texts more adequate to the user we need to know how they are currently organized in different linguistic communities and how the discursive devices evolved throughout various centuries. Only then can we set forth with psycholinguistic research to investigate which linguistic structures are particularly inadequate, difficult or 'unpragmatic' in text and hypertext. Let us therefore assume that contrastive textological studies based on corpora embody an effective and applied approach to answer fundamental questions on functional or dysfunctional elements of genres and allow us to map out our use of linguistic systems and devices from a cross-linguistic perspective and for very specific settings.

Notes

1 We primarily adhere to the empirically grounded branch of contrastive textology (cf. Spillner 1981, Arntz 1990, etc.) which since the early 1980s gains ground in the German-speaking community of text-linguists, but also integrate features of the programmatic approach by Hartmann (1980) when appropriate.

2 Even if in the context of contrastive textology we would refer to this type of corpus as parallel corpus, it is wise to refrain from applying this term in a corpus linguistic context. In corpus linguistics the term is traditionally employed to refer to bi- or multilingual (sentence-wise) aligned text corpora with text tokens which are translations of one another. Within a corpus linguistic framework our genre corpus is similar to a translation or comparable corpus which 'holds texts in at least two languages, none of which are translations but which are comparable in terms of being written in the same genre' (McEnery and Oakes 2000: 1 ff). Since there is no direct relation to translation issues we give preference to the term *(contrastive) genre corpus.*

3 The generic designations are extremely heterogeneous. Consequently we choose a very 'unspecified' expression that serves as 'superterm' for the manifold labels (e.g. medical handbook, treatise, folder, leaflet, brochure) changing in different periods.

4 It is crucial to distinguish the for the most part socially, pragmatically and semiotically grounded concept of (text) genre (*Textsorten*) from the purely linguistic concept of text type (*Texttyp*), particularly since one type of text may embrace a variety of genres (cf. for more details Dressler and Eckkrammer 2001).

5 According to her findings in the field of the ethnography of communication a linguistic community for the most part involves several communicative communities, which usually comprise several interpretational communities.

6 The lack of a consistent text typology has not impeded text and discourse studies from evolving considerably or producing reliable results.

References

Al-Sharief, Sultan (1996) 'Interaction in written discourse. The choices of mood, reference, and modality in medical leaflets', University of Liverpool, PhD dissertation.

Arntz, Rainer (1990) 'Überlegungen zur Methodik einer "Kontrastiven Textologie" ', in Arntz, Rainer and Thome, Gisela (eds) *Übersetzungswissenschaft. Ergebnisse und Perspektiven,* Tübingen: Narr, pp. 393–404.

Bazerman, Charles (1988) *Shaping written knowledge: The genre and activity of the experimental article in science,* Madison: University of Wisconsin Press.

Biber, Douglas (1993) 'Representativeness in Corpus Design', *Literary & Linguistic Computing* 8: 243–57.

Biber, Douglas, Conrad, Susan and Reppen, Randi (2000) *Corpus Linguistics: Investigating Language Structure and Use,* 2nd edn, Cambridge: Cambridge University Press.

Botley, Simon P., McEnery, Anthony M. and Wilson, Andrew (eds) (2000) *Multilingual Corpora in Teaching and Research,* Amsterdam/Atlanta, GA: Rodopi.

Clyne, Michael (1993) 'Pragmatik, Textstruktur und kulturelle Werte. Eine interkulturelle Perspektive', in Schröder, Hartmut (ed.) *Fachtext-pragmatik*, Tübingen: Narr, pp. 3–18.

Crowston, Kevin and Williams, Marie (1997) 'Reproduced and emergent genres of communication on the World Wide Web', in *Proceedings of the Thirtieth Annual Hawaii International Conference on System Sciences (HICSS '97)*, Maui, Hawaii, vol. VI, pp. 30–9.

Dressler, Wolfgang U. and Eckkrammer, Eva M. (2001) 'Functional Explanation in Contrastive Textology', *Logos & Language* 2(1), 25–43.

Eckkrammer, Eva M. (1996) *Die Todesanzeige als Spiegel kultureller Konventionen*, Bonn: Romanistischer Verlag (with coll. of Sabine Divis-Kastberger).

Eckkrammer, Eva M. (2002) 'LSP and electronic text: How to access hypertext from a contrastive viewpoint?', in Merja Koskela, Christer Laurén, Marianne Nordmann & Nina Pilke (eds) *Vaasan Yliopiston Julkaisuja. Porta Scientiae II. Lingua Specialis.* Vaasa: University of Vaasa, 583–596.

Eckkrammer, Eva M. and Eder, Hildegund M. (2000) *(Cyber)Diskurs zwischen Konvention und Revolution. Eine multilinguale textlinguistische Analyse von Gebrauchstextsorten im realen und virtuellen Raum*, Frankfurt a. M., etc.: Lang.

Eckkrammer, Eva M., Hödl, Nicola and Pöckl, Wolfgang (1999) *Kontrastive Textologie.* Wien: Präsens.

Fix, Ulla, Adamzik, Kirsten, Antos, Gerd and Klemm, Michael (eds) (2002) *Brauchen wir einen neuen Textbegriff? Antworten auf eine Preisfrage*, Frankfurt a.M.: Lang.

Gülich, Elisabeth and Raible, Wolfgang (eds) (1972) *Textsorten. Differenzierungskriterien aus linguistischer Sicht*, Frankfurt a. M.: Athenäum.

Halliday, Michael A. K. (1978) *Language as social semiotic*, London: Arnold.

Halliday, Michael A. K. and Martin, James R. (1993) *Writing Science: literacy and discursive power*, London, Falmer and Pittsburgh: University of Pittsburgh Press.

Hartmann, Reinhard R. K. (1980) *Contrastive Textology. Comparative Discourse Analysis in Applied Linguistics*, Heidelberg: Groos.

Ischreyt, Heinz (1965) *Studien zum Verhältnis von Sprache und Technik*, Düsseldorf: Pädagogischer Verlag Schwann.

Jakobson, Roman (1960) 'Closing statement. Linguistics and Poetics', in Seboek, Thomas (ed.) *Style in Language.* Cambridge, MA: MIT Press, pp. 350–77.

Kennedy, Graeme (1998) *An introduction to corpus linguistics*, London: Longman.

Kress, Gunther and Leeuwen, Theo van (2001) *Multimodality*, London: Arnold.

Lauridsen, Karen (1996) 'Text corpora and contrastive linguistics: Which type of corpus for which type of analysis?', in Aijmer, Karin, Altenberg,

Bengt and Johansson, M. (eds) *Languages in contrast. Papers from a symposium on text-based cross-linguistics studies*, Lund: Lund University Press, pp. 63–71.

McEnery, Anthony M. and Oakes, Michael P. (2000) 'Bilingual text alignment – an overview', in Botley, Simon P. *et al.* (eds) *Multilingual Corpora in Teaching and Research*, Amsterdam/Atlanta, GA: Rodopi, pp. 1–37.

Martin, James R. (1984) 'Language, Register and Genre', in Christie, Frances (ed.) *Children Writing: Reader*, Geelong, Victoria: Deakin University Press, pp. 21–30.

Oostdijk, Nelleke and Haan, Pieter de (eds) (1994) *Corpus-based research into language*, in honour of Jan Aarts, Amsterdam/Atlanta, GA: Rodopi.

Redder, Angelika and Wiese, Ingrid (eds) (1994) *Medizinische Kommunikation. Diskurspraxis, Diskursethik, Diskursanalyse*, Opladen: Westdeutscher Verlag.

Reiss, Katharina (1977) 'Textsortenkonventionen: Vergleichende Untersuchung zur Todesanzeige', *Langage et l'homme* 35, 46–54.

Rissanen, Matti, Kytö, Merja and Palander-Collin, Minna (eds) (1993) *Early English in the computer age: explorations through the Helsinki corpus*, Berlin: Mouton de Gruyter.

Salager-Meyer, Françoise (1989) 'Principal Component Analysis and Medical English Discourse: investigation into genre analysis', *System* 17(1), 21–34.

Sandig, Barbara (1983) 'Textsortenbeschreibung unter dem Gesichtspunkt der linguistischen Pragmatik', in *Textsorten und literarische Gattungen. Dokumentation des Germanistentages in Hamburg vom 1.–4.4.1979*, Berlin: Erich Schmidt, 91–102.

Saville-Troike, Muriel (1989) *The ethnography of communication*, Oxford: Blackwell.

Spillner, Bernd (1981) 'Textsorten im Sprachvergleich. Ansätze zu einer Kontrastiven Textologie,' in Kühlwein, Wolfgang, Thome, Gisela and Wilss, Wolfram (eds) *Kontrastive Linguistik und Übersetzungswissenschaft. Akten des Internationalen Kolloquiums, Trier/Saarbrücken, 25.–30.9.1978*, München: Fink, pp. 239–50.

Stolberg, Michael (1996) ' "Mein äskulapisches Orakel!" Patientenbriefe als Quelle einer Kulturgeschichte der Krankheitserfahrung im 18. Jahrhundert', *Kulturen der Krankheit. Österreichische Gesellschaft für Geschichtswissenschaften* 7(3): 385–404.

Storrer, Angelika (1999) 'Kohärenz in Text und Hypertext', in Lobin, Henning (ed.). *Text im digitalen Medium*, Opladen: Westdeutscher Verlag, pp. 33–65.

Swales, John M. (1990) *Genre analysis. English in academic and research settings.* Cambridge: Cambridge University Press.

Taavitsainen, Irma (1993) 'Genre/subgenre styles in Late Middle English?', in Rissanen, Matti, Kytö, Merja and Palander-Collin, Minna (eds) *Early English in the computer age: explorations through the Helsinki corpus*, Berlin: Mouton de Gruyter, pp. 171–200.

Ulijn, Jan M. and Gobits, Rudy (1989) 'The role of communication for disseminating scientific and technical innovation', in Bungarten, Theo (ed.) *Wissenschaftssprache und Gesellschaft. Aspekte der wissenschaftlichen Kommunikation und des Wissenstransfers in der heutigen Zeit*, Tostedt: Attikon, pp. 214–32.

3 Word meaning in dictionaries, corpora and the speaker's mind

Christiane Fellbaum with Lauren Delfs, Susanne Wolff and Martha Palmer

Introduction

Most Natural Language Processing (NLP) applications require large-scale, sophisticated lexical resources to enable successful word sense identification. Many efforts falter when they encounter polysemous words with related but distinct meanings. The most frequent words are also the most polysemous ones, so the problem must be addressed for even highly limited domains of application.

We consider the respective inadequacies of two types of off-the-shelf sources for lexical information (dictionaries and corpora/texts) and discuss the challenges for creating a resource that combines their strengths.

Dictionaries and corpora

Dictionaries are created for the purpose of helping their user identify the meaning of an unknown word or usage. The assumption is that the user has the context but needs to understand the word. For polysemous words, dictionaries list several senses with distinct definitions and distinct paradigmatic representations (e.g. different superordinates). Because of the way dictionaries are meant to be used, they often say little about the differences in the contexts with which each sense is compatible.

Miller and Gildea (1987) have demonstrated the limited use of dictionaries as a source for lexical knowledge; word-learning seems to proceed largely via context. Miller and Gildea got children to write sentences using novel words that the children had looked up in a dictionary. Their young subjects had clearly understood the dictionary definition but the sentences demonstrated that this information is not sufficient for learning a word's syntagmatic properties. The children wrote sentences like 'My family erodes a lot' (*erode* was glossed in the dictionary as 'eat out') and 'She was meticulous about falling off the cliff' (based on the dictionary definition of *meticulous* as 'careful').

By contrast, texts or corpora tell us a lot about how a word is used. Corpora have become important tools in the study of language, since they reflect speakers' linguistic performance. Corpora are based on naturally occurring texts or spoken language, which are created everyday by non-expert language users, whereas reference works like dictionaries and encyclopedias are artefacts, created by experts skilled in writing definitions.

An optimal lexical resource for NLP applications must contain information about frequently used, everyday words and their use in context. Merging a corpus and a dictionary produces such a resource for sophisticated applications.

Combining a dictionary and corpus into a semantic concordance

A semantically annotated corpus, or semantic concordance, contains links from all the content words in a corpus to a specific entry in a dictionary. A sufficiently large semantic concordance allows one to extract and compile contexts for specific word senses. Such data are useful for training an automatic system that learns how to recognize word senses and to distinguish them from other senses of the same word. For verbs in particular, a semantic concordance holds valuable evidence about the range of their syntactic realizations and the semantic nature of their noun arguments.

How to construct a concordance

It is easy enough to extract automatically from a corpus all the occurrences of a given word, but such a concordance does not distinguish between the different senses of the target word. A human annotator needs to inspect all the corpus lines and distinguish the different senses with respect to a dictionary; the annotator then records a link between a given occurrence of a word and the corresponding sense in the dictionary. This process of semantic annotation is also referred to as *tagging*.

Prior work

Miller *et al.* (1994 and Landes *et al.* 1998) report on the creation of a semantic concordance, dubbed *SemCor*. A large part of the *Brown Corpus* (Kucera and Francis 1967) was semantically annotated by native English speakers with no linguistic training. These taggers read the text files online, and, for each polysemous content word (noun, verb, adjective and adverb), selected the appropriate sense from the lexical database WordNet (Miller 1990; Fellbaum 1998).

Fellbaum, Grabowski and Landes (1997; 1998) and Fellbaum and Grabowski (2002) examine the annotations made by the Princeton taggers during their training session, where each tagger annotated the same text passage. They found that the taggers' annotations agreed with those of the two linguists supervising the project overall 74 per cent of the time; the agreement was highest for nouns and dropped off for verbs and adjectives. Agreement with the linguists' judgements decreased sharply as the degree of polysemy of the words to be tagged increased. Finally, taggers tended to prefer that sense of the polysemous word that was listed first in WordNet over senses in subsequent positions; we speculated that this might have been due to the fact that the first sense tends to be the most frequent, salient and perhaps the broadest and most inclusive one.

Fellbaum, Grabowski and Landes concluded that, while these results were not surprising, they called into question some of the tacit assumptions underlying the annotation task. Tagging relies on what one might call the *dictionary model* of word representation, namely, that word senses are discrete and enumerable. The dictionary model predicts that annotation is easy: taggers inspect the occurrences of a (polysemous) string in a corpus, interpret and determine its meanings, and match these against a dictionary entry. Tagging should be easy, since it should mimic our everyday behaviour of processing language input and looking up entries, as it were, in our mental lexicons. Under this model, tagging is also the inverse of corpus-based lexicography, where the lexicographer gathers the occurrences of a (polysemous) string from a corpus, interprets and determines its meaning(s), and creates an appropriate dictionary entry.

A comparison of different dictionaries, including WordNet, shows up significant differences with respect to entries for polysemous words. Firstly, not all senses are represented in each dictionary; lexicographers and editors presumably choose those senses they consider the most important and most frequent. Secondly, a single sense in one dictionary may be broken up into distinct subsenses in another dictionary. For example, *Webster's* and the *American Heritage Dictionary* distinguish a transitive (causative) and an intransitive sense for many verbs of change and motion, while *Collins Dictionary* merges them into a single sense. Finally, different dictionaries often cover the same semantic space in the entry for a polysemous word, but they carve it up into different and only partially overlapping senses. We must conclude from these facts that there is no unequivocal mental lexical representation that lexicographers, and by extension, all speakers, can consult in a straightforward look-up fashion.

Alternative models of meaning representation, such as prototype theory, are perhaps more realistic and could account better for speakers' capacity to interpret a large number of conventional and novel usages of polysemous words, but we have no way to represent such a model, which does not assume fixed correspondences between a word form and a meaning, in a dictionary that can be used in semantic annotation. An interesting theory of word meaning is represented by Pustejovsky's *Generative Lexicon* (1995). This model explores the systematic extension of underspecified senses based on the context. For example, sentence (1a) leaves open whether the book's contents or its physical make-up are of good quality; sentences (1b) and (1c) pick out only these specific meanings, respectively:

(1) a. This book is good.
b. This book is interesting.
c. This book is torn.

The *Generative Lexicon* theory suggests ways to represent word meanings more flexibly and allows for both broader, underspecified, as well as more specific senses. Such lexical representations might lead to higher annotation agreement and accuracy, but await large-scale implementation.

In the remainder of this paper, we discuss some initial results of the semantic annotation of the University of Pennsylvania TreeBank (the *Penn TreeBank*). This corpus has been syntactically tagged, and providing it with semantic annotations will make it a valuable tool for training automatic systems for sense identification that can exploit both semantic and syntactic clues.

Semantic annotation of the Penn TreeBank

The Penn TreeBank annotation project differs in several respects from the SemCor effort. Firstly, the annotators are linguistically trained. Fellbaum, Grabowski and Landes (1997) found statistically significant differences between the tags of the two supervising linguists and the naive tagger group.

Secondly, the Princeton taggers tagged running text. This required them to (a) familiarize themselves with many different lexical entries in each tagging session, and (b) refamiliarize themselves with the entry for a frequently occurring word each time it came up in the text, instead of considering multiple occurrences (with different senses) and weighing these against each other.

These considerations suggested, in hindsight, that serial tagging puts an unnecessary burden on the annotators. Targeted tagging, where all occurrences of one polysemous word are tagged at the same time, allows the annotators to familiarize themselves with the lexical entry for a given word, examining all occurrences of this word in the corpus, and analysing the entire dictionary entry in the light of the data. When all occurrences of one word are being tagged in one session, potential errors may be eliminated that arise merely from the fact that the taggers have to examine the entire verb entry each time they hit upon a given verb in serial tagging. In the case of targeted tagging, the annotators can learn, as it were, one dictionary entry at a time and have it at their fingertips.The Penn TreeBank was being tagged in a targeted fashion, for which, incidentally, the taggers expressed a strong preference.

Distinguishing senses

In the first phase of the tagging project, two linguistically trained annotators each tagged the same set of verbs independently of each other. The verbs included some of the most polysemous ones (such as *call* and *draw*). The taggers used a version of WordNet that is more recent (a pre-release version of 1.7) and improved than that used for SemCor.

After 30 verbs had been tagged, the annotations were compared and the discrepancies were examined. Our goal was to discern patterns of disagreement in the way the WordNet senses were interpreted against the tokens in the corpus. Specifically, we hoped to learn which senses the taggers interpreted as being semantically close or overlapping. Such senses should either be merged or grouped into clusters. Senses that are members of a cluster each represent a specific reading that arises from particular semantic or syntactic contexts. The cluster as a whole represents a broader, underspecified sense.

WordNet currently contains several thousand clustered verb senses. Clustering was done following both syntactic and semantic criteria. Verb senses related by syntactic alternations such as indefinite object drop, cognative object realization and causative/inchoative were grouped:

(2) a. We ate fish and chips.
 b. We ate at noon.
(3) a. They danced a wild dance.
 b. They danced.
(4) a. He chilled the soup.
 b. The soup chilled.

Syntactic clustering is uncontroversial, once the criteria have been laid down, but there are no equally clear criteria for semantic similarity that could guide meaning-based clustering. In WordNet, the semantic clusters were created without the benefit of a corpus and on the basis of lexicographic intuitions. An examination of the taggers' data should provide a firmer basis for capturing meaning similarity as the basis for clusters.

Inter-annotator disagreements and consequences

Contrary to the findings for SemCor, the rate of disagreement was not proportional to the number of WordNet senses. We find fairly high disagreement rates between the two taggers for words with both large and small numbers of WordNet senses. This indicates that the annotators' disagreements were due either to the impossibility of identifying an unambiguous match for a specific occurrence in the sense inventory of WordNet or to each tagger interpreting the occurrence in a different way.

For those verbs where inter-annotator agreements were examined, the average number of senses is twelve; the average rate of disagreement is 29 per cent. This high rate of disagreement may appear discouraging. However, many discrepancies were due to one tagger's disregard of syntactic distinctions among senses. When these errors were discounted, the remaining discrepancies showed some systematic patterns that we will discuss briefly.

The most obvious result was that one tagger turned out to be a *lumper*, who consistently selected fewer senses, while the other was a *splitter*, who chose several senses to the lumper's single sense. The lumper's choices often corresponded to a broader, more general sense that arguably includes the narrower senses selected by the splitter.

A case in point: use

The verb *use* was tagged 116 times by both annotators, producing 30 disagreements. The taggers could choose from the six senses of this verb in WordNet; all six senses were involved in the discrepancies. The lumper chose the following same sense in all but three of the discrepant cases:

1. use, utilize, utilise, apply, employ – (put into service; make work or employ for a particular purpose or for its inherent or natural purpose: 'use your head!'; 'we use Spanish at home'; 'use plastic bags to store food'; 'use a computer')

For the same 27 cases, the splitter selected four distinct senses:

2. use – (take or consume (regularly); 'She uses drugs rarely')
3. use, expend – (use up, consume fully)
4. practise, apply, use – (avail oneself of; 'use care when going down the stairs'; 'use your common sense')
5. use – (seek or achieve an end by using to one's advantage; 'use one's influential friends to get jobs'; 'use one's good connections')

Each of the senses selected by the splitter is in fact a more specific subsense of the one sense chosen by the lumper, but the sense distinctions involve two independent parameters. Senses 2 and 3 have specific aspectual properties (habitual and completive, respectively). Senses 4 and 5 impose specific selectional restrictions on their direct objects: behavioural or mental attributes, persons or abstract entities that can serve as the means to an end or goal, respectively. Both types of meaning components can co-occur in a single usage; the aspectual property of the verb is independent of its selectional restriction. An entity can be used for its inherent purpose (sense 1), and be fully used up (sense 2) or used regularly (sense 3). Many contexts leave the aspectual properties of the verb unclear and do not specify whether something is used up or used regularly. To account for occurrences where otherwise distinct meanings may overlap, an annotation referring several senses must be allowed. The dictionary must contain clusters of verbs combining aspectual distinctions and distinctions based on selectional restrictions.

Another example: live

Three senses of the verb *live* were involved in inter-tagger disagreements:

1. be, live (have life, be alive; 'Grandfather lived till the end of the war')

2. survive, last, live, live on, go, endure, hold up, hold out (continue to live; endure or last; 'The legend of Elvis lives on'; 'The racing car driver lived through several accidents')
3. exist, survive, live, subsist (support oneself; 'Can you live on $2000 a month in New York City?')

Sense 1 is the broadest sense and subsumes senses 2 and 3, which have an additional meaning component each: an aspectual meaning component in sense 2, and the specific *economic survival* meaning in sense 3. In some cases, the corpus sentences contained enough context to allow a match with one sense; in other cases, the context was simply not specific enough. The taggers' disagreements reflect this clearly. One tagger chose sense 2, where the other selected sense 3; other times, one annotator chose sense 3 and the other sense 1.

There is no reason to assume that an automatic system could discriminate the senses where the taggers could not due to a lack of context specificity. Therefore, clustering all three senses and allowing for annotations to the entire cluster seems like a good solution both for human and future machine annotation.

Conclusion

The traditional dictionary model of meaning representation, with its discrete senses, is clearly not adequate for semantic annotation by human taggers, and there is little reason to assume that automatic systems can map dictionary senses of polysemous words onto tokens in a corpus in a one-to-one fashion. Results from an annotation task performed by two trained humans show high rates of disagreements, but these annotation results can inform the makers of dictionaries that are intended for use in automatic word sense identification tasks. We saw that many natural occurrences of polysemous words are embedded in underspecified contexts and could correspond to several of the more specific senses. Annotators and automatic systems need the option to select either a cluster of specific senses or a single, broader sense, where specific meaning nuances are contained but hidden. Sense clustering, already present in much of WordNet's verb component, can be enhanced and guided by the analysis of inter-annotator disagreements.

Notes

This work has been supported by DARPA grant N66001-00-1-8915 to the University of Pennsylvania and by NSF grant II98-05732 to Princeton University.

Subsequent work on the semantic annotation of the Penn TreeBank is reported in Fellbaum *et al.* (2001) and Palmer *et al.* (submitted).

References

Fellbaum, Christiane (ed.) (1998) *WordNet*, Cambridge, MA: MIT Press.

Fellbaum, Christiane, Grabowski, Joachim and Landes, Shari (1997) 'Analysis of a Hand-Tagging Task', in Light, Marc and Palmer, Martha (eds) *Proceedings of the ACL/Siglex workshop, Association for Computational Linguistics*, Somerset, NJ: ACL, 34–40.

Fellbaum, Christiane, Grabowski, Joachim and Landes, Shari (1998) 'Performance and Confidence in a Semantic Annotation Task', in Fellbaum, Christiane (ed.) *WordNet*, Cambridge, MA: MIT Press, pp. 217–38.

Fellbaum, Christiane and Grabowski, A. (2002) 'The Representation of Polysemous Word Meanings', in Lenci, Alessandro and Di Tomaso, Vittorio (ed.) *Meaning and Computation*, Allessandria: Edizione dell'Orso, pp. 7–16.

Fellbaum, Christiane, Palmer, Martha, Hoa Trang Dang, Delfs, Lauren and Wolff, Susanne (2001) 'Manual and Automatic Semantic Annotation with WordNet', in *Proceedings of the SIGLEX Workshop on WordNet and other Lexical Resources (NAACL-01)*, Pittsburgh, PA.

Kucera, Henry and Francis, Nelson W. (1967) *The standard corpus of present-day American English* (electronic database), Providence, RI: Brown University.

Landes, Shari, Leacock, Claudia and Tengi, Randee (1998) 'Building a Semantic Concordance of English', in Fellbaum, Christiane (ed.) *WordNet*, Cambridge, MA: MIT Press, pp. 199–216.

Miller, George A. (ed.) (1990) 'WordNet', *Special issue of International Journal of Lexicography*, 3.

Miller, George A. and Gildea, Patricia M. (1987) 'How children learn words', *Scientific American* (September), 94–9.

Miller, George A., Chodorow, Martin, Landes, Shari, Leacock, Claudia and Thomas, Robert G. (1994) 'Using a Semantic Concordance for Sense Identification', *Proceedings of the Human Language Technology Workshop*, pp. 240–3.

Palmer, Martha S., Hoa Trang Dang and Fellbaum, Christiane (submitted) *Making fine-grained and coarse-grained distinctions, both manually and automatically*.

Pustejovski, James (1995) *The Generative Lexicon*, Cambridge, MA: MIT Press.

4 Extracting meaning from text

Gregory Grefenstette

Introduction

Everyone expects computers to be able to understand the meaning of the documents that they manipulate, and common users are disappointed and frustrated when computers do not live up to their expectations. The scientific community is, of course, aware that efforts to formalize knowledge and meaning largely predate the appearance of computers, and that these efforts, which gave rise to the fields of natural history and philosophy, have not been able to create any acceptable system for formalizing meaning, despite myriad propositions. When computer scientists decided to re-attack the problem of meaning representation, creating a subdomain called Artificial Intelligence, seconded by linguists in the subdomain of Computational Linguistics, they adopted two approaches to the problem. The first approach was to adapt or re-invent formal models of meaning, initially proposed by philosophers and logicians, and to try to make them useful by restricting the domain to which they applied (see Winograd 1972 for one of the earliest and most complete attempts). This approach led to a number of toy-systems developed in the 1970s and 1980s, followed by efforts to scale-up these solutions (Guha and Lenat 1990). A second approach taken was not to create an internal model of meaning which would then be used to demonstrate understanding through some application, but rather to try to create systems which accomplished meaningful tasks without necessarily referring to a sophisticated model of meaning (Hsu 1990; Nievergelt *et al.* 1995). In this paper, we present examples of the second approach to extracting meaning from text. We refer the reader to Bateman *et al.* (1990) for the first approach to modelling meaning in text.

Meaningful tasks

In this paper, we examine tasks that have been performed on text that simulate understanding the meaning of text. In this sense, we are not extracting meaning from text as something that can be shown independently of the task, but rather we are answering the question, for each task: if we were able to extract the meaning of this text, and use that meaning in order to perform this task, what would the result be? Here are some of the meaning-laden questions that people have built systems to answer: What kind of text is this? What other texts are like this? What is this text about? How good is this text? What is in this text? What can we learn from this sequence of texts? In the following sections, we will review these systems with an eye towards what information they used in the text as a substitute for creating an internal model of the text meaning.

These systems use three steps to simulate meaning: pattern recognition, counting and comparison:

- Pattern recognition means recognizing elements from a list in the text, or recognizing elements that match regular expressions, or recognizing elements that are accepted by some grammar.
- Counting means attaching a number to the patterns recognized in the first step. This number can be a simple frequency of how many times the pattern occurs in the text, or a relative frequency of how many times the pattern occurs divided by the total number of patterns recognized in the text. The list of recognized patterns and their counts can then be collected for the whole text, or part of it, into a vector that provides the profile of the text.
- The similarity of this profile to other stored profiles is calculated in order to make a choice that simulates understanding some of the meaning of the text.

Romesburg (1984) provides an excellent introduction to similarity calculations.

An illustrative of a meaningful task

As an example of such meaningful tasks, consider an automatic summarization system that, for example, reduces a 240-sentence text to 5 sentences. In the indicative summarization technique, first described in Luhn (1958), the purpose is to get an idea of what the document is about by reducing it to a few lines that capture the central meaning of the document. This is normally done by trying to extract the sentences that best characterize what the text means, without referring to any internal representation of meaning, in the following way. The main supposition is that the most characteristic sentences will contain the most important concepts in the document. Since we have no representation of meaning, we simulate recognition of the important concepts with a feasible calculation of the most common words, other than functional words called stopwords by Salton *et al.* (1975). That is, after a simple pattern-matching step which tokenizes (Grefenstette and Tapanainen 1994) the input text and removes stopwords, the remaining tokens are sorted and counted. The most common words are retained as the most important. Next the text is considered sentence by sentence, and each line is scored according to its position and the number of important words it contains. Sentences in the beginning of the document get some additional points to those in the middle. Words which appear in upper case (after the first word in the sentence) are taken to be proper names and give the sentence a few more points, as do sentences containing any key phrases from a list (e.g. 'in conclusion', 'in summary', etc.). Lastly, only sentences over a certain minimal length (e.g. 5 words) are considered for inclusion. Then the sentences are sorted from highest score to lowest score, and the top 5 or top 10 sentences are retained depending on the desired length of the summary, and re-presented in their original order. This technique often provides a satisfactory summary. From its description we see that an ersatz of meaning is found in the frequency of the words in the text, i.e. the counts of the most frequent words (other than stopwords) are used to simulate meaning. We will now briefly examine other meaningful tasks, and try to isolate where 'meaning' is approximated.

'Meaning-full' questions

What kind of text is this?

The following tasks try to answer the question what kind of text is this: genre identification (Biber 1993; Kessler *et al.* 1997) and authorship identification (Mosteller and Wallace 1964; Holmes 1994). In genre identification and authorship identification, the task is to decide whether a given document belongs to a certain genre of documents (such as Editorial, Scientific Paper, email) or whether it has been written by one of a small number of authors. In both tasks, we possess a large number of documents, called the training set, that are already classified as to genre, or that are known to have been written by the authors. Decision is based on the presence and frequency of stopwords. Full words are thrown out, and lists are made of all the stopwords. For example, one may count how many times a given author uses 'nonetheless' or 'notwithstanding'.

In this and many of the following techniques, the raw frequencies are not used but normalised by a formula (Salton and Buckley 1988) that weakens the weight of words that appear in many documents. Called TF-IDF for Term Frequency Inverse Document Frequency, the formula divides the number of times a word appears in a document by the number of documents that the word appears in. The idea is that words appearing everywhere are not discriminating. A common variant is to use the square root of the frequency in the document, and use the log rather than the absolute number of documents that a term appears in: SQRT(tf)*(1/log(df)). The only purpose of the square root and log is to attenuate the effect of raw frequency.

What other texts are like this?

Information retrieval (Salton *et al.* 1975), clustering (Jain and Dubes 1988; Pereira *et al.* 1993), classification (Fürnkranz *et al.* 1998) are three meaningful tasks which answer, in the same way, the question of when documents are alike. For all three tasks, stopwords are thrown out and the frequency of full words is used to characterize a class of documents. This characterization, or profile, is essentially a long list of words with their frequencies in the already-seen documents from each class. We generate a similar list of full words and weights for the new document to include in a cluster or in a class, or for a new question in the information retrieval task. This new list is compared against all the existing profiles of documents or classes, considering each list as a vector, in which each word defines a new axis and where the weight of the word (its frequency, or normalized frequency) defines the distance from the origin along this axis. Some calculation of the distance between the new document and the known documents allows us to choose which cluster to put them in, or which class to assign the document to, or to retrieve the closest documents in the information retrieval task. In all three tasks, meaning is being approximated by word frequencies of non stopwords.

What is this text about?

Another group of meaningful tasks attempts to show what a text is about: summarization (Luhn 1958; Paice 1990; Goldstein *et al.* 1999), topic detection (Hearst 1993; Allan *et al.* 1998; Hatzivassiloglou *et al.* 1999), entity recognition (McDonald 1996; Cucerzan and Yarowsky 1999; Riloff and Jones 1999), and question answering (Burke *et al.* 1997; TREC 1999). These tasks actually choose bits of a document text, and return this selection as a response. Summarization chooses N (e.g. N=5) sentences, or a percentage of sentences, from a text as a summary. Topic detection groups sentences, paragraphs, or documents into topics; entity recognition chooses strings from a text and types them (e.g. as people, places, companies, etc.); and question answering chooses 50 or 250 characters from a document that best answer a given question. In order to perform these tasks, both summarization and topic detection use profiles (e.g. lists of weighted full words) as described in the previous section. Summarization systems, as we have seen, create a profile for the whole document, and then go back and create a profile for each sentence. The sentences whose profiles best match the profile of the document (essentially, sentences which contain many words appearing often in the document) are chosen in the order they appear to form the summary. Topic detection produces profiles for each text segment (e.g. a paragraph) and then compares profiles between adjoining and previously seen segments to recognize a new topic (when the match is low) and group recurring topics when the match in profiles (i.e. many words are shared) is high. Meaning is simulated by word frequency and position in both summarization and topic detection.

Entity recognition uses lists of known entities (e.g. sports figures, banks) or lists of entity parts (e.g. Lake . . ., . . . River, . . . Corp.) and upper-case use to decide when an entity is found, and what type of entity it is. Question answering uses a combination of profile matching and entity recognition.

Questions are typed, so that a question beginning with, for example, 'Who was . . .?' means we want a text segment with a person in it. The remaining words of the question are used as in information retrieval and in topic detection to find the best matching document and then text segment. Within this segment, entities corresponding to the searched types are returned. In these last two tasks, lists of words and list of patterns associated with types (e.g. person, place, organization, money, etc.) are used to simulate meaning understanding.

How good is this text?

Two other tasks that would seem to necessitate some type of understanding are measuring authoritativeness of a text (Kleinberg 1998; Brin and Page 1999), and grading exam papers (Batten Page 1994; Larkey 1998). Authoritativeness, though, has been replicated by simply counting how many other documents refer to this document, and how many times this document refers to other authoritative documents. Only the first criterion is used in the www.citeseer.com, which ranks documents by presence of query words in the title, and by the number of articles which cite the document. Google uses both incoming pointers and outgoing pointers to judge the quality of a page. A page is considered authoritative if many authoritative pages link into it and if it links into many other authoritative pages. In this task, meaning is approximated by links into and out of the documents. Grading texts uses a set of graded texts, and then matches ungraded texts using full word profiles against the graded texts, assigning the grade from the closest matches. Such grading is another form of classification as in the section 'What is this text about?' (above) and uses word frequencies to simulate meaning.

What's in this text?

To find out what is in a text, in more linguistically oriented tasks, understanding is simulated by referring to lists: morphology (Carter 1995; Chanod and Tapanainen 1995); by referring to most likely patterns of part-of-speech sequences from a hand-tagged text: part-of-speech tagging (Church 1988, Brill 1992); to patterns of part-of-speech tags: noun phrase extraction and dependency extraction (with a marking of which elements are to be connected) (Abney 1996; Grefenstette 1996; Ait-Mokhtar and Chanod 1997); and by using lists (such as in entity recognition) and position information: anaphora resolution (Lappin and Leass 1994; Kehler 1997). Here, typed lists and patterns are used to extract meaning, with frequency being used by dependency extraction, and position being used by anaphora resolution.

What can we learn from this sequence of texts?

The behaviour of a word or group of words over a group of texts can be used to identify meaning. Trend analysis (Lent *et al.* 1997) uses text ordered by time. It counts words appearing at different points in time, and when the frequency of some words becomes much greater, or drops off, after a given time, then these words are isolated and displayed as trends. Terminology (Justeson and Katz 1995) also compares frequency of words between texts, but here the texts are grouped by subject or domain. Words or groups of words which have a higher frequency within the group than without are considered to be the terminological elements of that domain.

Thesaurus discovery (Grefenstette 1994) uses the words occurring with a term to create a profile for each term (as classification creates a profile for each document). Terms which have the same profile are considered as belonging to the same class, using the following technique: (i) identify terms via tokenization, part-of-speech tagging, lemmatization, noun phrase extraction, and/or dependency parsing; (ii) extract features for the terms over the collection of text. Features could be the document numbers, words appearing within a window of N words, or words occurring with the term in a syntactic dependency relation; (iii) create a term profile from the features and their frequencies. This is, as we have seen, a vector of terms and their weights; (iv) compare profiles, e.g. calculate the distance between vectors, (v) cluster terms. In these tasks involving behaviour over a group of texts, once again meaning understanding is simulated by shared frequency of occurrence.

Conclusion

Extracting meaning from text can be performed by modelling the domain and identifying elements of the domain in text, or, implicitly, by performing some task requiring what seems to be meaning understanding over a text. In this article, we have listed a number of 'meaning-full' questions that one might ask of a text, and have given a brief sketch of how these questions are answered, and what element operates as a substitute for meaning understanding. In most cases, meaning is found by extracting features (based on lists to extract, or to ignore), counting the number of times each feature appears and comparing these counts with each other to measure similarity or difference. That counting would be important seems evident, but the interesting thing about all these approaches involving counting is the appearance of a tremendously large and freely available corpus which is the WWW. It would seem that the amount of text available, and not yet exploited, on the web will give rise to better and better approximations of textual meaning as it is mined, and as statistics on word use are derived from it.

References

Abney, Steve (1996) 'Partial parsing via finite-state cascades', in John Carroll (ed.) *Workshop on Robust Parsing* (ESSLLI '96), 8–15.

Ait-Mokhtar, Salah and Chanod, Jean-Pierre (1997) 'Incremental Finite-State Parsing', in *Proceedings of ANLP-97*, Washington, 72–9.

Allan, James, Carbonell, Jaime G., Doddington, George, Yamron, Jonathan and Yang, Yiming (1998) 'Topic Detection and Tracking Pilot Study – Final Report', in *Proceedings of the Broadcast News Transcription and Understanding Workshop.*

Bateman, John A., Kasper, Robert T., Moore, Johanna D. and Whitney, Richard A. (1990) *A general organization of knowledge for NLP: the PENMAN upper model,* Technical Report, USC/Information Sciences Institute.

Batten Page, Ellis (1994) 'New Computer Grading of Student Prose Using Modern Concepts and Software', *Journal of Experimental Education,* 62(2), 127–42.

Biber, Douglas (1993) 'The Multi-Dimensional Approach to Linguistic Analyses of Genre Variation: Overview of Methodology and Findings', *Computers and the Humanities,* 26: 331–45.

Brill, E. (1992) 'A Simple Rule-Based Part of Speech Tagger', in *Proc. ANLP'92,* 152–5.

Brin, Sergey and Page, Lawrence (1999) 'The anatomy of a large-scale Web search engine', in *Conference Proceedings of the 7th International WWW Conference,* 101–17.

Burke, Robin, Hammond, Kristian, Kulyukin, Vladimir, Lytinen, Steve and Tomuro, Noriko (1997) 'Question answering from frequently-asked question files: Experiences with the FAQ Finder system', *AI Magazine,* 18, 57–66.

Carter, David (1995) 'Rapid development of morphological descriptions for full language processing systems', in *EACL-95,* 202–9.

Chanod, Jean-Pierre and Tapanainen, Pasi (1995) 'Creating a tagset, lexicon and guesser for a French tagger', in *ACL SIGDAT Workshop on From Texts to Tags: Issues in Multilingual Language Analysis,* Dublin, 58–64.

Church, Ken (1988) 'A stochastic parts program and noun phrase parser for unrestricted text', *Proceedings of the 2nd Conference on Applied Natural Language Processing,* 136–43.

Cucerzan, Silviu and Yarowsky, David (1999) 'Language independent named entity recognition combining morphological and contextual evidence', in *Proc. 1999 Joint SIGDAT Conference EMNLP & VLCE.*

Fürnkranz, Johannes, Mitchell, Tom and Riloff, Ellen (1998) 'A case study in using linguistic phrases for text categorization on the WWW', in *Proceedings of the AAAI-98 Workshop on Learning for Text Categorisation,* 5–12.

Goldstein, Jade, Kantrowitz, Mark, Mittal, Vibhu O. and Carbonell, Jaime G. (1999) 'Summarizing Text Documents: Sentence Selection and Evaluation Metrics', in *Proceedings of the 22nd International SIGIR Conference,* 121–8.

Grefenstette, Gregory (1994) *Explorations in Automatic Thesaurus Discovery.* Norwell, MA: Kluwer Academic.

Grefenstette, Gregory (1996) 'Light parsing as finite state filtering', in *Workshop on extended finite state models of language,* ed. A. Kornai, Budapest ECAI'96, 20–5.

Grefenstette, Gregory and Tapanainen, Pasi (1994) 'What is a word, what is a sentence? problems of tokenization', in *The 3rd International Conference on Computational Lexicography*, Budapest, 79–87.

Guha, Ramanthan V. and Lenat, Douglas B. (1990) 'Cyc: A Midterm Report', *AI Magazine*, 11(3) (Fall), 32–59.

Hatzivassiloglou, Vasileios, Klavans, Judith L. and Eskin, Eleazar (1999) 'Detecting text similarity over short passages: exploring linguistic feature combinations via machine learning', in *Proceedings of empirical methods in natural language processing and very large corpora* EMNLP'99.

Hearst, Marti (1993) *TextTiling: a quantitative approach to discourse segmentation*, Technical Report 93#24, Project Sequoia, University of California, Berkeley.

Holmes, David I. (1994) 'Authorship Attribution', *Computers and the Humanities*, 28(2), 87–106.

Hsu, Feng-Hsiung (1990) *Large scale parallelization of alpha-beta search: An algorithmic and architectural study with computer chess*, PhD thesis, Carnegie Mellon University, Pittsburgh, PA (February).

Jain, Anil K. and Dubes, Richard C. (1988) *Algorithms for Clustering Data*, Englewood Cliffs, NJ: Prentice Hall.

Justeson, John S. and Katz, Slava M. (1995) 'Technical Terminology: Some Linguistic Properties and an Algorithm for Identification in Text', *Natural Language Engineering* 1:9–27.

Kehler, Andrew (1997) 'Probabilistic Coreference in Information Extraction', in *Proceedings of the Second Conference on Empirical Methods in Natural Language Processing (SIGDAT)*, 163–73.

Kessler, Brett, Nunberg, Geoffrey and Schutze, Hinrich (1997) 'Automatic Detection of Text Genre', in *Proceedings ACL/EACL*, Madrid, 32–8.

Kleinberg, Jon M. (1998) 'Authorative Sources in a Hyperlinked Environment', in *Proceedings of the 9th ACM-SIAM Symposium on Discrete Algorithms*, ed. H. Karloff, 668–77.

Lappin, Shalom and Leass, Herbert J. (1994) 'An Algorithm for Pronominal Anaphora Resolution', *Computational Linguistics*, 20(4), 535–61.

Larkey, Leah (1998) 'Automatic essay grading using text categorization techniques' in *Proceedings of the 21st ACM/SIGIR (SIGIR-98)*, 90–6.

Lent, Brian, Agrawal, Rakesh and Srikant, Ramakrishnan (1997) *Discovering Trends in Text Databases, KDD-97*, 227–30.

Lewis, David D. (1995) 'Evaluating and Optimizing Autonomous Text Classification Systems', in *Proc. SIGIR-95*, 246–54.

Luhn, Hans P. (1958) 'Automatic creation of literature abstracts', *IBM Journal*, 159–65.

McDonald, David (1996) 'Internal and external evidence in the identification and semantic categorization of proper names', in Boguraev, B. and Pustejovsky, J. (eds) *Corpus processing for lexical acquisition*. Cambridge, MA: MIT Press, 21–39.

Mosteller, Frederick and Wallace, David L. (1964) *Inference and Disputed Authorship: The Federalist*, Reading, MA: Addison Wesley.

Nievergelt, Jurg, Gasser, Ralph, Mäser, Fabian and Wirth, Christoph (1995) 'All the Needles in a Haystack: Can Exhaustive Search Overcome Combinatorial Chaos?', *Computer Science Today: Lecture Notes in Computer Science 1000*, ed. J. van Leeuwen, Berlin: Springer, pp. 254–74.

Paice, Chris D. (1990) 'Constructing literature abstracts by computer: Techniques and prospects' *Info. Proc. and Management* 26, 171–86.

Pereira, Fernando, Tishby, Naftali and Lee, Lillian (1993) 'Distributional clustering of English words', in *30th Annual Meeting of the ACL*, 183–90.

Riloff, Ellen and Jones, Rosie (1999) 'Learning dictionaries for information extraction using multi-level bootstrapping', in *Proc. of the Sixteenth National Conference on Artificial Intelligence (AAAI-99).*

Romesburg, H. Charles (1984) *Cluster Analysis for Researchers.* Belmont, CA: Lifetime Learning Publications.

Salton, Gerald *et al.* (1975) 'A Vector Space Model for Automatic Indexing', *CACM*, 18(11), 613–20.

Salton, Gerald and Buckley, Christopher (1988) 'Term-Weighting Approaches in Automatic Text Retrieval', *Information Processing & Management*, 24(5), 513–23.

TREC (2000) Question answering track, http://trec.nist.gov/presentations/TREC9/qa

Winograd, Terry (1972) *Understanding Natural Language*, New York: Academic Press.

5 Translators at work: a case study of electronic tools used by translators in industry

Riitta Jääskeläinen and Anna Mauranen

Introduction

In this paper we report on a case study which was carried out in an international project called SPIRIT (Supporting Peripheral Industries with Realistic Applications of Internet-based Technology). The project was funded by the European Union's Multilingual Information Society (MLIS) programme and coordinated by the University of Ulster. The purpose of the Finnish part of the project was to find out the extent to which electronic tools (including electronic dictionaries, translation memory software, terminology management software, the Internet, electronic corpora and concordance software) are currently being used by translators in industry, and to try out the usefulness of corpus tools if these should turn out to be unknown or little used. The focus was on the Finnish export industry, or, more precisely, one sector thereof, i.e. the timber industry. The Finnish part of the SPIRIT project is reported in Jääskeläinen and Mauranen (2000).

The case study was partly motivated by a wish to test our own intuitions and experiences with translation students about the usefulness of corpora as a translator's tool. As translation teachers and researchers, we are convinced that corpora are useful for translators; however, instead of relying solely on our intuition, we wanted to carry out a field test with translators on the job. The field test, which we refer to as a 'corpus experiment', gave support to our intuitions, but it also brought forward new challenges.

The case study consisted of two parts: a needs analysis and a corpus experiment. We will first describe the findings of the needs analysis; then we will describe the corpus experiment and its findings; and, finally, we will discuss the implications of the research project.

Needs analysis

At the first stage of the research project we carried out a needs analysis among eastern Finnish translators (in-house and freelance) and small translation agencies. The purpose of the needs analysis was to acquire a more reliable picture of the extent to which electronic tools are being utilized by translators on the job and whether and in which ways such tools might be of more assistance to translators.

The needs analysis consisted of three parts: 1. interviews, 2. translation logs and 3. a questionnaire. The interviewees were five in-house translators and other language professionals (assistants, secretaries), from two fairly large Finnish export companies (in what follows, both groups will sometimes be referred to as 'translators'). The interviews were informal and they included questions about the translators' typical work assignments: text-types, languages, problems, tools (electronic or otherwise). On the basis of the interviews, a 'translation log' was created for the second stage of the needs analysis. A translation log is a kind of work journal with ready-made entries, in which the translators listed and described their work assignments during a two to three-week period. The logs contained sections similar to those in the interviews, i.e. the translators were asked to fill in details about their translation tasks and other tasks demanding language skills (foreign language writing tasks; language revision). A total of ten in-house translators and language professionals from the two companies participated in this part of the needs analysis. One of the most interesting findings (for our purposes at least) was that 76 per cent of the translation tasks during the logging period were done into a foreign language. To us, this indicated a need for monolingual target language corpora to help translators produce fluent and idiomatic texts in a foreign language.

The information collated from the interviews and the translation logs was used to formulate a questionnaire which was then distributed among freelance translators and translation agencies in eastern Finland. Regrettably, the large, telecommuting agencies did not reply, which makes the sample somewhat skewed as far as the distribution of electronic tools is concerned. Another reservation relates to the type of data: while the translation logs are fairly reliable records of the translators' daily assignments, the questionnaires represent the translators' estimates of their typical commissions (during the past two years). The questionnaire contained the following sections for describing the translators' typical commissions: language-pairs, topic areas (or special fields) and text-types, target groups, typical problems, traditional tools and electronic tools.

The replies showed that freelance translators and small translation agencies tend to specialize in relatively few languages (two to three foreign languages), whereas there is less opportunity to specialize in particular topic areas or text-types. The majority reported that their assignments deal regularly with four to seven special fields, and the text-types range from personal letters to research abstracts. This seems to point to a need for individual (tailored) special-purpose corpora and training in their use for freelance translators. Translating into a foreign language was reported to be very common; these tasks also included material for publication, such as tourist brochures or research abstracts. This, again, implies that there is a demand for high-quality FL text production and, as a consequence, a potential market for tools which help produce high-quality FL texts.

The replies to the questionnaire also show that electronic tools are not as widely used as we expected; while the Internet and electronic dictionaries (more precisely, the Finnish bilingual electronic dictionaries) were used by virtually every informant, tools like terminology management software, corpora and translation memory software were virtually unknown. (It must be remembered here that the large translation agencies did not reply which biases the findings.) To some extent this makes sense: e.g. translation memories, which depend on large masses of repetitious (mainly technical) texts, are not likely to be very helpful for a freelance translator who must have several specializations. On the other hand, even the large companies which participated in the earlier stages of the needs analysis (interviews and translation logs) did not use these tools, in spite of the fact that they already had a company intranet available. However, as was suggested above, even freelance translators could find uses for corpora, which motivated us to go ahead with the corpus experiment.

Corpus experiment

The purpose of the corpus experiment was to test the usefulness of corpora as a translator's tool with authentic translating tasks and real translators at work. Initially, the idea was to test corpora with freelance translators, but that turned out to be impossible. As was mentioned earlier, the sector of industry we were dealing with was the Finnish timber industry, but when it was time to start compiling 'a corpus on the timber industry', we realized that the designation 'timber industry' is not as straightforward as it seems. It is in fact a much more heterogeneous and nebulous entity than we had imagined. Therefore, creating a 'timber industry corpus' within the confines of the twelve-month research project turned out to be impossible. To be of any use to anyone, such a corpus should have been much larger than our resources allowed.

This point could be illustrated by an example from the replies to the questionnaire. The special field 'Timber industry' formed the second largest category (with eleven replies) of the typical commissions reported by the informants. (The largest category was 'Legal documents' with twelve replies.) However, the timber industry translations were further divided into the following sub-fields (the figures in parentheses represent the number of translators who reported commissions in these topic areas; there may be some overlap between 'Wood products' and 'Carpentry'):

- paper (3)
- pulp (2)
- sawmills (2)
- wood products (2)

- carpentry (1)
- mechanical wood processing (1)

The sector 'timber industry' thus covers a variety of narrower sub-sectors, which are easier to handle in terms of corpus development, for example. However, there were few freelancers specializing on the same sub-fields and, considering the nature of freelance work, it was highly unlikely that we would have managed to put our corpus to the test in the time available. As a result, we decided to ask one of our industrial partners from the first phase to take part in the corpus experiment. UPM-Kymmene/Schauman Wood Oy is a major Finnish plywood manufacturer and exporter, and they were able to provide us with a test group of nine translators and other language professionals.

For the experiment, we compiled a monolingual (English) plywood corpus. The interviews and translation logs had shown that English was the most widely used foreign language in the company. Furthermore, translators with no training in English have to use English at work, which is yet another indication of the need for monolingual corpora to be used by language professionals. The corpus was designed on the basis of the interviews, translation logs and consultations with the senior translator at Schauman Wood, as well as of extensive surveys of potentially relevant websites (due to the time pressure we resorted to using the web as the main source of texts). The test corpus was relatively small, about 0.5 million words, and it comprised product descriptions (265,290 words), testing and research reports (220, 550 words), and a small amount of the company's in-house material, revised at the company's UK branch (27,000 words).

The test group at Schauman Wood were then trained to use the corpora and concordance software. The training session consisted of a general introduction to corpora followed by individual hands-on training sessions with a general-purpose corpus of English. At a later date there were recap sessions with the plywood corpus. The concordance program we used was WordSmith Tools 1.0[1] which was chosen for its simplicity and reliability. After the training sessions, the test group were left to test the two corpora on their everyday translation and other foreign language tasks. The testing period was roughly three to four weeks, after which the test group gave feedback on their experiences. On the whole, the testers' feedback was positive: they found the corpora useful and interesting – but, to our surprise, they had found the concordance program difficult to use. The feedback will be discussed in more detail below.

The test group had used both the general-purpose and the plywood corpus for both comprehension and production purposes. That is, they had sought, and found, information about unknown expressions or terms in the corpora. They had also sought help with producing idiomatic foreign language texts: which preposition to use, which verb goes with a term, which is of course typical collocational information. Many translators reported using the plywood corpus together with special-field dictionaries, which are notorious for providing lists of potential equivalents with no definitions or context. The special-purpose corpus then provided the necessary context and other information.

However, two translators in the test group had not been able to test the corpora because they did not have any English tasks during the test period (German and Russian instead). This is one of the disadvantages of a real-life field test, and in the future it could be avoided by having a longer test period. More alarmingly, two translators reported having used the corpora only rarely because they felt they were not able to fit learning the new program into their busy schedule. This is of course understandable – during hectic times, one needs to rely on routines and put off learning new things – yet disappointing. In fact, only one translator said that using the concordance program was easy once she had learned the ropes; for the others, the concordance program was the main stumbling-block in the test.

Discussion

The survey of the use of electronic tools showed that electronic tools are not as widely used by the translation industry as we had expected. On the basis of the informants' comments in the questionnaire, it seems that in the case of freelance translators in particular, electronic tools are considered risky investments. For one thing, there is not enough reliable information available to translators. The test results of new products are usually published in forums targeted at programmers and other computer enthusiasts. There is an obvious demand for usability testing of language and translation software products, the results of which should be published in translators' journals.

Another problem is that language and translation software products are created and tested by programmers or computer linguists, and translators are not necessarily contacted or consulted at any point. In many cases translators are the end users of the software, but the differences between the programmers' and the users' needs and skills tend to be ignored. As our findings show, the level of computer literacy in the field can provide surprises. It is interesting that in our case study the Finnish bilingual electronic dictionaries, which are basically the same as the printed ones, and the web, were used by virtually all the informants. Obviously these can be considered as relatively risk-free investments. It seems that we would need more user-friendly software to lower the technological threshold which slows down the introduction of language and translation software to the translation industry at large.

The findings of our study suggest that the following kinds of corpora might find a market among translators:

1. general-purpose monolingual corpora (both source and target languages) of about five to six million words. Such corpora can be produced commercially and the same corpora may well have a world

market, particularly in the case of 'large' languages (English, German, French, Spanish, etc.)

2. highly specialized corpora, such as the plywood corpus in our case study, which need to be compiled for limited use by translators or companies themselves. To do this, guidelines and strategies need to be developed, but producing actual corpora commercially is hardly feasible. In addition, it is important to train translators on how to compile their own corpora and how to use them at work. Corpus training should be integrated into translator training at the undergraduate level, but courses should also be offered as continuing education to practising translators

On the whole, our case study highlights the need for more cooperation in research and development between those who make the software products and those who end up using them (here translators). For example, we recommend more field tests with different concordance programs to see if we can find a good 'translator's concordancer'; if not, one needs to be developed, preferably in cooperation with practising translators. In sum, we feel that observing translators at work and consulting their needs is an essential part of developing tools which meet the users' needs and which are more user-friendly.

Notes

1 WSTools is licensed to the Savonlinna School of Translation Studies and it was used here for in-house research purposes only; after the test the corpora and the concordancer were removed from the testers' computers.

References

Jääskeläinen, Riitta and Mauranen, Anna (2000) 'Project SPIRIT. Development of a Corpus on the Timber Industry'. Unpublished research report. University of Joensuu: Savonlinna School of Translation Studies.

6 Extracting meteorological contexts from the newspaper corpus of Slovenian

Primož Jakopin

Introduction

Meteorology is very close to everyone and every field of our life and weather is a popular topic to start even an uneasy conversation. A quantitative description of language connected to weather and its phenomena is an interesting problem, the solution of which depends on the feasibility of processing large amounts of text from a suitable text corpus. The obvious three steps required would be:

1. to identify and separate proven meteorological contexts
2. to perform quantitative analysis of this test sample
3. to extract significant data using the entire corpus as a control sample

Weather forecasts, typical contexts of meteorologic language, are published daily in newspapers all around the world. In this paper the newspaper text collection of the BESEDA corpus (Jakopin 2000) is used. It is available at the Internet site http://bos.zrc-sazu.si of the Fran Ramovš Institute of Slovenian Language ZRC SAZU in Ljubljana and contains an electronic version of the leading Slovenian daily (*Delo*, 6 times a week) as available to the visually impaired. The period from January 1998 to February 2000 (approx. 35 million words) is covered in the study.

The BESEDA text corpus

The term *beseda* in Slovenian means *word* in English. It is the first freely accessible text corpus and is used extensively for research and educational purposes (over 10,000 accesses in a little over a year of online use).

Besides the *Delo* newspaper text collection, BESEDA also includes 3.2 million words of Slovenian fiction, original and translations, as well as 2.6 million words of English fiction – the complete works of Walter Scott, Oscar Wilde and Mark Twain. If used with the example of the above common phrase: *of the weather*, the screen in Figure 6.2 results.

beseda

TEXT CORPUS at the F. Ramovš Institute of Slovenian Language, ZRC-SAZU

of the weather [Submit]

Search range:
- ☑ Entire corpus - 48 mill. words, or
- ☐ A - Fiction in Slovenian - 2.2 MWords
- ☐ B - Fiction Transl. to Slovenian - 1.0 MWords
- ☐ D - DELO Slovenian Daily - 42.0 MWords
- ☐ E - Fiction in English - 2.6 MW

What to do:
- ◉ Concordances
- ○ Word search
- ○ Word search, reversed

Examples: se je zdelo - all occurrences of the phrase "se je zdelo".
svetlob* - words beginning with "svetlob".

Word search:		
	verjetno	- words containing the string "verjetno".
	wo=besed*	- all the words beginning with "besed".
	wo=*etnik	- all the words ending with "etnik".
	fr>125000	- words with frequency over 125000
	lg=5 and wo:skl	- words 5 letters long which contain "skl"
	"and"	- words containing "and".
	a and e and o and i and u	- words which contain all the vowels
	lg>30 and not wo:.	- words longer than 30 letters, no URLs

Figure 6.1 BESEDA front page

beseda *of Slovenia*

of the weather (9)

just as one might speak	of the weather,	or any other common matter	E MT_CY 17
just as when people speak	of the weather --	that he did not notice	E MT_CY 18
standing rigging forward	of the weather-	gaskets. Yes, it was a	E MT_CY 1974
on account of the state	of the weather.	We now placed our men.	E MT_TA 669
strangers. Then they spoke	of the weather	and the roads.We also spoke	E MT_TA 1648
roads. We also spoke	of the weather	and the roads.Next, they	E MT_TA 1649
divorce suits, the state	of the weather,	and the like, while the	E OW_LS 537
does now, on the state	of the weather.	If a frost comes we shall	E OW_SM 25
to stop by the severity	of the weather,	which proved the safety	E WS_CC 2844

(left env. word(s) right env. author abbrev. title abbrev. sentence number)

Figure 6.2 BESEDA – *of the weather* concordances

The left and right environments are not cut in the middle of the words – the words which would surpass the given limit (22 characters is the default value) are shown complete, but in smaller print. The column on the right side shows the origins of every phrase instance: an abbreviation of the author (E for English part of the corpus, MT for Mark Twain. OW for Oscar Wilde, WS for Walter Scott), a text title abbreviation (i.e. TA for *Tramp Abroad*) and a sentence number within the text. A click on the reference **E_MT_TA_669** would bring up the screen seen in Figure 6.3.

beseda of Slovenia

Mark Twain: A Tramp Abroad, **sentence 669 in context:**

The loading process was done in the presence of duly constituted witnesses. **We considered it best to perform this delicate service with the assistance of a lantern, on account of the state of the weather.** We now placed our men.

Figure 6.3 BESEDA – example of a sentence in context

One of the frequently used features of BESEDA, besides concordances, is the word search. It reveals 18 words in the corpus which contain *weather* as a string of characters, either at the beginning, end or in the middle of a word (Figure 6.4).

beseda of Slovenia

Wordform Dictionary Search

weather (18)

(No.	**wordform**	frequency)	(No.	**wordform**	frequency)
1.	fairweather	1	10.	weatherly	1
2.	mayweather	3	11.	weatherman	1
3.	mayweatherju	1	12.	weathernet	1
4.	sweatherjih	1	13.	weatherpoonovo	1
5.	weather	205	14.	weathers	5
6.	weatherall	1	15.	weatherspoon	10
7.	weatherbeaten	4	16.	weatherspoona	2
8.	weatherbrain	1	17.	weatherspoonom	1
9.	weathercock	4	18.	weathervane	1

Figure 6.4 *weather* as a word particle in BESEDA

There are 18 such instances, some as could be expected from an English viewpoint, some not (all instances are shown in lower case). Some endings require a special explanation and in Figure 6.5 the concordances of *weatherspoona* are shown to make things easier.

beseda *of Slovenia*

weatherspoona (2)

krilnega centra Clarencea	Weatherspoona	in visokega branilca Jima	D 98219	2961
Caffeyja (Chicago), Clarencea	Weatherspoona	in Jima Jacksona (oba	D 98304	3023

(left env. word(s) right env. author abbrev. title abbrev. sentence number)

Figure 6.5 Concordances of *weatherspoona*

This is the case of the name *Weatherspoon* (a basketball forward for Philadelphia), inflected according to grammatical rules for Slovenian nouns with an -on (or -un) ending.

Identification of meteorological contexts

It turned out that all weather forecasts in the *Delo* newspaper begin with the heading: *Napoved za Slovenijo* (*Forecast for Slovenia*). The phrase never occurred elsewhere, not even as a part of a sentence. In Table 6.1 a typical weather forecast from late summer is shown. Headings can be translated as *Forecast for neighbouring regions* (Napoved za sosednje pokrajine), *The weather situation* (Vremenska slika), *How it looks* (Kako kaže), *Sea and lake temperatures* (Temperature morja in jezer) and a term which could be roughly put as *Bioweather* in English (Biovreme, the influence of weather on the well-being of humans).

The weather forecast extraction was carried out by software – the second paragraph after the *Bioweather* heading taken as the end of the forecast. As this heading was missing in some cases, overlong forecasts were manually trimmed to normal size. In all, 578 weather forecasts were identified and grouped into a separate file.

Quantitative description of the forecast sample

The forecast collection contains 9243 sentences and headings, 82,680 words with 1538 different wordforms (after the manual cleanup of 152 errors). 17 double-word units (Bela_krajina, Biskajski_zaliv, Blejsko_jezero, Britansko_otočje, Črno_morje, Dinarsko_gorstvo, Genovski_zaliv,

Table 6.1 Weather forecast example

Napoved za Slovenijo
Danes bo delno jasno, zjutraj in del dopoldneva bo po nekaterih kotlinah megla ali nizka oblačnost. V gorskem svetu so popoldne možne posamezne, kratkotrajne plohe. Najnižje jutranje temperature bodo od 8 do 14, najvišje dnevne od 19 do 24, na Primorskem do 27 stopinj C.

Napoved za sosednje pokrajine
Povsod bo jasno, le v Alpah bo zmerno oblacno, pojavljale se bodo tudi posamezne plohe in nevihte.

Vremenska slika
Nad zahodno Evropo je območje visokega zračnega pritiska, nad severnim Atlantikom, Skandinavijo in Turčijo pa so območja nizkega zračnega pritiska. Hladna fronta se severno od Alp pomika proti vzhodu. Nad naše kraje s severozahodnimi vetrovi priteka prehodno nekoliko toplejši in bolj suh zrak.

Kako kaže
V sredo bo spet več oblačnosti. V severnih krajih so popoldne možne posamezne plohe. Tudi v četrtek bo vreme podobno. Malo topleje bo.

Temperature morja in jezer
Koper 24, Bled 22 stopinj C.

Biovreme
Vremenski vpliv na splošno počutje in razpoloženje ljudi bo ugoden in vzpodbuden. Pri najbolj občutljivih ljudeh bo spanje v noči na sredo moteno.

---

v_glavnem, Gorski_Kotar, Iberski_polotok, Jonsko_morje, Julijske_Alpe, Kvarnerski_zaliv, Padska_nižina, Panonska_nižina, Pirenejski_polotok, Severno_morje), such as Black Sea or British Isles, were connected with hard-space characters and so 1424 entries remained before lemmatization. After lemmatization, for which the statistical POS-tagger was used (Jakopin and Bizjak, 1997), 737 lemmas remained. In Table 6.2 the most frequent lemmas are shown.

In the table lemmas are followed by their frequencies in weather forecasts, total corpus frequencies, the share of the forecast frequencies in the total corpus frequencies (in per cent), and approximate English translations. *Oblačno* (*cloudy*) is therefore the top contender – its frequency in the forecast collection is 927 and its frequency in the entire corpus 1064, i.e. the chance that *cloudy* will appear in a weather forecast and not somewhere else is 87.1 per cent. It is followed by *precipitation* (70.6 per cent), *Primorsko* (58.8 per cent), *forecast* (48.6 per cent), *morning* (adj.) and *weather* (adj.) (47.3 per cent).

Table 6.2 Top 20 word lemmas from weather forecasts

1. napoved	1179	2424	48.6	forecast
2. Slovenija	1051	60,054	1.8	Slovenia
3. vremenski	1008	2132	47.3	weather (adj.)
4. oblačno	927	1064	87.1	cloudy (adv.)
5. jasen	905	12,211	7.4	clear
6. Primorsko	881	1499	58.8	region 'By the sea', Coastal region
7. kraj	871	11,620	7.5	place
8. temperatura	863	2237	38.6	temperature
9. stopinje	856	1886	45.4	degrees (C)
10. sosednji	844	3390	24.9	neighbouring
11. pokrajina	824	4447	18.5	region
12. pretežno	779	1744	44.7	predominantly, mostly
13. območje	735	10,981	6.7	area
14. padavine	670	949	70.6	precipitation
15. morje	608	5565	10.9	sea
16. kazati	604	9963	6.1	to show
17. veter	591	2639	22.4	wind
18. delno	581	2779	20.9	partly
19. jutranji	576	1219	47.3	morning (adj.)
20. zračni	574	1602	35.8	air (adj.)

In Table 6.3 a representation of the 6 most significant words from Table 6.2 in several Internet search services is given. As could be predicted the term *weather* is a clear winner, yet there are some unexpected and hard-to-explain fluctuations. If the shares of the most significant single-word meteo-terms in the entire corpus are relatively modest (Table 6.2), the most significant word pairs in Table 6.4 reveal a far more compelling picture. Only for the top 8 word bigrams is the chance that they will be found in weather forecasts greater than 99 per cent.

Table 6.3 Frequencies of the most significant meteorological BESEDA words on the Internet

	Google	Lycos	Yahoo	Altavista	Excite	Infoseek
cloudy	1,240,000	634,681	411,000	294,515	59,030	127,020
precipitation	1,290,000	1,122,884	913,000	2,172,083	31,375	151,833
coastal	2,090,000	1,441,651	980,000	1,118,107	710,635	367,393
forecast	4,650,000	2,397,555	219,000	1,672,765	426,845	566,023
morning	9,670,000	8,549,604	4,550,000	4,745,998	547,425	2,590,316
weather	23,300,000	18,364,548	11,000,000	8,527,229	6,977,368	3,056,858

Table 6.4 Most significant word bigrams from the weather forecasts

vremenska slika	567	568	99.82	weather situation
zračnega pritiska	556	557	99.82	(of) air pressure
visokega zračnega	318	319	99.69	high air
območje visokega	316	317	99.68	area (of) high
vremenski vpliv	294	295	99.66	weather influence
delno jasno	419	421	99.52	partly clear
pretežno oblačno	527	530	99.43	predominantly cloudy
nad naše	319	321	99.38	over our
za sosednje	566	577	98.09	for the neighbouring
kako kaže	566	583	97.08	how it looks

The last two tables (6.5 and 6.6) show the most frequent sentences from the weather forecasts. The number of units in this sample (578) is limited and the number of sentences (9243) modest, but even so the top 15 sentences exceed a frequency of 10.

Where sentences only differ by an added word they are shown together with an additional word, and its frequency, shown in parentheses. The most repetitive part of the forecasts obviously is the *Bioweather*, with a positive influence in 54 instances and negative in just 12. It will be colder in 33 instances and warmer in 16. A third of the sentences in the table forecast the weather in a brief, 4 to 6-word statement: *It will be . . .*

Table 6.5 Weather forecasts – top 15 sentences with frequencies

1. Vremenski vpliv na splošno počutje in razpoloženje ljudi bo ugoden (in vzpodbuden). 33 (21)
2. (Nekoliko) Hladneje bo. 24 (9)
3. Pihal bo jugozahodni veter. 24
4. (Nekoliko) Topleje bo. 10 (6)
5. Ob severnem Jadranu bo pihala burja. 16
6. Danes bo pretežno jasno. 15
7. Zjutraj bo ponekod po nižinah megla. 15
8. Spremenljivo do pretežno oblačno bo. 14
9. Nad večjim delom Evrope je območje visokega zračnega pritiska. 12
10. Vremenski vpliv na splošno počutje in razpoloženje ljudi bo obremenilen. 12
11. Pretežno jasno bo. 12
12. Nad večjim delom Evrope je območje nizkega zračnega pritiska. 11
13. Danes bo delno jasno s spremenljivo oblačnostjo. 11
14. Danes bo spremenljivo do pretežno oblačno. 11
15. (Razmeroma) Hladno bo. 9 (2)

Table 6.6 Weather forecasts – approximate English translations of top 15 sentences

1. *The influence of the weather on the well-being of the population will be positive (and encouraging).* 33 (21)
2. *It will be (somewhat) colder.* 24 (9)
3. *The southwestern wind will blow.* 24
4. *It will be (somewhat) warmer.* 10 (6)
5. *The Bora will blow on the Northern Adriatic.* 16
6. *Today it will be predominantly clear.* 15
7. *In several low-lying areas there will be fog in the morning.* 15
8. *It will be variable to moderately cloudy.* 14
9. *An area of high air pressure extends over the larger part of Europe.* 12
10. *The influence of the weather on the well-being of the population will be depressing.* 12
11. *It will be predominantly clear.* 12
12. *An area of low air pressure extends over the larger part of Europe.* 11
13. *Today it will be partly clear with variable cloudiness.* 11
14. *Today it will be variable to predominantly cloudy.* 11
15. *It will be (relatively) cold.* 9 (2)

Conclusion

A sample of highly controlled language, as appeared in two years of weather forecasts in a Slovenian daily newspaper, has been statistically evaluated. It has been shown that the single-word level is not enough to reveal proper significance – with *cloudy* and *precipitation* the only true representatives. The word bigram level, however, brought to the surface a number of distinct meteorological terms.

References

Jakopin, Primož (2000) 'BESEDA – a text corpus of Slovenian', *Digital resources for the humanities: conference abstracts, University of Sheffield, 10–13 September 2000*, pp. 70–2.

Jakopin, Primož and Bizjak, Aleksandra (1997) 'O oblikoslovnem označevanju slovenskega besedila [Part-of-speech Tagging of Slovenian Language]', *Slavistična revija* 45(3–4): 513–32.

7 The Hungarian possibility suffix *-hat/-het* as a dictionary entry

Ferenc Kiefer

Introduction

In Hungarian, possibility is normally expressed by the suffix *-hat/-het* 'may, can' rather than by an independent word. It is attached to verbs without any morphological (or morphophonological) change, consequently it yields morphotactically completely transparent structures. The choice between the front and the back vowel variant is conditioned by vowel harmony, e.g.

(1) *énekel+het* 'He/she can/may sing'
sing can

(2) *tanul+hat* 'He/she can/may learn/study'
learn can

The possibility suffix may occur after any derivational suffix but it must precede the tense and person markers.

(3) *énekel+het+ né+ k* 'I could/might sing'
sing can cond. I

(4) *énekel+get+ het+ né+ nek* 'They could/might sing (dim.)'
sing dim. can cond. they

(5) *énekel+tet+ get+ het+né+ l* 'You could make (sb) sing'
sing fact. dim. can cond. you

where *cond.* stands for the conditional, *dim.* for the diminutive and *fact.* for the factitive suffix. The possibility suffix is more like an inflectional suffix since it can be attached to any verb (as can inflectional suffixes), and it never creates new words: the forms containing the possibility suffix never get lexicalized in contrast to the genuine derivational suffixes such as the factitive *-tat/-tet*, or the diminutive *-gat/-get.*

The possibility suffix is often listed in mono- and bilingual dictionaries in spite of the fact that it is not an independent word (in fact, it is the only suffix which occurs as a dictionary entry). The reason for this may be twofold: first, its semantics is in principle not distinct from the semantics of full words, and, second, these meanings can be related systematically to the meanings of modal verbs in other languages.

A traditional dictionary entry

As an illustrative example let us consider the dictionary entry for the possibility suffix in the *Concise Explanatory Dictionary of the Hungarian Language* (1975), in which four meanings are distinguished:

(6)(a)	<ability or the possibility of an action>	
	Nem szívlelheti.	'She cannot bear him'
	Itt nyugodtan alhat.	'You can sleep here'
(b)	<permission>	
	Munka után hazamehet.	'You may go home after work'
	<polite request>	
	Kaphatnék egy kávét?	'Could I have a cup of coffee'
(c)	<probability>	
	A lelet az ókorból eredhet.	'This find may date from antiquity'
(d)	<corollary of an action>	
	(Ha ezt megteszi,) szégyellheti magát.	'If you do it, shame on you'

By looking at the dictionary entry (6a,b,c,d) two questions arise immediately: first, is the semantic description of the possibility suffix (6a,b,c,d) theoretically adequate? second, is the dictionary entry descriptively adequate?

The theoretical adequacy of the lexical entry

As to the first question it should first be noted that it is arguable that ability/capability is not a modal notion though it is closely related to modality (Kiefer 1988). In some languages, such as Hungarian, ability and possibility are expressed by different lexical items. For example, 'Bill can play the piano' is rendered in Hungarian by the sentence *Bill tud zongorázni,* in which the verb *tud* 'know, be able to' occurs and which is not equivalent with *Bill zongorázhat* 'Bill can/may play the piano'. The latter sentence expresses possibility and can never be used to express ability. Notice, however, that possibility normally presupposes ability: if someone knows how to play the piano there must be occasions in which he/she has the possibility of playing the piano, in other words, ability conversationally implicates possibility. This being the case the gloss in (6a) is certainly inadequate. On the other hand, neither the first nor the second example in (6a) denotes ability. The first example is an example of dispositional ('someone's dispositions are such that . . .'), the second one an example of circumstantial possibility ('the circumstances are such that . . .'). Finally, neither 'to bear someone' nor 'to sleep' denotes an action: the former is a state, the latter an intermediary category between state and action.

Secondly, permission and polite request are pragmatic notions though both are based on the semantic notion of deontic possibility ('it is permitted that . . .'). The semantic meaning of *Munka után hazamehet* 'You may go home after work' can be paraphrased as follows: 'in view of what the norms are or what is expected it is possible for you to go home after work'. In order to get the 'permission' reading further conditions must be met: there must be – in the given speech situation – an authority who has the right to grant permission, there must be a hearer who is able to execute whatever is permitted, etc. Similar considerations hold for the second example in (6b). The sentence *Kaphatnék egy kávét?* 'Could I have a cup of coffee?' is a modalized yes–no question and could, in principle, be answered by a plain 'yes' or 'no'. Notice that the possibility suffix is accompanied here by the conditional suffix *-né*. The same content can also be rendered without this suffix: *Kaphatok egy kávét?* 'May I have a cup of coffee?'. Both questions express indirectly a request but the conditional makes the request more polite. Indirect requests are themselves more polite than direct requests. How do we know that we have to do with an indirect request? Let us contrast the question *Kaphatok egy kávét?* using the verb *kap* 'get, receive' with the question *Elvihetem ezt a könyvet?* 'May I take along this book?', which contains the verb *elvisz* 'take along'. By uttering this latter sentence the speaker asks for permission. The sentence cannot be used to express indirect request. Consequently, the pragmatic (speech act) meaning of an utterance is not independent of its semantics. All this is well-known from the literature (cf., for example, the papers in Cole and Morgan (eds) 1975), but what kind of conclusions can we draw from these observations with respect to the dictionary entry of the possibility suffix? First, it should be made clear that the first example in (6b) denotes deontic possibility with the speech act meaning 'permission', and, secondly, that the second example conventionally conveys an indirect request.

As to the third use of the possibility suffix, notice that the example in (6c) expresses probability only if the second constituent *az ókorból* 'from antiquity' is stressed. In that case it occupies the position immediately preceding the verb. On the other hand, the sentence, *A lelet eredhet az ókorból* 'It is possible (not excluded) that this find dates from antiquity', where the verb carries stress, means plain epistemic possibility ('it is not excluded that such and such a state of affairs holds'). Both probability and plain possibility are epistemic modals; the latter, however, is left unmentioned in the dictionary entry.

The last example (6d) is the most problematic one. It would seem that this sentence does not express modality at all: it is rather an idiomatic expression used in reproaches. Notice also that the English equivalent does not contain any modal. Similar examples are legion. It should also be noted that the English gloss 'corollary of an action' does not do justice to the Hungarian equivalent, which runs as follows: *Annak kifejezésére, hogy vkinek (helyzetéből adódóan) vmit tennie kell*, i.e. the suffix can be used 'to express the fact that someone must do something due to his/her position' and does not cover what is meant by the utterance in (6d) at all. In fact the utterance in (6d) is just one example of the many pragmatic functions which the possibility suffix may convey.

We may thus conclude that the lexical entry in (6a,b,c,d) is theoretically clearly inadequate.

The descriptive adequacy of the dictionary entry

It is easy to see that (6a,b,c,d) fails to satisfy the criterion of descriptive adequacy as well: the entry does not even cover the most important and salient uses of the possibility suffix (Kiefer 1983). It was already pointed out above that, though the probability sense figures in the dictionary entry, no mention is made of the plain epistemic sense ('objective epistemic possibility', Lyons 1977). Another example in which this sense can be found is the sentence *Bill can be at home but he can also be somewhere else.* In addition, theoretical works on modality (Kratzer 1978, 1981, Kiefer 1983, Öhlschläger 1989) also discuss the circumstantial ('the circumstances are such that it is possible that such and such a state of affairs holds'), dispositional ('the dispositions of the speaker are such that he/she can bring about such and such a state of affairs') and boulomaic ('in view of the speaker's wishes such and such a state of affairs can pertain'). The sentence (7a) is an example of circumstantial, (7b) an example of dispositional and (7c) an example of boulomaic possibility.

(7)(a)	*Itt pihenhetsz.*	'You may relax here' ('The circumstances here are such that . . .')
(b)	*Most énekelhetek.*	'I can sing now' ('The speaker's dispositions now are such that . . .')
(c)	*Bill lehetne a vezérünk.*	'Bill could be our leader' ('In view of the speaker's wishes . . .')

Theoretical work on modality may thus help us to identify further senses of the possibility suffix, but even without theoretical considerations, merely relying on intuition, we may easily come up with some more senses of *-hat/-het.* Let me just mention two of them. The first one may be termed 'dissociating possibility', exemplified in (8a), and the second one 'conformistic obligation', exemplified in (8b).

(8)(a)	*Tőlem elveheted Annát feleségül.*	'I don't care, you can marry Anna (if you want)'
(b)	*Most kezdhetem elölről.*	'Now I have to do it all over again'

The dissociating possibility meaning requires a special context or phrase (such as *tőlem* 'I don't care', German 'von mir aus') without which other modal meanings may become more salient. The sentence (8a), for example, if *tőlem* is omitted, would be taken to mean deontic possibility (permission). Typically, the sentence (8b) is uttered in a situation when something has misfired and therefore something must be done to repair it. In other words, (8b) expresses necessity rather than possibility. Once again, in order to get this reading a special context is called for. Typical sentences in which the conformistic obligation sense of *-hat/-het* prevails are conditionals ('if I do x, I must do y') and coordinated structures that admit the cause–effect interpretation ('A did x, therefore A must do y').

In sum, then, even without consulting a larger corpus, we must conclude that the traditional description is descriptively inadequate as well.

Next, let us see what the corpus can tell us about the possibility suffix.

The corpus

For the pilot study a smaller corpus containing approximately 15,000 running words was used. This corpus constitutes a subset of the corpus of the *Comprehensive Dictionary of Hungarian* (20 million running words). In the corpus 387 modal sentences were found, of which 82 were deontic, 46 epistemic and 77 circumstantial; the rest were other modal uses or idiomatic phrases containing the possibility suffix. No examples of dispositional or boulomaic possibility were found. In some cases the possibility suffix did not express modality (e.g. *Ugyan, mit akarhat?* 'I wonder what he wants?' – lit. 'what he can want?').

The use of the possibility suffix was analysed by using complete sentences however long they were. The longest sentence contained 62 words but also some one-word sentences were found (e.g. *Telefonálhatok?* 'May I make a phone call?', *Távozhatok?* 'May I leave?'). If the modal sentence was preceded by a question, the analysis was extended to the question–answer pair (e.g. *A Hiltonban lakik?* 'Does he stay at the Hilton?' – *Nagyszerű, gyalog átsétálhat* 'Excellent, then he can just walk over').

Special attention was paid to modal uses not mentioned in theoretical works as well as to the pragmatic functions of the possibility suffix.

Further uses of the possibility suffix

On the basis of the corpus some further uses of the possibility suffix could be identified. In doing so we found the description of the English modals *can* and *may* in the *Collins-Cobuild English Dictionary* particularly helpful.

In modal expressions such as *látható* 'visible', *használható* 'usable', *mosható* 'washable', *vasalható* 'suitable for ironing', *megmunkálható* 'workable', etc., a quality is mentioned people may make use of if they want to. Consider

(9)(a)	*Ez az anyag könnyen mosható.*	'This material can be washed easily'
(b)	*Ez a szerszám sok mindenre használható.*	'This tool can be used for quite a few things'

This use of the possibility suffix can be extended to certain types of facts. For example,

(10)(a)	*A kiállítás hétfőn nem látogatható.*	'The exhibition cannot be visited on Monday'
(b)	*A könyvklub a második emeleten található.*	'The book club can be found on the second floor'

The following use of the possibility suffix is related, but not identical, to its epistemic use. It is used to indicate that something may sometimes be the case.

(11)(a)	*A terápia több évig eltarthat.*	'The therapy may last several years'
(b)	*A főzelék odaéghet.*	'The vegetables may get burnt'
(c)	*A szívtrombózis hirtelen halált okozhat.*	'Coronary failure may cause sudden death'

As we saw above, the possibility suffix indicates necessity in the case of conformistic obligation, but this is not the only case when possibility is used to express necessity. Consider

(12)(a)	*Nemcsak a rangnak, hanem a tanult foglalkozásnak is búcsút mondhattak.*	'They had to renounce not only their ranks but also their professions'
(b)	*Legalább öt évig dolgozhatom éjjel-nappal, amíg kiheverem valahogyan ezt a csapást.*	'I must work day and night for at least five years to get over this misfortune'

In both (12a) and (12b) the possibility suffix occurs in a negative context. This observation may perhaps be generalized to the following statement: possibility means necessity whenever it occurs in a negative context.

To summarize, in the dictionary entry of the possibility suffix we must distinguish at least the following uses: (a) epistemic possibility including probability, (b) deontic possibility, (c) circumstantial possibility, (d) dispositional possibility, (e) boulomaic possibility, (f) dissociating possibility, (g) conformistic obligation, (h) to express a quality or a fact which people may make use of, (i) to express the fact that something may sometimes be the case, (j) possibility in negative context. These uses are all semantically distinct.

On the pragmatics of possibility

The expression of possibility can systematically be used to convey certain types of pragmatic meanings. The relationship between deontic possibility and permission has already been mentioned above. We repeat the example (6b) under (13a). (13b) is yet another example of permission.

(13)(a)	*Munka után hazamehet.*	'You may go home after work'
(b)	*Most már leülhet.*	'You may sit down now'

Correspondingly, the negation of (13a,b) means prohibition.

The pragmatic uses listed under 8 and 10 through 12 in the Collins-Cobuild dictionary are also attested in Hungarian. The possibility suffix can be used in questions in order to make suggestions or to offer to do something, e.g. *Segíthetek?* 'May I help you?' It can also be used in questions to start a conversation, e.g. *Kérdezhetek valamit?* 'May I ask you something?' As in English, the possibility suffix can be used with verbs such as *képzel* 'imagine', *hisz* 'believe', *gondol* 'think' in order to emphasize how you feel about a particular situation, e.g. *Gondolhatod, milyen boldog voltam* 'You can't think how glad I was'. And again, as in English, the possibility suffix in questions with *hogy* 'how' is used to indicate that you feel strongly about something, e.g. *Hogy mondhatsz ilyet?* 'How can you say such a thing?'. Polite requests, however (see the use under 9), are not always expressed by means of the possibility suffix in Hungarian. Compare *Megnézhetem?* 'May I have a look at it?' but *Tudnál segíteni?* 'Can you please help?' In the second example the conditional of the verb *tud* 'know, be able to' is used.

Idiomatic phrases containing the verbs *tud* 'know' or *mond* 'say' with pragmatic meanings are quite frequent. Such phrases must be listed separately, they cannot be brought under the heading of any of the more general pragmatic meanings.

(14)(a)	*Azt te sem tudhatod.*	'Don't be so sure'
(b)	*Azt én nem tudhatom.*	'How should I know'
(c)	*Tudhatja, hogy ki nem állhatom.*	'You should know that I cannot bear the very sight of him.'
(15)(a)	*Én mondhatom!*	'I can assure you'
(b)	*Na, mondhatom.*	'Well I never'
(c)	*Mondhatták az öreg asszonynak, hogy a fia rossz, ő tudta, hogy jó.*	'They were telling the old woman in vain that her son is wicked, she knew that he was a good boy'

All these phrases have particular discourse functions. Their analysis, however, would go much beyond the scope of the present paper.

Conclusion

The possibility suffix is notoriously polysemous. Starting out with a traditional dictionary entry for this suffix it was shown that the traditional description was neither theoretically nor descriptively adequate. We argued that theoretical considerations may help us to get rid of the theoretical shortcomings and that a higher descriptive adequacy may be attained by using corpora. However, the main point was that we needed both: a good theory and reliable material.

Theory helps us to characterize the various uses of the possibility suffix in a more precise way by making use of notions such as epistemic, deontic, circumstantial, boulomaic and dispositional modality and by distinguishing meaning and use, i.e. semantics and pragmatic function. On the other hand, the use of corpora is indispensable if one wants to get a wider coverage of the uses of the possibility suffix. Consequently, by combining theory and corpus work two important goals can be achieved: the description will be theoretically as well as descriptively more adequate, which may have important consequences for lexicography as well.

References

Cole, Peter and Morgan, Jerry L. (eds) (1975) *Syntax and Semantics 3, Speech Acts.* New York: Academic Press.

Juhász, József *et al.* (eds) (1975) *Magyar Értelmező Kéziszótár* ('Concise Explanatory Dictionary of the Hungarian Language'). Budapest: Akadémia Kiadó.

Kiefer, Ferenc (1983) 'What is possible in Hungarian?', *Acta Linguistica Hungarica* 33: 149–87.

Kiefer, Ferenc (1988) 'Ability and possibility: the Hungarian verb *tud* "to be able to" ', *Studies in Language* 12(2): 393–423.

Kiefer, Ferenc (1999) 'La modalité et la pragmatique', *Revue d'études françaises* 3: 25–31.

Kratzer, Angelika (1978) *Semantik der Rede. Kontexttheorie-Modalwörter-Konditionalsätze.* Königstein: Scriptor.

Kratzer, Angelika (1981) 'The notional category of modality', in Eikmeyer, Hans-Jürgen and Rieser, Hannes (eds) *Words, Worlds, and Contexts. New Approaches in Word Semantics.* Berlin: de Gruyter, pp. 38–74.

Lyons, John (1977) *Semantics,* Vols I-II. Cambridge: Cambridge University Press.

Öhlschläger, Günther (1989) *Zur Syntax und Semantik der Modalverben des Deutschen.* Tübingen: Niemeyer.

Sinclair, John (ed.) (1995) *Collins Cobuild English Dictionary.* London: HarperCollins.

8 Dictionaries, corpora and word-formation

Simon Krek, Vojko Gorjanc and Marko Stabej

Introduction

A lexicographer creating a list of possible words to be included in a comprehensive bilingual dictionary and producing corresponding dictionary entries might run into some difficulties when dealing with derivatives which are treated quite differently in monolingual dictionaries compared to bilingual dictionaries. While the latter provides translation equivalents for the entry word, monolingual dictionaries can use various strategies for presenting derivatives in their structure. If the derived form is not itself a headword, which is the case when its meaning cannot be directly associated with the primitive, one of the most popular techniques is to enter the derivative at the end of the corresponding entry as a non-defined run-on entry – tacitly suggesting that it takes all the senses of the primitive.

The problem of derivatives emerged during work on the new English-Slovene Dictionary. The task of deciding which derived form deserves to be included in the dictionary, and which of their senses should be taken into account, proved to be more difficult than expected. This paper presents some of the findings using the example of adverbs derived from adjectives and ending in *-ly*. Within the article, four English monolingual dictionaries will be examined more closely, two of them EFL dictionaries (CCELD, LDOCE) and two general-purpose dictionaries (CED, NODE), together with four bilingual dictionaries (CREFD, OHEFD, ODEGD, CESD) and data from corpora.

Microstructure

English monolingual dictionaries use the run-on entry technique quite frequently. The only monolingual dictionary of those mentioned above with a slightly different style is CCELD, which lists derivatives within their corresponding senses, thus indicating precisely in which sense they are used. It does not give a definition, but systematically provides an example of usage, which together gives more information than simply listing the derivative at the end of the entry. In certain (relatively rare) cases, LDOCE and NODE also provide an example within the run-on entry.

As Adam Kilgarriff (1998: 51) reports in his survey, among the tasks that monolingual lexicographers find the most difficult or hardest, deciding on run-on entries ends up in the last place as the simplest task. It seems that in monolingual lexicography, morphology is not considered to be a very exciting issue. However, there are quite a number of examples that show how derivatives do not take all the meanings of the primitives or that these are distributed differently. EFL dictionaries – especially CCELD – are generally more sensitive to the nuances of sense distribution in derivatives than the general-purpose dictionaries. Bilingual dictionaries, on the other hand, compelled to show the senses of derivatives more explicitly because of the necessity to provide translation equivalents, are faced with two pitfalls if they rely on information from monolingual dictionaries: (a) a derivative may take only some of the senses of the primitive which may be (b) arranged differently according to frequency. Below an example for each of the problems can be found and in Appendix 1 entries from the relevant dictionaries are reproduced.

Senses not transferred

affected – affectedly: CED and NODE agree on three senses of the adjective – 1. (detrimentally) changed/influenced (by an external factor); 2. artificial, pretentious, designed to impress; 3. (archaic) disposed or inclined in a specified way; – while CED identifies two more senses – 4. deeply moved; 5. feigned. LDOCE and CCELD recognize only the most frequent sense: not sincere, unnatural (in behaviour). Bilingual dictionaries take a different approach: CREFD and ODEGD follow EFL dictionaries and provide translation equivalents only for the most frequent sense of the adjective while OHEFD and CESD also take into account less frequent senses, which results in a drastic difference in sense distribution between the adjective and the derived adverb since the latter preserves only the most frequent sense, which is also confirmed by the data from the British National Corpus (BNC) (five hits).

Different sense distribution

awkward – awkwardly: monolingual dictionaries differ greatly in the semantic analysis of the adjective. However, one can roughly identify some of the more general senses: 1. difficult, hard to deal with, inconvenient; 2. embarrassing, uncomfortable, clumsy, shy; 3. unhelpful, uncooperative. While the adverb is unyieldingly treated as a run-on entry in the monolingual dictionaries, the bilingual dictionaries seem to show that the adverb is more frequently used in the second sense, which is also confirmed by the most frequent verbal collocates in the BNC (say, stand, fall, smile, shuffle, scramble, sit, shift, rise, etc.).

One could, therefore, conclude that the run-on entry technique found in monolingual dictionaries sometimes obscures latent differences in sense distribution between the primitive and the derivative, while bilingual dictionaries are forced to make these differences more explicit. The real issue in this context is probably the reasoning behind the run-on entry technique. By listing derivatives as run-on entries, also in cases where they do not take all the senses of the primitive or where these are distributed differently according to frequency, monolingual dictionaries, and especially desk dictionaries, show that – in the case of derivatives – they are primarily concerned with the form, not the content. As long as the factual senses of the derivative remain within the span of derivable senses of the primitive, it seems not to matter whether all of the implied senses are realized or realizable at all and which of them are the most frequent. While a great space-saver, the run-on entry technique can therefore also be a bit deceitful and somewhat unfairly leaves the interpretation of the sense to the dictionary user. Particularly in cases when the derivative is in itself a fairly frequent lexical item, relying solely on the form is a bit dangerous from the lexicographer's point of view as dictionaries are primarily concerned with the meaning, and such items tend to develop their own independent life in specific contexts, attract different collocates, etc. There is no inherent reason why the primitive should get the full treatment – in contrast with the derivative – except for space-saving reasons and dictionary users would probably profit from a more moderate use of the run-on entry technique.

Macrostructure

When looking for possible candidates to expand the headword list, again one has to take into account the indiscriminate policy of English monolingual desk dictionaries regarding run-on entries.

It has been noted more than once that at the core of lexicography there lies 'an ill-acknowledged, subjective notion of importance. Important words need fuller treatment' (Kilgarriff 1994: 101), but the problem is how one knows which lexical items are more important. With the advent of corpora, the answer seemed to be firmer: those that are more frequent. Yet, the notorious question of corpus representativeness and size poses itself immediately. A lot of effort was put into designing the criteria for corpus representativeness, with the British National Corpus as probably the most prominent example of this approach. On the other hand, it was also argued that 'corpora of finite size were inherently deficient because any corpus is such a tiny sample of a language in use that there can be little finality in the statistics. [. . .] At this stage we simply do not know how big a corpus needs to be for general or particular purposes' (Kennedy 1998: 68), or 'experience has shown that even when working with corpora that are all based on the principle of representativeness, different corpora will present the lexicographer with different frequencies for words and repeated strings' (Summers 1996: 261) and 'even on the basis of very large corpora, word counts for all but the few thousand most frequent words are highly unstable' (Kilgarriff 1997: 150).

In the last years, corpus linguists have turned to the web as 'the corpus of the new millennium' (Kilgarriff 2001: 344). Software which extracts linguistic information from the web has emerged (http://www.webcorp.org.uk) but as one of the explorers of this trend put it, 'compared to the web, the BNC is an English country garden' (Kilgarriff 2001: 342). And indeed, statistics will show later on that it is hard to reach any sensible conclusions out of the results of a simple web search, except that whichever item is looked for, it usually can be found.

To get a clearer picture of the status of derived adverbs ending in *-ly* in dictionaries and corpora, three tables comparing the existence or non-existence of these items in different dictionaries and corpora were prepared. Table 1 in Appendix 2 shows adverbs ending in *-ly* (letter A) from the OHEFD headword list. The adverbs are listed according to the numbers in the second column which contains the number of hits in the BNC. Other columns provide information from two bilingual dictionaries, two EFL monolingual dictionaries and two desk monolingual dictionaries for native speakers of English. The results could be summarized as follows:

Monolingual desk dictionaries strictly follow their policy of incorporating derivatives as run-on entries regardless of their frequency. Thus we can find adverbs with more than one thousand hits in the BNC (approximately, automatically, actively, accurately, abruptly, etc.) having the same status as those with one hit or no hits (abstemiously, antithetically, attributively, etc.). Only a strikingly significant shift in meaning brings them headword status (actually, absolutely, accordingly, admittedly, awfully, etc.), mostly when they function as intensifiers or sentence adverbs. In CED there are also some allegedly frequent items missing (additionally, approvingly).

EFL dictionaries also follow the run-on status policy but different approaches bring about different results. As CCELD always provides an example of usage, it cuts off the derivatives at a higher point – at 11 hits in the BNC. What seems particularly interesting is that in spite of being based on a different corpus (the Bank of English), the dividing line is quite sharp with only one additional item below the line (atrociously) and two missing above (austerely, agitatedly). LDOCE continues further down the list, but also pays more attention to frequency information, confirming the declared policy that 'a word should only be entered as a run-on if, among other things, it was less frequent than the headword and was not in itself a frequent or important word' (Kilgarriff 1997: 146). Thus, some of the more frequent adverbs with the run-on status in desk dictionaries become headwords in LDOCE (automatically, allegedly, acutely, aptly, absurdly, etc.). Furthermore, it can be noticed that also in LDOCE some allegedly frequent items are missing (avidly, avowedly, agitatedly), but these are rare and in general EFL dictionaries show remarkable compliance with the frequency data from the BNC.

The other two bilingual dictionaries show somewhat similar patterns to CCELD, with a far less sharp breaking point at approximately 10 hits in the BNC. Quite a few allegedly frequent items are missing (adversely, appreciatively, appallingly, administratively, architecturally, arrogantly, adamantly, etc.)

Table 2 in appendix 2 shows the collection of adverbs ending in *-ly* listed as derivatives in NODE whose primitives appear in the OHEFD headword list. The adverbs are listed according to the numbers from the BNC starting from the most frequent item. One extra column is added which shows the number of hits produced by the Google web search engine in November 2001. Again, some generalizations:

Monolingual desk dictionaries show more dissonance on that list, especially with less frequent items in the BNC (adaptably, adiabatically, adoptively, adultly, agronomically, etc.). Of the more frequent ones, some of them are again missing in CED (anecdotally, aerobically, amusedly).

EFL dictionaries show the same pattern as on the previous list. CCELD lists some isolated items from the beginning of the list but, nevertheless, a number of adverbs with more than 10 hits in BNC are 'missing' (aerobically, anomalously, analogously, alertly, anecdotally). LDOCE continues further down the list with sporadic hits but also misses quite a few allegedly frequent items (analytically, aerobically, anciently, etc.).

The two bilingual dictionaries analysed differ greatly, with CREFD listing only one item and ODEGD recording eight.

Google shows an interesting picture:

1. all the items can be found on the web, starting with 23 (annalistically) to more than 100,000 hits (analytically)
2. some of the highest scores can be attributed to technical material (analytically, algebraically, anomalously, algorithmically, etc.)
3. very roughly the numbers from the web follow the pattern from the BNC, with quite a few exceptions

When expanding a headword list with derivatives, one has to take into account several factors. The analysed dictionaries show considerable consensus about the list of derivatives which are frequent in the available balanced corpus of 100 million words. Since this list coincides with the usual size of EFL dictionaries and bilingual dictionaries (40–60,000 entries in total), one could conclude that the derivatives found in these dictionaries are all feasible candidates for expansion. The dissonance begins with items which are rare in that type of corpora. Therefore, the logical answer is in expanding the balanced corpus beyond the limited size while keeping its characteristics intact. The web, however, with its massive and chaotic collection of lexical material will probably always vastly surpass any balanced corpus in size and once the relevance of a lexical item is established through a more reliable source, it can provide more information about it.

Conclusion

On the basis of the analysed data, it can be concluded that in English monolingual dictionaries the information about derivatives is to some extent imprecise, concentrating on the form rather than on the content. The data from corpora helps but since also in large corpora derivatives are usually not very frequent, the maxim is: the bigger the corpus, the better. The web is becoming the biggest corpus available and even though frequency counts produced by search engines are unreliable, they can help to assess the importance of lexical items where data from other sources is scarce.

References

CCELD (1995) *The Collins Cobuild English Language Dictionary*, 2nd edn. London: HarperCollins.

CED (1994) *The Collins English Dictionary*, 3rd edn. London: HarperCollins.

CESD (unpublished) *The Comprehensive English-Slovene Dictionary*. Ljubljana: DZS.

CREFD (1995) *The Collins-Robert English-French Dictionary*, 4th edn. Birmingham: HarperCollins.

Kennedy, Graeme (1998) *An Introduction to Corpus Linguistics*. London: Longman.

Kilgarriff, Adam (1994) 'The Myth of Completeness and Some Problems with Consistency,' in Martin, Willy *et al.* (eds) *Euralex '94 Proceedings*, Amsterdam, pp. 101–6.

Kilgarriff, Adam (1997) 'Putting frequencies in the dictionary', *International Journal of Lexicography* 10(2): 135–55.

Kilgarriff, Adam (1998) 'The hard parts of lexicography', *International Journal of Lexicography* 11(1): 51–4.

Kilgarriff, Adam (2001) 'Web as corpus', in Rayson, Paul *et al.* (eds) *Proceedings of the Corpus Linguistics 2001 Conference*, Lancaster: UCREL, pp. 342–4.

LDOCE (1995) *The Longman Dictionary of Contemporary English*, 3rd edn. Harlow: Longman.

NODE (1998) *The New Oxford Dictionary of English*. Oxford: Oxford University Press.

ODEGD (1996) *The Oxford Duden English-German Dictionary*, 2nd edn. Oxford: Oxford University Press.

OHEFD (1994) *The Oxford-Hachette English-French Dictionary*. Oxford: Oxford University Press.

Summers, Della (1996) 'Computer lexicography: the importance of representativeness in relation to frequency', in Thomas, Jenny and Short, Mick (eds) *Using Corpora for Language Research: Studies in honour of Geoffrey Leech*. London: Longman, pp. 260–6.

APPENDIX 1

AFFECTED–AFFECTEDLY

NODE

affected
adjective
1 influenced or touched by an external factor: *affected areas.*
2 artificial, pretentious, and designed to impress: *the gesture appeared both affected and stagy.*
3 [PREDIC.] archaic disposed or inclined in a specified way: *you might become differently affected towards him.*
DERIVATIVES
affectedly adverb.

CED

affected 1 *adj.* (*usually postpositive*)
1. deeply moved, esp. by sorrow or grief: *he was greatly affected by her departure.*
2. changed, esp. detrimentally.

affected 2 *adj.*
1. behaving, speaking, etc., in an artificial or assumed way, esp. in order to impress others.
2. feigned: *affected indifference.*
3. *archaic.* inclined; disposed.

— **affectedly** *adv.*
— **affectedness** *n.*

OHEFD

affected *adjective*
1 (influenced) (by event, change, decision) (adversely) **touché (by par)**; (neutrally, positively) **concerné (by par)**; affected by the disaster **sinistré**;
2 (emotionally) **ému (by par)**; (adversely) **affecté (by par)**;
3 medicine [*part*] **infecté (by par)**; [*person*] **atteint (by de)**;

4 pejorative (mannered) **affecté**;
5 pejorative (feigned) **affecté**.

affectedly *adverb* [**behave, speak**] **avec affectation**.

CESD

affected *prid.* **1** slabš. izumetničen, zaigran, prisiljen, afektiran; hlinjen, lažen; **that affected accent of hers** ta njen izumetničeni naglas; **affected politeness** hlinjena vljudnost **2** prizadet; podvržen, pod vplivom; **those affected by the disaster** tisti ki jih je prizadela nesreča **3** ganjen; prizadet; **she was greatly affected by his departure** njegov odhod jo je globoko prizadel **4** obolel; **it may cause pain in the affected part** povzroči lahko bolečine v obolelem predelu **5** zastar. nastrojen, razpoložen

affectedly *prisl.* izumetničeno, zaigrano, prisiljeno, afektirano; hlinjeno; **they spoke so affectedly** govorili so na tako izumetničen način

AWKWARD–AWKWARDLY

OHEFD

awkward *adjective*
1 (not practical) [*tool*] **peu commode**; [*shape, design*] **difficile**; /. . ./
2 (clumsy) [*person, movement, gesture*] **maladroit**; [*prose, style*] **gauche**;
3 (complicated, inconvenient) [*arrangement, issue*] **compliqué, difficile**; [*choice*] **difficile**; [*moment, day*] **mal choisi**; /. . ./
4 (embarrassing) [*question*] **embarrassant**; [*situation*] **délicat**; [*silence*] **gêné**;
5 (embarrassed) **mal à l'aise, gêné**; /. . ./
6 (uncooperative) [*person*] **difficile** (about **à propos de**); /. . ./

awkwardly *adverb*
1 (inconveniently) awkwardly placed/designed **mal placé/conçu**; /. . ./
2 (clumsily) [*move, hold, express oneself*] **maladroitement, avec maladresse**; [*fall, land*] **lourdement**;
3 (with embarrassment) [*speak, apologize*] **d'un ton gêné**; [*behave*] **d'une manière embarrassée**.

CREFD

awkward *adjective*
a (inconvenient, difficult etc)
tool **peu commode, peu maniable, mal conçu**
path **difficile, malaisé**
(Aut) bend **difficile** *or* **malaisé à négocier**
problem, task **délicat**
question **gênant, embarrassant**
silence **gêné, embarrassé**
situation **délicat, gênant**
b (clumsy)
person **gauche, maladroit, empoté***

movement, gesture **maladroit, peu élégant**
style **gauche, lourd, peu élégant**

awkwardly *adverb*
a speak **d'un ton embarrassé** or **gêné**
b behave, handle **gauchement, maladroitement**
move, walk **maladroitement, peu élégamment**
awkwardly placed **placé à un endroit difficile** *or* **gênant**
awkwardly expressed **gauchement exprimé, mal dit**

awkward *prid.* **1** mučen, zoprn; nelagoden, neprijeten; neroden, kočljiv; **an awkward pause** mučen premor; **awkward questions** neprijetna vprašanja; **to make life awkward for sb** komu zagreniti življenje **2** neugoden, nepravi, neprikladen, neprimeren, neroden; **at an awkward time** ob neugodnem času; **it's a bit awkward: I'm so busy** nekoliko nerodno je veliko dela imam **3** okoren, neroden, nespreten; nepriročen, nepraktičen; **to be sitting in an awkward position** sedeti v nerodnem položaju; **the device was awkward to use** naprava je bila zelo nepriročna; **with this toothbrush you can get at all the awkward corners** s to zobno ščetko je mogoče doseči najbolj nedostopne predele; **the room has awkward proportions** soba ima nepraktične dimenzije **4** v zadregi, nelagodno, neprijetno; **she felt awkward about leaving** nerodno ji je bilo ker je morala oditi **5** težaven, težek; problematičen; nekooperativen; **she's a very awkward girl to be with** z njo je težko; zelo težavna je; **he's being awkward about the whole thing** pri vsej stvari ni čisto nič v pomoč **6** težek, tvegan, nevaren; **an awkward ascent of the ridge** nevaren vzpon na gorsko sleme **7** *zastar.* perverzen

IDIOMI: the awkward age telečja leta; **an awkward customer** čuden tič; težaven človek; **the awkward squad** *pog. šalj. VB* nergači; (v vojski) novinci

awkwardly *prisl.* **1** neugodno, neprikladno, neprimerno, nerodno; **awkwardly for me he was only free at 10 o'clock** na mojo smolo je imel čas samo ob desetih **2** okorno, nerodno, nespretno; nepraktično; **he fell awkwardly** nerodno je padel; **awkwardly designed** nepraktično oblikovan **3** v zadregi, nesproščeno; **she patted my shoulder awkwardly** v zadregi me je potrepljala po rami

APPENDIX 2

TABLE 1

OHEFD	BNC	CREFD	ODEGD	CCELD	LDOCE	NODE	CED
abstemiously		–	–	–	R	R	R
antithetically	**1**	+	–	–	–	R	–
attributively	**1**	+	–	–	R	R	R
accommodatingly	**2**	–	+	–	–	R	R
adverbially	**2**	+	+	–	–	R	R
allusively	**2**	+	–	–	R	R	R
appositely	**2**	–	+	–	R	R	R
adjectivally	**3**	+	–	–	R	R	–
angelically	**4**	–	–	–	R	R	R
affectedly	**5**	+	+	–	–	R	R
arduously	**5**	+	+	–	R	R	R
auspiciously	**5**	+	+	–	–	R	R
amorously	**6**	+	+	–	R	R	R
antagonistically	**6**	–	–	–	R	R	R
allegorically	**7**	+	–	–	R	R	R
atrociously	**7**	+	+	RE	R	R	R
articulately	**8**	+	+	–	R	R	R
abrasively	**10**	–	–	–	R	–	–
abusively	**11**	–	–	–	R	R	R
artlessly	**11**	+	+	–	R	R	R
audaciously	**11**	+	+	RE	R	R	R
adoringly	**18**	+	–	RE	–	R	R
astronomically	**18**	+	R	RE	R	R	R
abysmally	**20**	+	–	RE	RE	R	R
abjectly	**21**	+	+	RE	R	R	R
abominably	**22**	+	+	RE	RE	R	R
affirmatively	**24**	+	+	RE	R	R	R
austerely	**25**	+	+	–	R	R	R
advisedly	**27**	+	+	+	+	+	R
advantageously	**29**	–	+	RE	R	R	R
astutely	**29**	+	+	RE	R	R	R

TABLE 1—*continued*

OHEFD	BNC	CREFD	ODEGD	CCELD	LDOCE	NODE	CED
agitatedly	**32**	+	–	–	–	R	R
appealingly	**32**	+	+	RE	R	R	R
acceptably	**33**	–	+	RE	R	R	R
ambitiously	**35**	+	+	RE	R	R	R
animatedly	**36**	+	+	RE	R	R	R
affably	**37**	+	+	RE	R	R	R
ambiguously	**37**	+	+	RE	R	R	R
annoyingly	**37**	+	–	RE	RE	RE	R
avowedly	**37**	+	+	RE	–	R	R
abstractedly	**38**	+	R	RE	R	R	R
amusingly	**40**	+	R	RE	R	R	R
ardently	**40**	+	+	RE	R	R	R
adroitly	**42**	+	+	RE	R	R	R
acoustically	**44**	–	+	RE	R	R	R
artfully	**46**	+	+	RE	RE	R	R
audibly	**46**	+	+	RE	R	R	R
absent-mindedly	**51**	+	+	RE	R	R	R
archly	**55**	+	+	RE	RE	R	R
assuredly	**57**	+	+	+	+	RE	R
adamantly	**61**	+	–	RE	R	R	R
arrogantly	**61**	–	+	RE	RE	R	R
architecturally	**68**	+	–	RE	RE	R	R
agreeably	**69**	+	+	RE	+	RE	R
amicably	**86**	+	+	RE	R	R	R
artistically	**86**	+	+	RE	R	R	R
administratively	**87**	+	–	RE	R	R	R
airily	**87**	+	+	RE	+	R	+
admiringly	**89**	+	R	RE	R	R	R
alphabetically	**89**	+	+	RE	R	R	R
apprehensively	**90**	+	+	RE	RE	R	R
accusingly	**94**	+	+	RE	R	R	R
ably	**97**	+	+	+	+	+	+
amiably	**99**	+	+	RE	R	R	R
attentively	**104**	+	+	RE	R	R	R
appallingly	**108**	+	–	RE	RE	R	R
aimlessly	**109**	+	+	RE	R	R	R
anonymously	**109**	+	+	RE	R	R	R
aesthetically	**110**	+	+	RE	RE	R	R
avidly	**112**	+	+	RE	–	R	R
appreciatively	**115**	+	–	RE	R	R	R
assiduously	**119**	+	+	RE	R	R	R
approvingly	**121**	+	+	RE	RE	R	–
appreciably	**137**	+	+	RE	RE	R	R
abnormally	**149**	+	+	RE	+	R	R
academically	**176**	+	+	RE	R	R	R
attractively	**177**	+	+	RE	R	R	R

TABLE 1—*continued*

OHEFD	BNC	CREFD	ODEGD	CCELD	LDOCE	NODE	CED
abundantly	**180**	+	+	+	+	+	R
absurdly	**183**	+	+	RE	+	R	R
apologetically	**188**	+	+	RE	RE	R	R
absently	**198**	+	+	RE	+	R	+
amply	**199**	+	+	RE	RE	R	+
affectionately	**203**	+	+	RE	R	R	R
astonishingly	**205**	+	+	RE	RE	RE	R
alarmingly	**212**	+	+	RE	R	R	R
alternately	**229**	+	+	RE	RE	R	R
arbitrarily	**229**	+	+	RE	RE	R	R
aptly	**239**	+	+	RE	+	R	R
admirably	**246**	+	+	RE	R	R	R
aggressively	**284**	+	+	RE	R	R	R
artificially	**320**	+	+	RE	RE	R	R
awkwardly	**361**	+	+	RE	RE	R	R
amazingly	**367**	+	+	RE	RE	RE	R
awfully	**378**	+	+	RE	+	+	+
acutely	**406**	+	+	+	+	R	R
adversely	**417**	–	+	RE	R	R	R
accidentally	**531**	+	+	RE	+	R	R
additionally	**570**	+	+	RE	+	+	–
anxiously	**603**	+	+	RE	RE	R	R
arguably	**628**	+	+	+	RE	+	R
admittedly	**708**	+	+	+	+	+	+
appropriately	**878**	+	+	RE	RE	R	R
allegedly	**1039**	+	+	RE	+	RE	R
angrily	**1041**	+	+	RE	RE	R	R
annually	**1094**	+	+	RE	R	R	R
adequately	**1134**	+	+	RE	RE	R	R
abruptly	**1159**	+	+	RE	R	R	R
accurately	**1402**	+	+	RE	RE	R	R
actively	**1488**	+	+	RE	RE	R	R
alternatively	**1729**	+	+	+	RE	+	R
accordingly	**2286**	+	+	+	+	+	+
automatically	**2748**	+	+	RE	+	R	R
approximately	**2826**	+	+	RE	RE	R	R
absolutely	**5672**	+	+	+	+	+	+
apparently	**7600**	+	+	+	+	+	R
actually	**25454**	+	+	+	+	+	0

TABLE 2

NODE	BNC	OHEFD	CREFD	ODEGD	CCELD	LDOCE	CED	Google
analytically	**87**	–	–	+	RE	–	R	100,000
aerobically	**31**	–	–	–	–	–	–	13,200
agonizingly	**26**	–	–	–	RE	R	R	19,000
algebraically	**25**	–	–	–	–	R	R	42,000
anciently	**20**	–	–	+	RE	–	+	17,800
anomalously	**20**	–	–	+	–	R	R	15,000
analogously	**19**	–	–	+	–	–	R	53,600
alertly	**14**	–	–	+	–	–	R	8,180
anecdotally	**10**	–	–	–	–	–	–	19,000
alluringly	**8**	–	–	–	RE	–	R	4,710
amateurishly	**8**	–	–	–	–	R	R	2,070
anaerobically	**7**	–	–	–	–	–	R	8,900
anally	**7**	–	–	–	–	–	R	17,600
altruistically	**6**	–	–	R	–	R	R	4,570
amusedly	**6**	–	+	–	–	–	–	5,660
anachronistically	**6**	–	–	–	–	R	R	3,250
aggrievedly	**5**	–	–	–	–	–	R	347
absorbedly	**4**	–	–	–	–	–	R	595
absorbingly	**4**	–	–	–	–	–	R	1,250
algorithmically	**4**	–	–	–	–	–	R	17,600
angiographically	**3**	–	–	–	–	–	–	3,980
affectingly	**2**	–	–	+	–	–	R	1,780
affectively	**2**	–	–	–	–	–	–	6,320
aggravatingly	**2**	–	–	–	–	R	–	1,640
amenably	**2**	–	–	–	–	–	R	335
adorably	**1**	–	–	R	–	–	R	8,980
adulterously	**1**	–	–	–	–	–	R	443
adventitiously	**1**	–	–	–	–	R	R	1,150
adversarially	**1**	–	–	–	–	–	–	520
aetiologically	**1**	–	–	–	–	–	R	407
affluently	**1**	–	–	–	–	–	–	437
alliteratively	**1**	–	–	–	–	–	–	641
amorphously	**1**	–	–	–	–	R	R	878
analogically	**1**	–	–	–	–	–	R	4,170
anarchically	**1**	–	–	–	–	–	R	817
angularly	**1**	–	–	–	–	–	R	3,290
adaptably		–	–	–	–	–	–	171
adhesively		–	–	–	–	–	R	3,570
adiabatically		–	–	–	–	–	–	7,060
adoptively		–	–	–	–	–	–	1,020
adultly		–	–	–	–	–	–	174
advisably		–	–	–	–	–	R	543
agronomically		–	–	–	–	–	–	4,880
allowably		–	–	–	–	–	R	547
ambidextrously		–	–	–	–	–	R	421
amphibiously		–	–	–	–	–	R	384
annalistically		–	–	–	–	–	–	23
annularly		–	–	–	–	–	R	332
allowedly		–	–	–	–	–	+	202

Legend: + – full entry; – – no entry; R – run-on entry; RE – run-on entry + example

9 Hidden culture: using the British National Corpus with language learners to investigate collocational behaviour, wordplay and culture-specific references

Dominic Stewart

Introduction

Preliminary remarks

In a previous article (Stewart 2000) I examined issues of conventionality and creativity in the area of Corpus Linguistics and Corpus Translation Studies. Some of the topics discussed therein offer a useful preamble to the present work, and may be summarized as follows. It was suggested that arguably the most telling evidence electronic corpora have provided so far is that human beings are linguistic creatures of habit. While it is true that the importance of collocation and idiomaticity in language have frequently been emphasized in modern linguistics, it is only in recent times that corpora have become substantial enough to confirm the extraordinary pervasiveness of repeated patterns in language. Patrick Hanks (1996: 85) observes that 'the creative potential of language is undeniable, but the concordances to a corpus remind us forcibly that in most of our utterances we are creatures of habit, immensely predictable, rehearsing the same old platitudes and the same old clichés in almost everything we say'.

A number of translation scholars and corpus linguists, however, have assured us that, notwithstanding the prevalence of conventional patterns, this does not mean that creative flair and imaginative verve are completely swamped. As Dorothy Kenny notes (1998: 515), 'routine is not such a bad thing . . . It is what allows the creative use of language to be identified as such', while Mona Baker (1998: 483) offers the proviso that 'bien que les études basées sur le corpus s'intéressent d'abord aux régularités, elles ne s'intéressent pas moins à la créativité'. In the same vein John Sinclair (1996: 81) has underlined that the focus on recurring usage 'does not mean that unique, one-off events are necessarily ignored, but rather that they cannot be evaluated in the absence of an interpretative framework provided by the repeated events'.

It was further underlined (Stewart 2000) that the idea of identifying predictable language events in order to gain insights into the workings of unpredictable, imaginative usage lies at the heart of the notion of semantic prosody, defined by Bill Louw (1993: 157) as 'a consistent aura of meaning with which a form is imbued by its collocates'. In this connection it had previously been noted by Sinclair (1991) that almost all collocates of verbs such as *happen* and *set in* represent unpleasant things or events, a co-occurrence so powerful that any 'pleasant' collocates of these verbs are to be considered departures from recurrent patterns.

Wordplay in newspaper headlines

Departures from recurrent patterns are commonplace in newspaper headlines. The following headline from *The Times* newspaper introduces an article concerning the decision by the Ulster Unionist Council (the ruling body of the Ulster Unionist Party) to endorse George Mitchell's proposal for a power-sharing executive:

PEACE IS BREAKING OUT

The unusual co-occurrence of *peace* with the phrasal verb *break out,* which habitually collocates with unpleasant things and events such as *disease, riots* or *war,* not only attracts the reader's attention, but also serves to emphasize the difficulty in finding a peace agreement for Northern Ireland. Such collocational clashes, often adopted with ironic intent, are studied by Alan Partington (1995), who shows how linguistic creativity so often depends upon an upsetting of our collocational expectations. In a subsequent work, Partington (1998: 121–43) explores the way in which newspaper headlines not only play with semantic prosodies but also, and much more commonly, distort proverbs, quotations and idiomatic expressions, with journalists exploiting the 'framework of habit that collocation imposes on language' (ibid.: 121).

An interesting example of such phenomena is the following headline, particularly rich in wordplay:

THE MERCY BEAT FOR 'MAC DAD'

The article concerns a former policeman from Liverpool who at the time of writing was teaching computer literacy to Albanian children. There are fairly transparent references to the policeman's 'beat', to Mackintosh computers, and to the fact that the subject of the article is like a father ('Dad') to his pupils. Perhaps slightly less evident is the veiled allusion to the 'Mersey Beat', a term used to describe popular music in the Liverpool area (i.e. around the River Mersey) in the early 1960s, with 'mercy' (presumably to be interpreted as something to do with a mission of mercy) replacing 'Mersey'. This kind of substitution abounds in newspaper headlines, yet although it involves a capsizing of collocational expectations it is not so much an example of departure from semantic prosody as of a more general deviation from a norm. It is precisely this type of phenomenon that I intend to focus upon in the present paper.

Aims and methodology of the present work

As mentioned above, it has been claimed that corpora are particularly useful in providing a backdrop of repeated language events against which to identify and assess departures from conventional usage, providing insights which Louw (1993: 157) claims 'have been largely inaccessible to human intuition about language'. In the same way one wonders how accessible to intuition the 'Mercy Beat' type of newspaper headline might be, above all to non-native speaker intuition, and how effective or ineffective a corpus of English might be in helping to identify such deviations from conventional patterns. With the purpose of investigating precisely this question I decided to make it the theme of a final year module I taught recently in Linguistics at the School for Interpreters and Translators, University of Bologna. I selected around 60 headlines, with accompanying articles, from British and American newspapers and magazines, submitting these to groups of (Italian) students for analysis. The headlines were not chosen at random: I sifted out those which seemed to be of linguistic and cultural interest to the group. I devoted one lesson a week to this activity, and for each meeting two students were asked to prepare beforehand a number of headlines, usually four, and to submit their findings to the rest of the class.

Similar to the 'Mercy Beat' headline, all the headlines contained aspects of cultural and linguistic interest, usually involving variations upon idioms, culture-specific references, quotations, etc., the majority of which would be hidden to non-native speakers of English, even very proficient non-native speakers, without recourse to linguistic resources (though it should be emphasized from the outset that some of the more subtle and ingenious examples would also be hidden to the average native speaker of English). While a few of the headlines were fully understood by the students either with no resources at all or with the use of bilingual and monolingual dictionaries alone, other headlines remained quite beyond the scope of conventional learning aids. When this was the case, students were obligatorily required to consult for further information the British National Corpus (BNC),[1] which I had trained them to use and which is available on all the computers at our school. Naturally the students were free to consult other resources too, e.g. dictionaries of idioms, dictionaries of quotations and popular sayings, the World Wide Web, encyclopaedias, etc.

Types of deviation

Before reporting classroom feedback relating to the degree of usefulness of the BNC in attempts to 'solve' the kind of wordplay typical of newspaper headlines, it is perhaps worth pausing to examine some examples of the types of deviation featured (see also the classifications proposed by

Partington 1998: 125–8, and Moon 1998: 120–77). In each case the 'solution' is provided below the headline cited.

Inversion of key elements

NOT WITH A WHIMPER BUT A BANG

Original: 'This is the way the world ends
Not with a **bang** but a **whimper**'.

A line from T.S. Eliot's *The Hollow Men*, 1925.

Omission of original element

POLICEMAN'S LOT A HAPPY ONE

Original: 'When constabulary duty's to be done, A policeman's lot is **not** a happy one'. From the Gilbert & Sullivan opera *The Pirates of Penzance.*

Substitution of key element

SPIES IN THE WORKS

Original: the idiomatic expression *put/throw a* ***spanner*** *in the works.*

Insertion of new element (+ substitution)

A STAIRCASE TO INTERNET HEAVEN

Original: *Stair**way** to Heaven.* Title of a song by Led Zeppelin.

Orthographic alteration

DON'T LET THE BUGS BYTE

Original: 'Sleep tight, and don't let the bugs **bite**'. Line from a nursery rhyme.

Some headlines were slightly more complex:

HAYS' SHARES MAKE THE MOST OF THE SUNSHINE

Original: the proverbial expression *make hay while the sun shines.*

The article focuses on the fortunes of the financial group Hays.

REPAIRING JACK'S HOUSE

Original: *This is the House that Jack Built.* Title of a nursery rhyme.

The article discusses matters relating to the British Home Secretary Jack Straw.

A handful of the headlines examined were not deviations from a norm at all, appearing in their original, integral form, though in the following headline a bracketed exclamation is added:

LONG TO REIGN OVER US (SIGH!)

Original: 'Long to reign over us, God save our queen'. A line from the National Anthem.

Resources used

Obviously certain resources were more useful than others in individual cases, e.g. the *Cambridge International Dictionary of Idioms* for idiomatic expressions, the *Oxford Concise Dictionary of Quotations* for popular sayings. A pleasant surprise was that the *Cambridge International Dictionary of English*, a learner dictionary, was extremely helpful in tracing the source of not only idiomatic expressions but also popular sayings, e.g.

DON'T SHOOT THE PIANIST

In the entry for 'shoot' (and perhaps surprisingly not for 'pianist') is included:

> *Please don't shoot the pianist. He is doing his best* (Sign in a bar reported by Oscar Wilde in *Impressions of America*, Leadville, 1883) (*Cambridge International Dictionary of English*, p. 1319).

However, our main concern in the classroom was to test the usefulness of the BNC in revealing the original form of the type of headlines reproduced above. With this in mind, the following section reports student feedback, offering illustrations of how helpful or unhelpful the BNC proved to be in certain cases.

The BNC as an aid to comprehension

Cases where the BNC was unhelpful or not particularly helpful, with other resources proving more useful

PRIOR JOINS UP WITH THE ROYLE FAMILY

Original: *The Royle Family*. The title of a British TV soap.

The article in question discusses the transfer of the footballer Spencer Prior to Manchester City, whose manager is Joe Royle. Apart from the transparent punning on the Royal Family, there is also the said culture-specific reference to the hugely popular British TV series *The Royle Family*. The reason no trace is to be found of this show in the BNC is exclusively chronological: it first appeared on television in the mid/late 1990s and is therefore not captured by the BNC, whose most recent texts date back to 1994.

In the following case, on the other hand, it is regional factors which are decisive:

THE SECOND SHOE DROPS

Original: 'Wait for the other shoe to drop'. An idiom meaning 'wait for something bad to happen' (*Cambridge International Dictionary of Idioms*, p. 285).

This headline, introducing an article concerning political questions in Germany, represents a variation upon the entry in the *Cambridge International Dictionary of Idioms* inasmuch as it focuses upon the moment 'something bad' actually happens. The expression appears to be used more in American English, and has perhaps passed into popular British usage only recently. It is therefore no surprise that just one example is retrievable from the primarily British texts of the BNC. The query builder 'shoe|shoes # dropVERB', with a span of five, produced 18 concordance lines, of which the only relevant example was:

There's still another shoe to *drop* on whether they can survive the maelstrom

For the two headlines given above, the World Wide Web proved to be by far the most productive resource. The respective searches 'royle family' and 'shoe drops' produced a whole host of web pages with related titles, from which the 'puzzle' of the headline could be solved at once.

Cases where the BNC was just one of various resources able to reveal the hidden reference

VICAR WITH MOBILE PHONE DEFENDS BT IN THE BELFRY

Original: 'have bats in the belfry'. A dated idiomatic expression meaning 'be crazy'.

The article concerns the proposed installation of a British Telecom transmitter in a church belfry.

A BIT OF A CAMP SQUIB

Original: 'a damp squib'. An idiom used to describe something which is 'expected to be interesting, exciting or impressive, but fails to be any of these things' (*Collins Cobuild English Dictionary for Advanced Learners*, p. 1512). The review in question criticizes a disappointing musical featuring an abundance of camp characters.

In each of the two headlines above the words which turn out to be the unaltered nodes – *belfry* in the first case and *squib* in the second – do not belong to a high frequency lexical band, and do not appear in large numbers of idiomatic expressions. As a result the students were able to trace the original idiom in conventional resources (i.e. by looking up *belfry* and *squib* in a monolingual or bilingual dictionary or dictionary of idioms). In these cases the BNC was by no means crucial in identifying the source of the modified expression, though it was certainly useful for further exemplification and typical patterning. For instance, out of the 22 concordances featuring *damp squib*, seven contained the string *of a damp squib*:

But was it art, or just a bit *of a damp squib*? Video-taped reports
first week looks a bit *of a damp squib*, the full moon on
'Well, they're a bit *of a damp squib*!' We are really struggling
that it seemed more *of a damp squib* than a big band!
turned out to be something *of a damp squib* for the Slough, Berkshire
turns out to be something *of a damp squib*. I finished third in the
trading proved something *of a damp squib* as the stock added

Moreover a further five of the 22 concordances of *a damp squib* were immediately preceded by *like* or *as*, leaving the overriding impression that this expression prefers some sort of immediately preceding qualifier.

Cases where the BNC was crucial in revealing the hidden reference

Simple searches

SPECIAL QUEUE

Original: 'special brew'. A brand name of Carlsberg lager + title of 1980s pop song by Bad Manners.

The article reports that 50 people have applied for ten jobs as beer tasters at the Bass brewery in Staffordshire, England.

STARE CRAZY STARS SHOULD REFLECT ON FAME

Original: 'stir crazy'. An idiomatic expression meaning 'upset, angry and disappointed because you have been prevented from going somewhere or doing something for a long time' (*Cambridge International Dictionary of English*, p. 1427).

The article explains that the singer Madonna does not relish being stared at by flight attendants when she travels by aeroplane, and that as a result the cabin crew are under instructions to avoid eye contact with her.

CELL MATES

Original: 'soul mate'. An expression describing 'a person with whom one has a deep lasting friendship and understanding' (*Oxford Advanced Learner's Dictionary*, p. 1135).

The article concerns two men who fell in love after sharing a prison cell.

In each of the three cases above the unaltered nodes – *special, crazy* and *mates* respectively – belong to fairly or very high frequency lexical bands, and commonly occur with many different collocates. This renders the task of locating likely-looking 'original' collocates in the dictionary rather arduous. Under *mate*, for instance, in the *Cambridge International Dictionary of English*, the examples provided of collocates immediately preceding *mate* are *best, running, ship's, flat, team* and *work*, with no sign of *soul mate*. Looking up *special* in particular proved to be a futile enterprise, not only because it is an extremely common word with all manner of diverse collocates, but also because in the case in point the hidden expression is a brand name (*Special Brew*) and is therefore unlikely to feature in the dictionary.

The absence of tangible clues also made the concealed allusions impossible to find with search engines on the World Wide Web. Searches in the BNC, however, turned out to be more productive. A simple query for *special* retrieved 22,000 occurrences. These were too many to download in one go, but random searches of smaller numbers of concordance lines made visual scanning more manageable. After sorting alphabetically in descending order by the first word to the right of the node, and after exercising a good degree of patience, students finally hit upon an occurrence of *special brew*, which rhymed with *special queue* and seemed to match the context of breweries and beer-tasting. This was swiftly followed by a phrase query search 'special brew', of which there were nine occurrences:

A *Special Brew* was produced by Moor
loads of hippies going with cans of *Special Brew*, but that's not true,' he
a splashing can of Carlsberg *Special Brew* and asking me the time.
dogs on strings, and cans of *Special Brew*.'
launch of Gales Festival Mild, a *Special Brew* available for a limited period
violently sick. For the ten pints of *Special Brew* and vindaloo crowd only.
Centre all day with a can of *Special Brew* in your hand. Or perhaps
to women than the Carlsberg *Special Brew* brigade, something more
afterwards re-sold them as *Special Brew*. It was perhaps no wonder

Similarly the quick query 'crazy' produced 1760 concordance lines, which this time were sorted alphabetically to the left. After a number of wild-goose chases the students in question eventually hit upon two examples of *stir crazy*, for which there was no obvious connection with aeroplanes, Madonna or popular music, but whose phonetic similarity to *stare crazy* made it the likeliest candidate:

out of the house. You must be *stir crazy*.' She wandered over to the
some money out I'm gonna get *stir crazy* not being able to play badminton

The query 'mate' produced analogous results. There were 1877 concordances with *mate*, of which two featured a collocation with *soul* after sorting to the left. In this case the connection with *cell mate* was not only phonetic but also semantic, in that the two prisoners allegedly built up a very close relationship. Interestingly the students failed to notice that the *Oxford Advanced Learner's Dictionary* (p. 1135) is also of assistance, in that it provides a cross-reference to the expression *soul mate* under its entry for *mate* (i.e. 'See also SOUL MATE').

More complex searches

The BNC proved absolutely crucial when there was no key word with which to begin investigations, but only a structural pattern, for example:

OUT OF THE JUNGLE INTO THE POT

Original: 'out of the frying-pan into the fire'. An idiomatic expression meaning 'from a bad situation to one that is worse'.

The accompanying article deals with the question of meat for human consumption derived from wild animals, and in particular how some local economies in Central Africa rely for their income on the sale of bushmeat. Although one would certainly expect a native speaker of English to spot the disguised idiom, not one of my group of students was able to recognize it spontaneously. Nevertheless it was clear that some sort of wordplay was going on.

Unsurprisingly, dictionary and web searches for the keywords *jungle* and *pot* proved fruitless, as did those for the prepositions *out of* and *into*, both belonging to high frequency lexical bands. It was here, however, that the BNC came into its own, inasmuch as its 'query builder' option enables the user to look for key *patterns* rather than key terms. The following query builder,

('out of') ('the') (_) ('into') ('the')

with the so-called 'any node' in the middle representing any single word form, produced 71 concordances, of which three featured the hidden expression:

'So you're going *out of the frying-pan into the* fire?' Dr Abraham
perfect example of jumping *out of the frying-pan into the* fire. 'And I suppose
off.' That's it, then: *out of the frying-pan into the* fire; here's awful

Aside from the identical structural patterns, the semantic similarity between the *pot* of the headline and the *frying-pan* of the concordances also suggested that the correct solution had been found. A simple query 'frying-pan' then revealed further instances:

and said farewell. Out of the *frying-pan*, into the fire. Now all she
when they say, 'Out of the *frying-pan*, into the fire'? What do

In these two cases it would appear that the presence of the comma after *frying-pan* prevented the query builder from capturing them in the original search. Also worth noting in passing is that a greater number of relevant concordances would have been captured had it not been for the fact that *frying-pan* is often written as two words, i.e. *frying pan*.

The BNC: a backdrop of conventionality?

As mentioned in the Introduction above, corpora have been described as providing a backdrop of conventionality, of conventional language events, against which to measure creativity. Our investigations would suggest, however, that this is true only up to a point. Consider some further concordances generated by the query 'frying-pan':

jump from the frying-pan into the *frying-pan*, is there?' There you see
That would be jumping out of the *frying-pan* into a raging inferno.

Here the concordances in question already furnish evidence of creative variation upon an original form. Now while in the case in point the original form *out of the frying-pan into the fire* appeared in other concordance lines, and thus students were able to unearth the hidden phrase, in other cases the already modified usage in the BNC actually impeded the resolution of the problem. Consider the variation in the following headline, introducing an article from the beginning of 2000 concerning President Clinton's intention to step up his travelling plans:

COMING TO AN AIRSTRIP NEAR YOU

Original: 'Coming to a cinema near you'. A typical expression used to introduce trailers to forthcoming films.

Although the wordplay is perhaps fairly transparent – most of the students understood it more or less immediately – the source expression is actually quite difficult to trace in the BNC. The following query builder,
('coming to') ('a'|'an') (_) ('near you'),
produced 3 concordance lines:

Variety Spectacular' is *coming to a college near you.* Forget your Roller
by a band called Fuel – *coming to a shop near you* just about now
is on tour and will be *coming to a town near you,* where you can

(There is in fact one example of the unmodified form in the BNC, though the concordance in question is interrupted after *near,* and is therefore not captured by the above search.)

Here of course it could be argued that the chances of finding a cinema trailer of this kind in the BNC are limited anyway. The following headline was more problematic in that its origin was not clear to the students at all, and once again, for the same reasons as above, the BNC did not prove helpful:

YOUNG, GIFTED AND BACKS

Original: 'Young, gifted and black'. A popular saying/The title of an album by Aretha Franklin/A film title.

Native speakers of English consulted were in agreement that this represented a variation upon *young, gifted and black*; *backs* is a technical term used in the game of rugby, to which the article in question refers. The phrase query 'young, gifted' produced two occurrences:

New Musical Express. Young, gifted and plaque Fair and
thing today. Er Let's have *young, gifted* and demanding it says.

It may be that in such cases the original saying, quotation or whatever has become engulfed by the deviation (there is currently a British television programme entitled 'Young, Gifted and Broke') and may in the course of time disappear altogether. This phenomenon also extends to common abbreviations such as *When in Rome . . .* in place of *When in Rome do as the Romans do* (explainable in terms of the Gricean maxim of quantity, i.e. 'do not make your contribution more informative than is required'), where the abbreviation would appear to be in the process of usurping the full form. What is particularly interesting is that if this phenomenon is proved to be widespread it could hold profound implications for language description, particularly lexicography. The author of the present article is currently conducting and supervising research in this area at the School for Translators and Interpreters, University of Bologna.

Conclusions

One of the principal objectives of the activities described above was to encourage use of the BNC as a source of both linguistic and cultural data, in that it contains a wealth of information which is beyond the remit of more conventional resources. Such resources, along with the World Wide Web, are already well exploited by students, but in my experience the extraordinary possibilities offered by electronic corpora still 'blush unseen', whether owing to lack of opportunity, to inadequate training or simply to natural reticence. However that may be, the study of newspaper headlines proved a good way of introducing learners to the idea of using corpora for problems of comprehension, in so far as headlines are particularly rich in wordplay, veiled references, departures from standard linguistic patterns, etc.

Further, the initiative was well-received in that the students were highly motivated to find a given solution. In my experience it can happen that students, even after receiving adequate training, remain somehow reluctant to exploit corpora, falling back a little too readily on more familiar resources. However, the fact of giving them a specific 'puzzle' to solve, combined with the fact that their usual resources were sometimes of little assistance, gave them a tangible, compelling reason to consult the corpus. Moreover, the fact that they were seeking not just linguistic but encyclopaedic information seemed to make the whole thing more challenging and stimulating.

Aside from the BNC's obvious merits as an important source of examples in context and of statistical, collocational, encyclopaedic, etc. information, in the investigations conducted the BNC tended to prove (i) extremely helpful in those instances where the unaltered constituent of the collocation sought belongs to a high frequency lexical band (*special queue*), and (ii) crucial where the *structural pattern* of the source expression had been preserved rather than the content words (*out of the jungle into the pot*). It was inevitably less useful in those cases where (iii) the source expression lies beyond the usual scope of the BNC (non-British usage; references to aspects and events subsequent to 1994), (iv) the source expression has apparently been ousted by variations upon it (*young, gifted and x*).

Notes

1 The BNC is a 100-million-word general language monolingual corpus of contemporary, original (i.e. not translated) English, consisting of 90 per cent written texts and 10 per cent spoken. It was completed in 1994, and first released a year later, by an industrial/academic consortium led by Oxford University Press. It is encoded, and is a sample corpus, i.e. new texts are not added to it. See Aston and Burnard (1998: 28–40). Further information is available at the BNC website (http://info.ox.ac.uk/bnc).

References

Aston, Guy and Burnard, Lou (1998) *The BNC Handbook: Exploring the British National Corpus with Sara.* Edinburgh: Edinburgh University Press.

Baker, Mona (1998) 'Réexplorer la langue de la traduction: une approche par corpus', in Laviosa, Sara (1998), pp. 480–5.

Hanks, Patrick (1996) 'Contextual Dependency and Lexical Sets', *International Journal of Corpus Linguistics* 1(1): 75–98.

Kenny, Dorothy (1998) 'Creatures of Habit? What Translators Usually Do with Words', in Laviosa, Sara (1998), pp. 515–23.

Laviosa, Sara (ed.) (1998) *L'Approche Basée sur le Corpus/The Corpus-Based Approach.* Special edition of *Meta* 43: 4.

Louw, Bill (1993) 'Irony in the Text or Insincerity in the Writer? The Diagnostic Potential of Semantic Prosodies', in Baker, Mona, Francis, Gill and Tognini-Bonelli, Elena (eds) *Text and Technology: In Honour of John Sinclair.* Amsterdam/Philadelphia: John Benjamins, pp. 157–76.

Moon, Rosamund (1998) *Fixed Expressions and Idioms in English.* Oxford: Clarendon Press.

Partington, Alan (1995) 'Kicking the Habit: The Exploitation of Collocation in Literature and Humour', in Payne, J. (ed.) *Linguistic Approaches to Literature. English Language Research Journal.* Birmingham: University of Birmingham 17: 25–44.

Partington, Alan (1998) *Patterns and Meanings: Using Corpora for English Language Research and Teaching.* Amsterdam/Philadelphia: John Benjamins.

Sinclair, John McH. (1991) *Corpus Concordance Collocation.* Oxford: Oxford University Press.

Sinclair, John McH. (1996) 'The Search for Units of Meaning', *Textus* 9: 75–106.

Stewart, Dominic (2000) 'Conventionality, Creativity and Translated Text: the Implications of Electronic Corpora in Translation', in Olohan, Maeve (ed.) *Intercultural Faultlines. Research Models in Translation Studies 1: Textual and Cognitive Aspects.* Manchester: St Jerome Publishing, pp. 73–91.

Dictionaries consulted

Cambridge International Dictionary of English (1995). Cambridge: Cambridge University Press.

Oxford Advanced Learner's Dictionary (1995). Oxford: Oxford University Press.

Collins Cobuild English Dictionary for Advanced Learners (2001). Glasgow: HarperCollins.

Oxford Concise Dictionary of Quotations (1997). Oxford: Oxford University Press.

Cambridge International Dictionary of Idioms (1998). Cambridge: Cambridge University Press.

10 Language as an economic factor: the importance of terminology

Wolfgang Teubert

Why terminology is becoming more important

We have come to regard our languages, the languages spoken in the country or region where we live, as cultural assets, contributing to our heritage and identity in the same way as all the cultural artefacts we find in our environment. Our languages have not just evolved: they have been moulded by generations of writers, poets, speakers and critics, until they have become something to be proud of. We want to preserve them, and we want to keep them from being corrupted. Many think, however, that the omnipresent English will eventually put most other languages, Western languages in particular, in jeopardy. For more than a hundred years now English, the new global interlingua, has been putting its stamp on almost all languages as only Latin and later French were able to do in early modern times. A few of us non-native speakers of English welcome this development; it helps facilitate international communication, but others are concerned that our mother tongues are gradually losing their individuality. This is a problem that concerns all of us. Like our cultural heritage, our native language belongs to the language community as a whole; it is no one's private property; it is not something you can buy or sell. Ordinary language is not a major factor when it comes to the gross domestic product.

Things are different when it comes to languages for special purposes (LSP). Their vocabularies differs from ordinary, general language. The terminologies of LSPs are quickly becoming a precious commodity. There is a growing market for termbanks and the modern highly controlled languages for special purposes. As we all know, each domain tends to develop a terminology of its own, which makes it possible for experts to communicate verbally with each other. In principle, it works the same way with apiculture as with computer science, even though, to take an example, the German terminology of apiculture is derived from ordinary words of German origin, whereas in the case of computer science the German terminology uses primarily words of English origin, which do not belong to the ordinary German vocabulary. Learning this kind of terminology that we now find in many modern scientific and industrial domains takes a much greater effort than the terminology of a traditional domain like apiculture. Indeed, terminology today is becoming a serious problem in vocational training. Still, public interest in these languages for special purposes is poor. Therefore, it is not surprising that we are hardly aware how terminology, while constantly evolving into more specialized, more complex systems, has grown into a commercial commodity, an important economic factor. Smaller companies pay large sums of money for multilingual terminologies describing the products they sell; large companies spend even more money on creating, developing and standardizing the LSP they use themselves and want to force their competitors to use. For a long time, academic language studies have taken little account of terminology. This is still largely true for Germany. In France and Britain, courses on LSP and terminology are now becoming a part of linguistic curricula.

Why do more and more big businesses establish their own terminology departments? Why is there a rapid growth of agencies that offer terminological databases? Why does the Commission of the European Union massively support the creation of a European infrastructure for terminology work and the development of procedures for automatic terminology processing? What makes LSP so important?

Technology rules our modern world, more precisely, the kind of technology that becomes more and more complex and is, at the same time, becoming less and less illustrative. Traditional crafts were, to a large extent, self-explanatory. In order to understand apiculture, one must watch an apiculturist doing his work. The art of apiculture was learning by doing. Apiculture is illustrative. What counts is the practical work. Experience is the master. Of course, domain-specific knowledge concerning apiculture does exist. Textbooks and special journals are available. But one can be a good apiculturist and continue to be one without reading apiculturist journals. Texts in this case only complement experience. They cannot substitute for it.

This is different in computer science. What happens in a computer cannot be experienced. In order to become a computer scientist, one must first and foremost communicate with other computer scientists, talk to them, read their texts. Only then it will start making sense to watch them doing their work. In order to implement new software, one must have read the description of the product, the installation procedures and the user instructions. Without these texts, software is useless. The more comprehensible the user manual is for the user, the more use he will be able to make of the product. Everyone knows the complaints about insufficient instructions, for example, for text-processing systems. The more functions they contain, the more overwhelming the flood of new terminology becomes for the user. While the terminology of apiculture may not exceed some hundred terms, the terminology of computer science comprises many thousands of units, and new ones are established daily.

The concepts denoted by the apiculture terms often can be explained by illustration. In comparison, terminology concerned with computer science remains abstract, regardless of all the inventive struggles of the authors, and it takes much effort and differentiation work to describe the relations and hierarchies between the concepts in a precise, transparent and understandable way. A honey extractor can also be used when the instructions have been lost, but we cannot extend the principle of trial and error to the operation of video recorders and much less of computers. Without instructions detailing the elements, functions and operation steps clearly, the user is lost. It is only communication, verbal exchange which makes domains such as computer science, nuclear technology, biochemistry and even modern tool construction possible. Communication between developer and user can only work if the text author and the text recipient share the same terminology, i.e. if a given term denotes exactly the same concept for author and reader. Language, and primarily written language, is the prerequisite for our modern technology. You can become an apiculturist without reading texts, but not a computer scientist (or a car mechanic or an electrical engineer). The more complex, the less illustrative a subject is, the more the expert must rely on texts, on descriptions, user manuals and instructions.

Vocabulary and terminology

The vocabulary of ordinary, general language consists of words which have more or less a clear meaning. A *tiger* is *a catlike animal with a yellow to red colouring and black stripes.* The term *tiger* can be found in many languages, and it may be assumed that the words which denote the concept *tiger* in these languages carry more or less the same meaning. This is different for a word like German *Kummer* (English: *grief*) which denotes a kind of *distress caused by misfortune or worry which has taken hold of a person.* Our German word *Kummer* is subtly distinct from the German words *Trauer* (in English roughly: *mourning/grief*) and *Leid* (in English roughly: *sorrow/grief*), and none of these words has exact English or French counterparts. How are we supposed to convey to a non-native speaker when we use the word *Trauer,* when *Leid* or when *Kummer*? Many words in our ordinary language have unspecific meanings which cannot be described without referring to the context in which they occur, but this is what dictionaries, due to their constraints in space, cannot do effectively. Therefore, they try hard to decontextualize the meaning of words, to describe the words in virtual isolation. Dictionaries do not list the meaning or meanings of a word; at their best, they give us a rough, incomplete and subjective sketch; they record the lexicographer's understanding of the meaning(s), which cannot be more than a limited picture. What dictionaries tell us is often no more than a first orientation.

This is quite different with terminology. With terminology, we are not confronted with meaning; rather, terms denote concepts which, in principle, are defined independently of any particular language. That is true for *tiger*, and indeed, *tiger* is not only a word belonging to the general language but at the same time a term used in zoology. The German word *Kummer*, however, is not a term; it does not denote a concept that would exist independently of the language to which it belongs. As opposed to the indications of meaning we find in dictionaries, the definitions of concepts are (or, in principle, should be) complete, unambiguous and exhaustive. They enlist all essential properties of a concept. What is not part of the definition remains contingent, i.e. arbitrary. For example, the concept *tiger* does not tell us anything about the number of black stripes, because it is not relevant for the definition. The term *tiger* shows something else: concepts are elements of a domain-specific taxonomy, listing all its concepts in a hierarchical structure and defining the relationships between them. As we know, in our Western world, the plant and animal world is ordered according to Linnaeus's system. There are generic concepts such as *catlike animals* and subsumable concepts such as *lions* and *leopards*. A conceptual system like this, a taxonomy, defines the concepts of a subject field strictly independently of any context or other collateral information; in principle, the concept *tiger* will remain unchanged regardless of whatever is being said in texts about tigers. To change the definition of the term *tiger*, the community of tiger experts would have to agree to dismiss the old and adopt a new definition.

Communication and the standardization of terminology

You can be an apiculturist by yourself, but no one can build an aeroplane, a computer or a simple television set by themselves. Someone intending to achieve any of these objectives has to rely on the cooperation with others, for example, suppliers. This interaction presupposes communication. Descriptions for essential parts, supplied by a third party, will be needed; the documentation of the functionalities of tiny electronic chips, used in almost every device these days, can be a document of many pages. In modern technology, the brilliant inventor as a single human being no longer exists. Nothing happens without teamwork. To solve complex tasks, many teams scattered in distant locations, often in different countries, work together. If interfaces are not clearly defined, nothing works. Modern technology is based on the principle of division of labour. The more labour is divided up, the more important becomes language, more precisely, terminology. Modern technology does not work without verbal communication. Successful verbal communication depends on unambiguous texts. Texts are unambiguous if the language community has successfully negotiated the meanings of their elements, and if the domain experts have agreed on the definitions of the concepts they use.

Even today, an apiculturist reading his monthly journal may be quite happy with a fifty-year-old glossary of apiculture. There is no such thing as a fifty-year-old special dictionary on computer science. The domain simply did not exist fifty years ago. Yet even a ten-year-old special dictionary on this subject would be quite insufficient today. The more rapid the development of a subject, the quicker its terminology becomes outdated.

Technological change manifests itself in new concepts for which new expressions must be found. Each domain must develop its own infrastructure for coordinating this terminology work. Without such concert, everyone would speak their own LSP, and communication among experts would become virtually impossible. Procedures accepted by the expert community must exist to secure the success and acceptance of the established terminological practice. Standardization is indispensable if the readers of product documentation, patents, user manuals, etc. are to understand the authors. For the new technologies exhibiting rapid change, this means that we have to develop new forms of terminology work. Today, one can no longer wait until some responsible semi-annually convening committee works on proposals, then discusses objections, reworks drafts and eventually passes a standardized terminology. It may well happen that the concept to be standardized has become irrelevant by then. This also means that the printed special domain dictionary, which was traditionally used to ensure the standardization of terminology, has had its day. Only terminology databases can, at least under adequate conditions, keep pace with the technical change today.

The task of standardization, therefore, is not only to make sure that the threads of screws fit the nuts, but also that terminology denoting standardized items and procedures (by naming the according concepts) is understood in exactly the same way within a given domain, within a given LSP. The procedure for terminology standardization must therefore become an item of standardization itself. In Germany, a standardization committee for terminology (Normenausschuss Terminologie: NAT) at the Deutsche Institut für Normung (DIN) was established a long time ago in which engineers, lexicographers, linguists, translators and other experts have been busy developing standards, i.e. general principles of terminology work, thus trying to meet the challenges of our technical era. Germany was not alone. Other industrialized nations established comparable institutions. Today, most countries have bodies responsible for regulating the terminology in their national languages. On the international level, the work is coordinated by the Technical Committee of the International Standardization Organization (ISO TC 37). Recent standards guarantee that terminological data (i.e. the names as well as the very complexly structured definitions) developed for a particular application, for example, for the user manual of a new type of car, can be migrated automatically from the termbank of the team involved in its development into the terminological database for motor vehicle technology, even if this database is structured quite differently. It should be noted that *data migration* itself is a relatively new term in data processing.

Multilingual terminology work and its localization

Not only since *globalization* has become a powerful key word, we owe the existence of many terminology databases first of all to the needs of translators. The translation of terminological texts, i.e. texts written in a LSP, is (or should be) highly paid specialist work, and often translators are the first to have to find terminological equivalents in the target language for new concepts or, if they cannot find them in existing documents, they have to invent them. A prerequisite for this is the thorough knowledge of the terminology in the source as well as in the target language, in order to avoid the creation of neologisms and confusing duplicates where adequate translations already exist. Translators have an ever-growing part in the task of looking after the homogeneity of terminologies.

Globalization is accompanied by the hegemony of English. Especially in the new technologies, concise terminologies are often only available in English. More and more frequently, experts, regardless of their individual mother tongues, are forced to communicate with each other in a jargon which comes closer to English than to their mother tongue. Even widespread regional languages such as Spanish, French or German have to fall back onto public support if they do not want to run the risk that in the near future terminological texts can no longer be written in them. Economically, the most sensible thing would be to subsidize the translation of relevant innovative texts from English and, at the same time, to create an infrastructure which allows for the extraction of the terminology used within the translated texts, with the goal of processing and unifying the terms for the target language. As soon as a national terminology has been brought into existence via translations, experts who prefer to write in their native language, rather than clumsily having to use a foreign language, will confidently have their word in it. Supporting terminology work therefore also means supporting national research and development by providing the means of horizontal and vertical information exchange. Countries not wishing to give up the goal of their national terminology must be aware that this is a public task in the national economic interest. It is due to the frenzy for regulations for which the European institutions are notorious that producers are obliged today to deliver descriptions and instructions in the national languages along with the devices that they sell and that they are made liable for the correctness of their contents. This initiative can offer valuable support for the establishment of a national terminology.

No hi ha poble sensa cultura ni cultura sense llengua. There is no people without a culture, and there is no culture without a language. This aphorism by the Catalan poet Benjamin Vautier is also valid for terminology. It has become an accepted truth for the countries which used to be part of or live under the hegemony of the former Soviet Union. The small Baltic states view the development of a national terminology as essential for their survival. Precisely because they have experienced that the renunciation of an independent terminology went together with economic dependency, they do everything to avoid that, on the national level, English terminology replaces Russian terminology. Countries wanting to exercise their sovereignty also in economic matters must pursue the goal of developing terminologies in their national languages.

Without a national terminology, countries also give up having an active, independent part in the design and further progress of a technological domain. Although internationally the scientific language will be English and English only, only those who can refer to a national discourse are able to take a credible and successful part in the international discourse. French research and development will only be taken seriously internationally as long as it manifests and presents itself as genuine French research, in its independence, first and foremost linguistically, via texts written in French. Without a national discourse in research and technology, one remains dependent on texts whose relevance and quality is not being discussed here but elsewhere. Smaller European countries such as the Baltic states and also Hungary, Slovenia and Scandinavian countries have been following the German example concerning terminology work. They hope that national terminology centres will remain in existence in our changed world and that they will play a leading role again in building up a European infrastructure for terminology. Research and development cannot be carried out in the isolation of academic ivory towers or industrial management floors where knowledge of English is the rule: the basis of successful research and development is the practical training and qualification of skilled workers, technicians and engineers, a kind of training which today and in the future will continue to be carried out in the national languages. National terminology is imperative to safeguard the communication between skilled workers, engineers and researchers. Staking everything on the English card means to sever science from its base in engineering and in a skilled workforce, with disastrous consequences. The European nations assert their positions as economically strong countries mainly through the combination of academic science with a strong industrial base, a combination made possible by a national discourse using the national terminology. Theory and practice need this discourse. In order to understand each other, they must speak the same language and have a reliable terminology.

Corpus linguistics

There are two ways to standardize terminology. One is to prescribe the correct usage. This works if there is a body legitimized to make such prescriptions. For French terminologies, the body is AFNOR. In it, there are committees consisting of specialists deciding which term will denote a certain concept. The procedure is time-consuming. From the first draft of a standard supposed to regulate the terminology of a given domain up to the final implementation of the finalized text can take years.

Someone wanting to introduce a new product on the market together with product descriptions and instructions in all the national languages of the EU cannot wait until the terms of the new concepts which characterize the product are standardized in the traditional way. Instead they will have to come up with new terms whenever they cannot refer to existing terminology. If translators are looking for an appropriate term for a new concept, they will search the latest texts, preferably on the Internet, to find out if the term they need already exists. They cannot wait with their translation until a terminology standard has been decreed through traditional procedures. If the component or feature to be described is so new that the target language offers no equivalent for it, it is necessary to invent new terms in analogy to other terms which denote similar concepts. The kind of terminology work which is based upon current language use is descriptive terminology.

In the new technologies, marked by rapid change, the trend goes in the direction of descriptive terminology. So far, no reliable standardization method for descriptive terminology exists, but terminology work can profit from recent development in linguistics, where there has been relevant progress when it comes to observe and describe lexical change. With corpus linguistics as a new discipline, new instruments have been developed which can be applied to descriptive terminology work.

One main goal of corpus linguistics consists of extracting meaning from texts by looking at the way words (or larger lexical units) are used in sentences and texts. For example, by analysing the contexts of the German word *Schloss* in as many citations as possible, it will become evident that in perhaps 50 per cent of the contexts aristocrats and in the other 50 per cent doors are mentioned. Obviously, there are two usages and consequently two meanings of *Schloss*, namely, *palace* and *lock*. Texts from which meaning is extracted constitute the corpus. For the field of terminology, this means that we can systematically search in terminological texts for terms denoting new concepts. This is because these concepts do not occur in isolation. If translators look for equivalents for *(data) migration*, they can assume that it is likely to be found in the context of terms such as *file, data structure, database, data medium.* It must be texts with a high degree of saturation concerning the relevant terminology, and it must be relatively new texts reflecting the latest technological change. The traditional concept of a finite corpus is not applicable here. The corpus used for terminology work is dynamic and will be continually enriched by new texts documenting technological innovation linguistically. Such corpora are called monitor corpora.

Besides traditional corpora consisting of printed texts, the Internet as virtual corpus becomes more and more important; from it, domain-specific special corpora can be derived and continuously updated (in the sense of a monitor corpus) using thesaurus-based filtering techniques. By comparing newer texts with older ones, neologisms can be identified, that is, words (in our case, terms) that have not been found or have only been found in different contexts so far. When they appear for the first time in a certain text, they are often introduced in the form of a definition: 'We call this invention ABC in the course of xyz' or the like. This is the terminological material which is needed by translators specializing in LSP texts of a given domain and by authors of such texts intent on using the latest terminology.

Hard and soft terminology

So far, we have been mostly talking about 'hard' terminology, that is, terminology in the classical sense which made the modern industrial production process possible. Standardized concepts enable the division of labour and cooperation in the production process; they guarantee the flow of communication between producers and users. They supply, independently of language, author and addressee with unambiguous information. In the framework of 'hard' terminology, terms denote exactly described concepts which are static and unchangeable within fixed limits. Precisely in this normative claim lies the success of classical terminology work. Once the development of a new product or procedure is completed and has reached the status of a final definition (e.g. patents), production (product descriptions) and application (user manuals), the definition work on the terminological vocabulary has also come to an end, either by general acceptance or by decree. The relevant terms are listed in accordingly marked parts of texts (e.g. in indexes) and in special glossaries where the concepts they denote are explicitly defined. They are now standardized.

Scientific terminology and the terminology used in the exploration of new technological ideas cannot be treated like 'hard' terminology. Research and development aim at innovation and are, in principle, dynamic. What was state of the art yesterday is out of date today. Something which functions as a salient feature in a received theory may be a contingent feature in a new approach. For example, it is controversial in modern linguistics whether semantic cohesion has to exist or not between the elements of a *collocation* (i.e. a group of words occurring more often in a corpus than statistically expected). The concept of *collocation* has been given a great deal of attention recently and is particularly fiercely discussed by linguists of different schools. There is no generally accepted definition of *collocation.* Only when it results in a concrete design, for example a dictionary of collocations, the will concept *collocation* be strictly defined for this product, that is, it will be standardized.

In scientific discussions as presented in journals, in lectures at conferences and, more recently, also massively on the Internet, we find 'soft' terminology. Especially in fields that are subject to intensive research, the permanent elaboration of definitions and of the relationships between concepts are a relevant part of the development of theories. Here, we normally do not find binding definitions but contextually constrained attempts at definitions of temporary validity, and these are often scattered throughout texts in unpredictable places. To standardize 'soft' terminology would make no sense because it would freeze all ongoing research together with the scientific discussion. If the focus in terminology work is on 'soft' terminology today, this is the case because people have realized that the methodology of corpus linguistics offers an ideal platform to detect the latest state of the art of research in a specific domain by extracting citations containing definitions from a corpus. By looking at terminological change, researchers can learn which views are predominant in different theories and schools that are important for relevant phenomena.

Knowledge extraction

Knowledge describes the state of being aware of something being the case. If someone claims to know that the earth is a disc, they tell us that they have interpreted sensorial data and now are conscious that they have found the correct interpretation. Interpretation is an activity, and consciousness is an intentional state. Computers carry out procedures, but do not act on their own, and certainly they are not conscious of the data they have stored in their memories. There is no automatic knowledge extraction in this sense. Computers, once they are properly programmed, can only detect certain formally describable phenomena in texts. If the phenomena they are trained to detect are candidates for terms, preferably in connection with candidates for definitions of these terms, then they provide the information a terminologist needs for establishing terminological knowledge. For 'hard' terminology, this is simple enough and not very fruitful. There already exists a glossary of terms together with their definitions as they are confirmed by the community of experts. Detecting 'hard' terms in texts does not yield any new or useful information. You cannot find new 'hard' terms, and if you find a definition not agreeing with the one in the glossary (termbank), it must be wrong.

Filtering terminological data from texts only makes sense for 'soft' terminology, for new terms not yet listed in termbanks or glossaries and for tentative definitions not yet sanctioned by the authorities. Texts full of 'hard' terminology describe what we know already. Texts full of 'soft' terminology describe new hypotheses and potential new knowledge that someone has already, that is not shared yet, and that we can find nowhere else outside of this text. Mining 'soft' terminology means extracting data that we can analyse. 'Soft' terminology can indicate texts and text segments full of innovation. It is dependent on our interpretation if we accept this data as new knowledge. Only in this wider sense, corpus linguistics provides the methodology for knowledge extraction, for extracting data that may enrich our knowledge. Where new terms are being introduced and new definitions are proposed, there we can be sure to find new concepts, new ideas and new visions. This is why 'soft' terminology is so much more important than 'hard' terminology: it shows us the current state of the art. If we can filter out the 2 or 3 per cent of texts full of 'soft', provisional terminology, then we do not have to deal further with the 97 per cent of texts repeating only what we have always known.

The procedures for automatic knowledge extraction in this restricted sense detect the citations in texts in which the relevant units (unregistered terms, collocations, set phrases) occur in a previously defined frequency. If these procedures are combined with a corpus-based thesaurus, they will not only identify terms, but also their synonyms and, where applicable, higher and lower order concepts. Corpus linguists are developing software that will identify neologisms and differentiate between different usages of 'soft' terms. Without being forced to digest intellectually the endless flow of primarily repetitive information, without this extremely costly exercise, we can use the methodology of corpus linguistics and its procedures to lead us directly and specifically to the text passages we are interested in. This shows another reason why terminology has become such an important economic commodity. Terminology work based on corpus linguistics thus can pave the way for the development of cutting-edge technology for small and medium-sized enterprises (SMEs), companies that cannot afford the expensive research labs of their global competitors. If they know the current state of the art, they can proceed from there and develop innovative products.

Fortunately, national infrastructures for terminology have been existent in Western European countries, and it is an important asset for the role of Europe in the emergent global market. Small and medium-sized businesses will have the premier benefit from the corpus linguistics approach to knowledge extraction. In view of globalization, the development of a dependable European infrastructure has to be established and incorporated into international terminology work. Here, too, the course is set.

What is necessary now is the development of robust procedures for mining soft terminology. Such procedures are being jointly developed by corpus linguists, terminologists and computer scientists. Fast access to soft terminology facilitates communication among experts in a given domain. It is a precondition of national research and development discourses. Only where access to soft terminology exists is the necessary vertical information exchange between science and technology on the one hand and engineering and skilled labours on the other hand possible. Soft terminology lets us participate in the latest innovations, thus giving SMEs a chance to compete with much larger competitors. Modern text-based terminology work is becoming an economic factor. Today it can be carried out almost automatically with a limited amount of manpower and with measurable results. It is time for us to take up the challenge.

11 Lemmatization and collocational analysis of Lithuanian nouns

Andrius Utka

Introduction

In corpus studies when analysing a word, it is often convenient to see all or several grammatical forms of this word as one group. Such a group is referred to as a *lemma*. Traditionally the lemma is seen as a group of words that share the same stem and belong to the same part of speech, however their endings or spelling differ. Therefore *lemmatization* is a practice of conflating constituents of such a group into one single form.

Lemmatization is not an uncomplicated matter. Sinclair (1991: 41) has aptly described lemmatization as a 'subjective judgement by the researcher', where thousands of subjective decisions are made. Lemmatization also brings technical problems, since it is not only about stripping off prefixes and inflections, which can be done automatically by a computer, but it is also about dealing with 'open-ended linguistic material', which makes lemmatization rather more challenging (Federici and Pirrelli 1992: 123).

We can also view lemmatization as a kind of convenient generalization about relationships between the lemma and its forms. As a result, however, such a generalization can hide important linguistic information about individual constituents of the lemma. The preference of form to lemma is especially emphasized in John Sinclair's works, who claims that 'each distinct form is potentially a unique lexical unit, and that forms should only be conflated into lemmas when their environments show a certain amount and type of similarity' (Sinclair 1991: 8). This assumption is also supported and exemplified in studies by Stubbs (1996: 172–3) for English, and by Tognini-Bonelli (1996: 124–31) for Italian.

In spite of criticisms, lemmatization is often considered to be a useful method used in various statistical counts (especially counts of word frequencies), concordancing, collocational analysis and other areas.

This paper questions the practice of lemmatization for the Lithuanian language. More specifically it deals with lemmatization of nouns in collocational analysis.

The special importance of lemmatization for Lithuanian

Lithuanian is a strongly inflected language. Most Lithuanian nouns have seven grammatical cases (Nominative, Genitive, Dative, Accusative, Locative, Instrumental and Vocative) both in the plural and in the singular, and, thus, studying one wordform will often mean studying less than one fourteenth of the lemma (see Table 11.1). In contrast, most English nouns have just a singular and a plural form, and lemmatization is simply realized through associating, for example, the word *computer* with its plural form *computers.*

The multitude of wordforms is even more characteristic of Lithuanian verbs, for example the full paradigm of the verb 'to be' consists of 307 different wordforms. The extent of the contrast between English and Lithuanian languages can be demonstrated by word counts in George Orwell's famous book *1984* (see Figure 11.1).

In Figure 11.1, the bigger columns represent the size in words (or tokens) of the original book and the Lithuanian translation, and the smaller columns stand for the different words (or types). It is evident that even though the Lithuanian translation is shorter than the original, it contains many more different words. The type/token ratio gives the exact proportion of this difference. On average each wordform is repeated approximately twelve times in the English version and just six times in Lithuanian.

As a result, our software is commonly confronted with a large variety of wordforms, which means that we need to run complicated searches and deal with wordlists of enormous size (for example the Lithuanian corpus of 60 million words contains 1.2 million types). Reducing the number of wordforms with the help of lemmatization may seem a panacea for this problem.

However, as has been mentioned previously, there are some good grounds to assume that the practice of lemmatization in collocational analysis may bring a loss of important linguistic information. This

Table 11.1 Lithuanian cases

	Singular		*Plural*	
	'man'	*'way'*	*'men'*	*'ways'*
Nominative	*vyras*	*kelias*	*vyrai*	*keliai*
Genitive	*vyro*	*kelio*	*vyrų*	*kelių*
Dative	*vyrui*	*keliui*	*vyrams*	*keliams*
Accusative	*vyrą*	*kelią*	*vyrus*	*kelius*
Instrumental	*vyru*	*keliu*	*vyrais*	*keliais*
Locative	*vyre*	*kelyje*	*vyruose*	*keliuose*
Vocative	*vyre*	–	*vyrai*	*keliai*

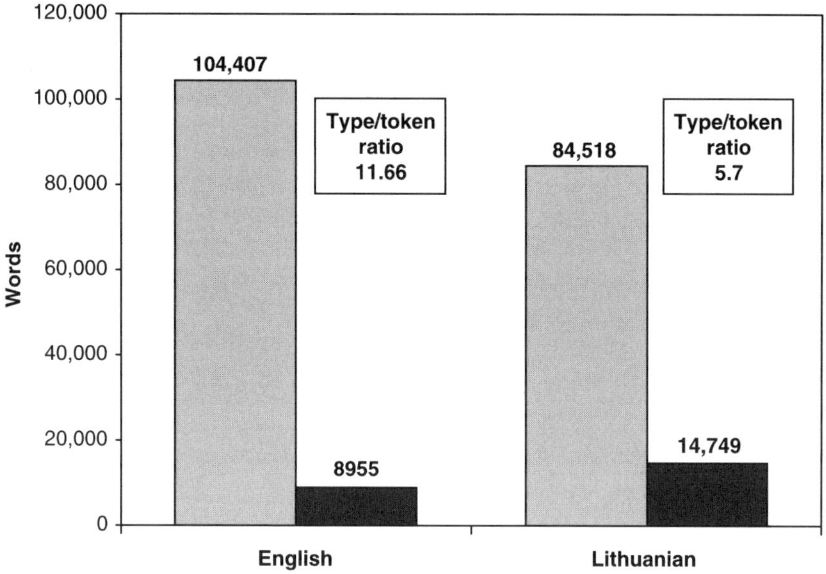

Figure 11.1 Tokens and types in George Orwell's *1984* in English and Lithuanian versions

assumption is based on two considerations. First, different grammatical cases of words have specific meanings expressed in them, that is, a word has its own lexical meaning plus the grammatical meaning (in English this is done with the help of prepositions). Thus we can expect that a word in different cases will occur in different contexts. Secondly, Lithuanian grammatical cases have very different frequencies of occurrence. If we consider a collocational profile for the whole lemma of a word, we will disregard collocational profiles of individual cases. As a result of this, the collocational profile for the whole lemma will largely reflect the profiles of more frequent grammatical cases, while the possibly interesting information related to less frequent cases may remain unnoticed. In the sections below we will try to demonstrate the validity of these considerations.

The case of the noun *teisybė* (truth)

We will look more closely at the Lithuanian noun *teisybė* ('truth'). This small experiment is run on a 10 million-word subcorpus, which has been specially created for it. Texts for the subcorpus have been taken from the largest Lithuanian corpus (Marcinkevičienė 1997). In order to make the subcorpus more balanced, we have included 50 per cent of periodicals and 50 per cent of books. The idea of the experiment is as follows: lists of collocates for different cases of *teisybė* are compared with the total list of collocates for the whole lemma. Such a comparison will reveal how well the lists of collocates of separate cases are reflected in the total list of collocates.

Composition of the lemma

First of all let us consider the composition of the lemma of the noun *teisybė*. All wordforms of *teisybė* have occurred 1271 times in total. As had been expected, not all of the grammatical cases have an equal share in this number.

Figure 11.2 shows that the Singular Nominative, Singular Genitive and Singular Accusative make up 96 per cent of all occurrences, while the Singular Dative, Singular Instrumental, Plural Nominative, Plural Accusative and Plural Genitive are very poorly represented, and some other cases do not appear at all. This distribution is partly due to the nature of this word. This is an abstract noun and thus it is rarely used in the plural, but it also represents the general situation in the Lithuanian language, which is that Nominative, Genitive and Accusative are by far the most frequent cases in the Lithuanian language.

This uneven distribution alone suggests that in the total list of collocates of the lemma frequent cases are more likely to be better represented than rare ones.

Lemma v case. Ranks of collocates

Let us consider the lists of collocates themselves. Lists of collocates based on the frequency of co-occurrence within the five-word span have been generated and analysed for the whole lemma of *teisybė*, and for the separate cases. As a result, nine lists have been produced: eight for the different cases and one for the whole lemma. In order to find out how the total list of collocates reflects the lists of collocates of specific cases a measure of ranking has been applied, so that each collocate in lists of separate cases has been given a rank in the total list of collocates (see Table 11.2).

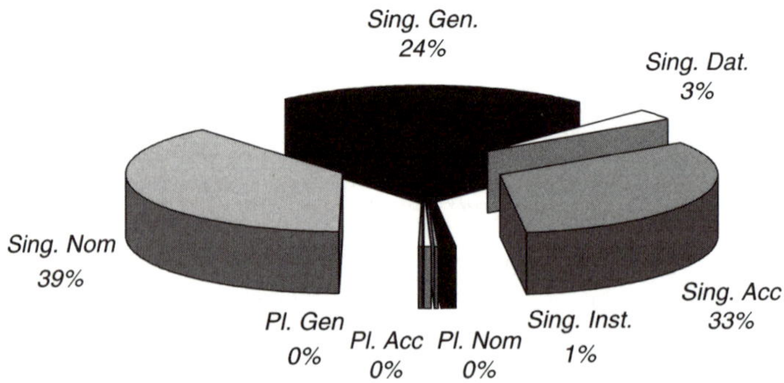

Figure 11.2 Composition of the lemma of the noun *teisybė*

Table 11.2 Ranks of collocates of *teisybė* in Singular Nominative and Singular Instrumental as opposed to their ranks in the total list of collocates

Ranks	*Singular Nominative* (39%)	*Ranks in total list*	*Singular Instrumental* (1%)	*Ranks in total list*
1	*ir (and)*	1	*kad ((that)*	2
2	*tai (it)*	3	*nei (neither)*	38
3	*kad (that)*	2	*ar (or)*	6
4	*ar (or)*	6	*iš (from/out)*	7
5	*bet (but)*	10	*ir (and)*	1
6	*ne (no)*	5	*jie (they)*	71
7	*yra (is)*	11	*jis (he)*	18
8	*buvo (was)*	12	*niekuo (nobody)*	203
9	*aš (I/me)*	4	*savo (his)*	15
10	*iš (from/out)*	7	*aš (I/me)*	4
11	*taip (yes)*	29	*dar (else)*	28
12	*jau (already)*	20	*geriau (better)*	173
13	*mano (my)*	21	*kitu (other)*	759
14	*į (in/into)*	8	*man (for me)*	31
15	*kas (who/what)*	19	*melo (lie)*	153
16	*kur (where)*	26	*ne (no)*	5
17	*čia (here)*	17	*nebus (will not happen)*	324
18	*kaip (how)*	16	*nebūsi (you will not be)*	325
19	*o (and)*	13	*netikės (will not believe)*	881
20	*tik (only)*	9	*netiki (does not believe)*	333

In Table 11.2 we can see the difference immediately. The first 20 collocates of the more frequent case (Singular Nominative) and their ranks in the total list are enumerated in the left column, and the less frequent case (Singular Instrumental) is represented in the right column. All the top collocates of *teisybė* in the Singular Nominative also have a high ranking in the total list, while the top collocates of *teisybė* in the Singular Instrumental are not so highly ranked in the total list. In the next section we will try to evaluate this difference by a numerical value with the help of a statistical procedure.

Pearson's correlation coefficient as the measure of linearity

Pearson's correlation coefficient has been chosen for this experiment in order to compare series of ranks of collocates for separate cases with their ranking in the total list of collocates. This coefficient is a measure of the linear association between two data series. The idea is that a series of ranks of collocates for a specific case (which for all cases is 1, 2, 3, 4, . . . n) is compared to the ranks of these words in the total list (for example for Singular Nominative 1, 3, 2, 6, . . . m, Table 11.2). If these ranks are all mixed up in the total list then there will be no linear association between these two data series and the Pearson's coefficient will be low, but if the total list more or less resembles the order of ranks, then the coefficient will be closer to one (see Table 11.3).

Table 11.3 Pearson's coefficient for different cases of *teisybė*

		Pearson's coefficient
Sing. Nominative	39%	0.7790
Sing. Genitive	24%	0.7467
Sing. Dative	3%	0.4547
Sing. Accusative	34%	0.7745
Sing. Instrumental	1%	0.4348
Pl. Nominative	0%	0.4246
Pl. Genitive	0%	–0.3249
Pl. Accusative	0%	–0.3876

In Table 11.3 Pearson's coefficients for lists of collocates of specific cases clearly show that the total list much better resembles the more frequent cases of the lemma. It is 0.7 for frequent cases, 0.4 for less frequent cases, and even negative for very rare cases.

Representation of nominal collocates

In collocational analysis there is a tendency to pay special attention to the most frequent nominal collocates in the list of collocates, as these collocates are usually the most important carriers of meaning. For example, considering the top nominal collocates for the whole lemma of *teisybė*, we find such words as *žmogus (man), Lietuva (Lithuania), metų (year), akis (eye),* and others (see Table 11.4). Consequently, we would want to generalize, and claim things of the kind that *teisybė* is a most significant collocate to *žmogus (man)* and to nouns that denote time, and that there is an interesting occurrence of the collocate *akis*, etc. However, these claims may not be valid for all grammatical cases of *teisybė*. In order to test this, we took 15 top ranked nouns from the total list of collocates, and determined how they occur in the lists of specific cases (see Table 11.4).

The results of the test are presented in Table 11.4. If a noun occurs at least once in the list of collocates of a specific case of *teisybė* then this is represented by a white square, while if it did not occur at all, this is represented by a shaded square. The table once again shows that nominal collocates for specific cases of *teisybė* are misrepresented in the total list of collocates. At the top of the list of collocates of the whole lemma we mostly find the collocates from the more frequent cases, meanwhile there are almost no collocates from the lists of Plural Nominative, Plural Genitive and Plural Accusative.

Table 11.4 Representation of most frequent nominal collocates of the lemma *teisybė* in specific cases

List of nominal collocates	Occs	Sin. Nom 39%	Sin. Gen 24%	Sin. Dat 3%	Sin. Acc 34%	Sin Instr 1%	Pl. Nom 0%	Pl. Gen 0%	Pl. Acc 0%
1. *m̌ogus (man)*	**21**	7	3	1	9	0	1	0	0
2. *m̌onęs (men)*	**16**	3	8	0	4	1	0	0	0
3. *kartą (time)*	**15**	5	8	0	1	1	0	0	0
4. *Lietuvos (Lithuania)*	**13**	1	7	0	5	0	0	0	0
5. *metų (year)*	**13**	4	9	0	0	0	0	0	0
6. *m̌ogaus (man)*	**13**	6	4	0	2	1	0	0	0
7. *akis (eye)*	**12**	6	1	2	3	0	0	0	0
8. *tęvas (father)*	**11**	4	1	0	5	1	0	0	0
9. *dievo (god)*	**10**	3	4	0	2	1	0	0	0
10. *gyvenime (life)*	**10**	2	6	1	0	1	0	0	0
11. *metu (year)*	**9**	5	2	0	2	0	0	0	0
12. *motina (mother)*	**9**	2	2	0	5	0	0	0	0
13. *melo (lie)*	**8**	0	6	0	0	2	0	0	0
14. *rusai (Russians)*	**8**	3	2	0	3	0	0	0	0
15. *tiesa (truth)*	**8**	5	3	0	0	0	0	0	0

Conclusion

The paper has tried to show that in the Lithuanian language a collocational analysis for the whole lemma of a noun tends to give 'pro-frequent case results', while disregarding minor grammatical cases. As a result, idiosyncrasies of individual cases remain unnoticed. In other words, we tried to show explicitly that form and context are closely related, so that each form (each specific grammatical case) occurs in different collocational environments. However, the practice of lemmatization in collocational analysis can be partly justified by the fact that it gives a generalized collocational profile of a word accounting for the majority of occurrences, and at the same time it saves time and energy. The ideal analysis, however, would be a context analysis for each separate form, which for a Lithuanian noun would make up to 14 different analyses and even more for a verb. While such a study is more complicated, it may also lead to some new insights and findings.

References

Federici, Stefano and Pirrelli, Vito (1992) 'A Bootstrapping Strategy for Lemmatisation: Learning Through Examples', *Proceedings of the 2nd*

International Conference on Computational Lexicography, COMPLEX '92. Budapest: Hungary: 123–36.

Marcinkevičienė, Rūta (1997) 'Tekstynų lingvistika ir lietuvių kalbos tekstynas', *Lituanistika* 1(29): 58–78.

Sinclair, John (1991) *Corpus, Concordance, Collocation.* Oxford: Oxford University Press.

Stubbs, Michael (1996) *Text and Corpus Analysis: Computer-assisted Studies of Language and Culture.* Oxford: Blackwell.

Tognini-Bonelli, Elena (1996) 'The Role of Corpus Evidence in Linguistic Theory and Description'. PhD thesis. Birmingham: University of Birmingham.

12 Challenging the native-speaker norm: a corpus-driven analysis of scientific usage

Geoffrey Williams

Introduction

Publication is an absolute necessity for all researchers; for many this means publication in English, especially in sciences where high impact requires recourse to international, hence English language, journals. This requirement often raises the spectre of language skills taking precedence over information content so that the request to 'get this checked by a native speaker' is far from infrequent. The problem is that the native speaker is a commodity in short supply. As has recently been pointed out by Graddol (1999), while there has been a steady rise in the number of users of English as an international language, the proportion of native, first-language, speakers is declining. This would seem to imply that the remaining few are doomed to correct the English of an ever-increasing majority. Another approach to assisting Non-Native Speaker (NNS) researchers might be to develop computerized tools based on specialized corpora.

The research article genre has been well researched on small text collections (Swales 1990) and increasingly on 'small' corpora (see Ghadessy *et al.* 2001). Constructing balanced specialized corpora presents particular problems of representativity, although to some extent these can be overcome by explicit external and internal selection criteria. However, one aspect that is often overlooked is the status, NS or NNS, of the authors included, a crucial point if the corpus is to be used to typify the grammatical norms of a genre. Whereas in large corpora, 'anomalies' may disappear in the mass of data, this cannot be true of small corpora. Studies in learner English, such as those based on the International Corpus of Learner English (Granger 1998), take a corpus of Native Speaker (NS) writing as a benchmark against which to measure Non-Native Speaker (NNS) production. While this is feasible for learner corpora based on controlled groups, this is much more difficult for specialized corpora where selection is based on relevance to the domain. Attempts to subcategorize a corpus on the basis of NS and NNS sources is far from a simple matter as to do this raises the question as to what a native speaker is.

The present study is based on a single language corpus, the BIVEG corpus (Williams 1998, 2001), for which the input comes from a wide variety of language backgrounds. The study is part of a larger project[1] that aims to study NS and NNS usage in writing research so as to build genre-specific tools for writer assistance. The part of the project described here is designed to look at a given range of known problem areas within a corpus of published scientific research to see whether variations in usage are related to NS or NNS usage. The methodology adopted is that of corpus-driven research (Tognini-Bonelli 2001), that is to say that no a priori decisions are taken as to the provenance of the concordance lines studied. The analysis is based entirely on corpus evidence.

This paper deals with the use of *which/that* relatives in a corpus of plant biology research articles. The aim is not to give a definitive answer to the problem of relatives in research writing, or even to approach an answer, but purely to experiment a corpus-driven methodology for the exploration of syntactic or lexical usage in specialized corpora. The paper proposes a potential solution for overcoming avoidance strategies through specialized dictionaries based on in-depth studies using specialized learner corpora and domain-comparable corpora.

Adopting a methodology

One obvious solution to the study of NS and NNS usage is the corpus-based approach. If we start with the hypothesis that NNS writing may be ill-formed or syntactically poor due to avoidance strategies, we would first classify the files by first-language origin of author and then carry out a comparative study. Two problems arise with this approach: that of defining who is, and who is not, a native speaker, and the danger, inherent in all hypothesis-based approaches to corpora, that if you set out to look for something, you will almost certainly find it, but pass by all the interesting details on the way. First we shall address the question of native-speaker status and then introduce the corpus-driven methodology that has been adopted.

The nativeness of native speakers

When marking up a corpus in XML using the TEI guidelines (Sperberg-McQueen and Burnard 2002) a lot of information appertaining to the authors can be listed in the header and re-used when classifying texts. This, however, leads to highly subjective decisions as to native and non-native speaker status. The most obvious problem that arises is as to what varieties of English will be accepted in the benchmark corpus. Australian, British and American English may seem obvious candidates, but by what right do we discount other varieties. If we take Commonwealth countries for example we must accept the Indian subcontinent as English-speaking, after all English is the lingua franca of the subcontinent and the population is much higher than that of the UK. However, not everyone has the same level of competence. It is no more possible to know from a name or place of work whether an Indian-sounding name was brought up speaking Hindi or English, or whether educated in India or in England, than to know whether someone going under the surname of Williams, for example, was born and bred outside of the UK and with no contact with the English language other than through secondary schooling.

Another problem that arises when dealing with science research articles is that of multiple authorship. Many scientific publications are the work of a research team, so it is impossible to know which one wrote the text, the native or non-native, and whether the text was heavily corrected afterwards. This is compounded by scientists working away from home, especially frequent in the world of post-doc research contracts. In this case the location of the laboratory tells us nothing about those working and publishing there.

Apart from isolating the NS and NNS we must decide whether the 'native writer' should be accepted as representing the norm. After all, how do we measure language competence? In many cases, the educational systems of some countries give a much more rigorous training in grammar than that received by the average English student. It is quite conceivable that in some cases the grammatical variants, one of the defining characteristics of a so-called sublanguage, are not simply bad English.

Given the difficulties inherent in dividing NS from NNS writers in a specialized corpus this research adopts a corpus-driven approach accepting that published research is an accepted norm. Instead of making a subjective classification beforehand we look at who does what, and why, within a corpus of published scientific research to find out just how reliable a corpus of published material may be as a benchmark for 'correct' scientific usage.

Corpus-driven approach

In a corpus-driven perspective classifying of texts by presumed first-language origin of author is clearly a bad solution in that it starts with the hypothesis that non-native speakers are less competent than native speakers and will automatically produce material that is either syntactically or pragmatically incorrect or more simplistic in structure.

Rather than attempting to isolate what is native and non-native speaker writing, we start with a quantitative analysis so as to group texts without reference to authors' linguistic origins, but only as a function of linguistic strategy. At a later stage we do refer to NS production, but only after texts have been classified on usage patterns and only referring to authors known to be of British, American or Australian origin. This is only possible if in close contact with the producing community, as is the case here.

The project

The project consists in exploring usage within a corpus of international scientific English by looking at usage first, before seeing who produced the individual texts. The aim is to bring together linguists working from different perspectives, syntacticians, pragmaticians, corpus linguists, to look at scientific writing with the view to building a computer-based tool to assist with the writing process. It seeks to analyse certain grammatical factors within a corpus for frequency, well-formedness and pragmatic usage so as to isolate potential avoidance strategies and suggest alternatives. The texts are analysed using corpus tools to discover regularities, the results are then analysed by a syntactician with reference to accepted norms and by a pragmatician to study for what reason the norms may be adapted or flouted. This is a deconstructive stage that must be carried out before a reconstructive approach assisting with research writing can be envisaged.

The problems faced by non-native writers of English are relatively well known: despite a knowledge of the genre-specific norms, they still face both structural and grammatical problems. Structural problems are often essentially pragmatic and are expressed through organization of information, essentially theme–rheme structure. Grammatical problems include the use of relatives, determiners, compounding and tense choice. These have been well documented in the literature from Barber (1962) onwards. Such difficulties are not just grammatical, but are largely pragmatic in nature in that they relate to choices within a restricted socio-rhetorical context. This brings in the problem of typifying the norms of a genre.

Lexico-grammatical factors have been used to typify different genres (Biber 1986, Nakamura 1993). However, while factorial analysis can be used to categorize it still fails to address the pragmatic questions as to why and where within a text such choices are made (Gledhill 2000: 33). In this study, rather than just quantifying discrete factors, we use the relative frequency of given features so as to group the texts in which they occur by order of frequency in order to isolate high, low and mid frequency users. These subsets would then be studied to see how and to what purpose the factors were being used and what alternative strategies are being adopted. In such an inductive approach we can then go back to the initial corpus subset to look at the frequency of alternative rhetorical and syntactic strategies so as to see to what extent avoidance strategies are being used. Further work will be required to see whether it is the high-frequency groups that are using avoidance strategies to avoid, for example, compounding. As an example of the approach adopted we shall look at *that* and *which* as markers of relativity in a corpus of research articles.

The corpus

The BIVEG Corpus (Williams 1998, 2001) was built to carry out essentially lexicographic research with a corpus-driven approach. It was expanded from a very small pre-study corpus into a corpus that seeks to demonstrate language use in a particular scientific community, that of parasitic plant research. For this study it was decided to divide it into two subsets that cut across disciplinary boundaries: articles published in a number of specialized scientific journals, the *Plant Biology Journal* (*PBJ*) set and the proceedings of a conference on parasitic plant biology, the Parasitic Plant Conference (PPC) set.

The reason for this breakdown is simple, the reputed international journals are noted for nitpicking on grammatical details and so it may be presumed that peer-reviewed articles will be relatively well-formed. On the other hand, the peer-review process for conferences may be based more on relevance to the theme so that norms of well-formedness may not be so rigorously applied.

Lexical analyses of the two subsets did reveal a tremendous difference in terminological density between the two subsets in that one is addressing a field-specific community through a peer-reviewed journal, the other a topic-based community which is multidisciplinary. The question which we have set out to look into here is whether there are more syntactic infelicities in the topic-based PPC subset, which would then be reflected by syntactic poverty in the other subset when NNS writers are forced to use avoidance strategies to get round difficulties of expression.

Relative use of relatives

In looking at *which/that* relatives a number of questions may be asked:

- How frequent are these clauses?
- What are they used for?
- Is there a difference between the choice of *which* over *that*?
- What other strategies are used?

If we start with the PPC set we find that there is a wide variation of occurrence of both *which* and *that*, measured in terms of relative frequency, with three texts not using *which* at all. As Graph 1 shows the texts with a high frequency of *which* may have a low frequency of *that*, which could lead to the question of interchangeability with a preference for one above the other, or at least some degree of confusion between restrictive and non-restrictive clauses.

If we take both the high and low-scoring groups, the five texts with the highest and lowest frequencies, we find an equal use of restrictive and non-restrictive clauses. In the low-frequency group, it is rare to find *that* used incorrectly in non-restrictive clauses. On the other hand, incorrect use of punctuation is frequent, as can be seen in the following examples:

> The parent line *N-13 which* is known to possess moderate resistance to Striga under field conditions (!REF), had high-stimulant characteristics

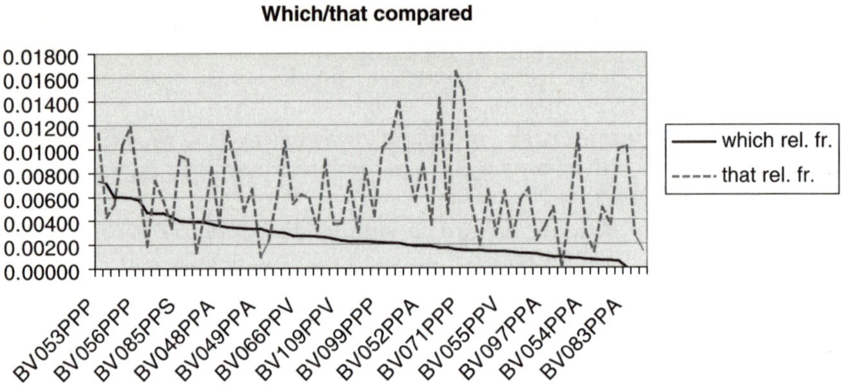

Graph 1 Comparative usage of *which* and *that*

> The infestation totals less than *3000 m2 which* we fumigated with methyl bromide

> Nuclei of Striga were predominantly euchromatic in contrast to those of *Vicia which* appeared heterochromatic

What is more significant, however, is the difference in usage. The texts with low relative frequency are all descriptive, factual texts; they are simply reporting. Closer inspection of the source texts shows that this does not necessarily equate with NNS usage as all the texts make use of complex sentence structures. However, three of them display a poor degree of cohesion; the two of known NS source use more complex structures and show greater cohesiveness.

We can then tentatively conclude that low frequency of *which* relatives arises not from a lack of rhetorical strategies – there is a wide use of non-finite clauses – but from text type. The problems that are encountered are those of more general textual cohesion.

Table 12.1 PPC set. Texts with low relative frequency of *which*

Low relative frequency		Source
BV054PPA	descriptive, factual, complex juxtaposition, poor cohesion	
BV067PPV	descriptive, factual, complex juxtaposition	
BV074PPA	descriptive, factual, complex structures, cohesive	NS
BV090PPP	descriptive, factual, complex structures, cohesive	NS
BV101PPV	descriptive, factual, complex juxtaposition, poor cohesion	

If we now turn to the group with a high relative frequency of *which* relatives (Table 12.2) a different picture can be found. Here the texts are no longer simple description, but adopt a much more discursive style. Some texts still have difficulty with cohesive devices, but on the whole we find a more evolved style.

It would be hasty to draw conclusions from such a small sample, but two facts seem to be coming clear: use of relatives is linked to text purpose, purely factual to the descriptive. There does however remain the possibility that some NNS are deliberately adopting this reporting strategy to avoid complications in a more discursive style.

Table 12.2 PPC set. Texts with high relative frequency of *which*

High relative frequency		Source
BV053PPP	classifying by comparison, high use of adverbials, cohesive	NS
BV059PPV	descriptive discussion, poor punctuation of non-restrictives	
BV060PPP	descriptive discussion, high use of adverbials, cohesive	NS
BV069PPV	classifying by comparison, well-structured, cohesive	
BV096PPV	experimental, well-structured, cohesive	NS

Turning to the *PBJ* set (Tables 12.3 and 12.4) we find a similar story as to usage – texts with low frequency tend to be more descriptive and factual, often using non-restrictive clauses to comment. Again in the high-frequency texts we find a more discursive style with mostly non-restrictive clauses, which explains the low usage of *that*. Somewhat surprisingly we also find very poor punctuation showing a confusion as to the use of restrictive and non-restrictive clauses. However, the overall picture is that this corpus is not concerned with defining, and hence uses less restrictive clauses, unless of course other strategies are being used.

Problem-solving

What we are beginning to find is that we must differentiate two problems:

- ill-formed phrasing
- avoidance strategies

The former could be treated through some form of grammar checker that has been calibrated to take into account usage in the field of the writer. Unfortunately a corrector only looks at what is 'wrong', not what is missing,

Table 12.3 *PBJ* set. Texts with low relative frequency of *which*

Low relative frequency of *which*	Relative frequency of *which*		Relative frequency of *that*		Source
BV012PBJ	0.0005	Prep+which, Non-restrictive	0.0029	Descriptive, factual	
BV015PBJ	0.0006	Non-restrictive	0.0010	Descriptive, poor cohesion	
BV033PBJ	0.0007	Restrictive	0.0017	Descriptive, cohesive	
BV119PBJ	0.0007	Non-restrictive	0.0007	Descriptive, hypothetical	NS
BV125PBJ	0.0007	Prep+which	0.0015	Discussion, well-structured	NS

Table 12.4 *PBJ* set. Texts with high relative frequency of *which*

High relative frequency of *which*	Relative frequency of *which*		Relative frequency of *that*		Source
BV034PBJ	0.0067	Non-restrictive, incorrect punctuation	0	Discursive, cohesion and punctuation poor	
BV111PBJ	0.0006	Non-restrictive, incorrect punctuation, restrictive	0.0004	Discursive, cohesive	
BV126PBJ	0.0007	Non-restrictive and restrictive	0	Descriptive, cohesion and punctuation poor	
BV152PBJ	0.0007	Non-restrictive and restrictive	0.0004	Discursive, cohesion poor	
BV154PBJ	0.0007	Non-restrictive and restrictive	0.0230	Discursive, cohesive	NS

so linked to the grammar checker we should have a tool that will offer reformulations. Such a tool would have to be rendered aware of specificities of subgenre in research writing. However, before we can build our tool, we must clarify some aspects of usage.

The *which/that* choice

> Restrictive relative clauses are closely connected to their antecedent or head prosodically, and denote a limitation on the reference of the antecedent.
>
> Quirk *et al.* (1985, 6.33: 366)

As we have seen, the problem with restrictive/non-restrictive clauses is one of punctuation: the choice of non-restrictive clauses forces the choice of *which.* This then leaves restricted clauses for which the two relatives might be seen as interchangeable.

One theory is that the difference of use between the two pronouns is pragmatic, an anaphoric/cataphoric opposition. This may be the case theoretically, but there is little evidence of this in the corpus examples so that in practice the choice appears completely open. The fact that a word processor prefers *that* for *which* in its grammar corrector may only reflect American usage in that the preference among British or British-educated sources is very much for *which.* Part of the choice may be simply due to colligation, restricted uses.

Quirk *et al.* (1985) report no difference of use in general restricted clauses, but a number of differences in certain precise cases (ibid., 17.15: 1250). It is then necessary to see whether these restrictions are respected or whether the form is avoided.

In theory *that* or 'zero' is preferred for non-personal antecedents such as *all, everything . . ., that* being preferred when the antecedent is modified by a superlative or by the post-determiners *first, last, next, only.* In practice only two examples of the former are found in the entire corpus. The first is a mistake in an NNS text where *much less* is followed by *that* rather than *than,* the second '*Anything which can reveal allelic*' is a NS production. In theory, superlatives are followed by *which,* which was not the case in the only example found:

> figure 1 represents the most parsimonious tree that was constructed . . .

With only single examples no conclusions can be drawn, so it is difficult to say whether lack of data corresponds to an avoidance strategy, or that these formulae have no place in scientific writing. The only way to know whether potential avoidance strategies are present is to have recourse to a larger corpus. This will be discussed later. On the other hand, if it is an avoidance strategy, means should be found to exemplify usage so as to widen the rhetorical arsenal of the NNS writer.

One obvious difference in usage of *which/that* is between relative and appositive clauses. The latter do not seem to be a problem as there is no element of choice, these are lexical phrases in their own right of the form *the fact that, there is evidence that,* etc. This concerns a relatively closed set as indication, observation(s), speculation, suggestion. However, in noting patterns we must beware of traps as in *the observation that* and *an observation which/that,* which brings us to the related problem of determiners, and in particular the definite article. As Quirk *et al.* (*op. cit.*) do point out there can be an ambiguity between relative and appositive, but it is rare in that misuse of an appositive would be immediately noticed and corrected by reviewers.

Relatives in this corpus are mostly used to refine rather than define an idea. If the anaphorical/cataphorical opposition is real and can explain preferences for one or other form, then we are going to have to find out how this is expressed, as there is no point in explaining this to the user. This all goes to prove that you cannot teach by theory or rule, but only by example, and to do that we come back to the dictionary as a teaching tool and the representation of grammar within the specialized lexical context. This would mean the development of specialized pedagogical ESP dictionaries which, instead of seeking to define, would exemplify usage in domain-specific contexts. This in turn will lead to a problem of presentation, classifying related grammatical and pragmatic functions – an example of this might be seen with the problems of what Quirk terms 'relative as adverbial'.

Relative as adverbial

Proof of a potential avoidance strategy does appear with preposition + *which* forms, Quirk's 'relative as adverbial'. In the high/low groups of the PPC set the texts using adverbials all fell into the higher group, the most frequent usage being exclusively among NS writers. Faced with the question as to how to exemplify, these the answer seems to be through the head noun or its hypernym.

Prepositions in relative clauses are fulfilling precise functions relating to the means whereby something happens, as in 'by', relating to time or duration, as with 'after' and 'during', etc. Within the BIVEG corpus these functions are often related to a limited lexis, for instance 'by' occurs with mechanisms and processes, so the clause could be introduced through the hyponym 'process'. Similarly 'at *which*' occurs with frequency, temperature and place, 'of *which*' with numbers so that the following patterns would have to be demonstrated:

- at which
  - 'frequency' at which x occurs
  - 'temperature' at which x occurs
  - 'place' at which x occurs
- by which
  - 'process' by which x happens

- of which
  - 'number' of which

Such formulae would then have to be demonstrated along with the other grammar patterns found with the headword and the headwords linked through their classifier to demonstrate the regularity of the pattern.

This is only a passive offer – it goes without saying that a more active reformulation process offering greater assistance to the apprentice science writer is desirable. However, while terminological extraction tools can locate terminological reformulation, a corpus-driven analysis is necessary to locate potential problem areas.

Putting the cart before the horse

The obvious outcome of this very small corpus-driven study is that we must be very careful when claiming that a corpus represents usage within a given genre, and that in consequence these are the strategies and functions to be taught. At a recent, 1999, meeting in Marburg, the chairman announced that 'The English of Science is bad English'. Given the examples taken from the BIVEG corpus this pessimistic viewpoint could well be thought to be true. It is perhaps inevitable in the development of World Englishes where the aim is above all to communicate. However, this poverty may reflect avoidance strategies which are used to raise texts to a publishable standard, but which are a cause of frustration for the NNS writer who would like to express him- or herself better. Dealing with avoidance and 'incorrect' usage also raises questions as to the benchmarks against which to measure publishable standards in science writing.

If we draw up a list of grammatical functions that 'typify' science writing we cannot be sure that we are reflecting a developing socio-rhetorical strategy adopted for reasons of precision and scientific rigour, or simply a series of avoidance strategies that reflect the needs of NNS scientists to get their word in edgeways. If the latter is the case then the answer may be to look at corpora to identify avoidance strategies and seek ways to alleviate them, within the norms of science, and not try to impose the model of literary practice. The answer may well be to tease out a selection of NS articles as a benchmark, but here we come back to subjective judgements as to what is and what is not NS, and what is an acceptable standard given that the NS texts are not error-free if we measure them by currently accepted norms.

Part of the answer may lie in building a comparable corpus using known NNS research papers, at various stages of elaboration, and a benchmark corpus from known NS sources, provided of course that we wish to accept British or American usage as the standard to be adopted.

Once patterns have been isolated on such specialized learner corpora, it will be necessary to see whether generalizations can be drawn. BIVEG, like most specialized corpora, is small, so it would be useful to look at other corpora for comparative purposes. However, recourse to large reference corpora is not necessarily the answer given their heterogeneous nature, but on the other hand, in making the small corpora bigger their specificity is lost, and we run the risk of losing the wood in the trees. One solution being developed to overcome this is a comparative study through the Corpus of Scientific and Medical English (CorpSE) Initiative.

This initiative seeks to associate researchers working on scientific and medical topics so as to build a series of specialized corpora that can be used in comparative studies. The aim is not to standardize the corpora, but to have clearly defined external and internal selection criteria and a standardized system of mark-up so as to facilitate exchange of data. It is accepted that researchers working on small corpora are frequently impeded by copyright restrictions from handing over the documents themselves, but that the data from search routines can be shared. It is hoped that this will get round some of the difficulties of the large/small corpus barrier by allowing researchers access to greater amounts of comparative data within a given genre.

The research outlined here is of necessity ongoing. This paper only demonstrates an approach to the complexity of judgements as to well-formedness in specialized corpora. The research is also ongoing as language learners and users have always made mistakes, and always will. There can never be a definitive solution, just a usable solution within the constraints and technical possibilities of the moment, and that means continuing to look at corpora.

The problem with corpus-driven approaches is that they are uncomfortable; you look but do not know what you will find. Corpus-driven research will raise ever more questions, which must be better than just coming in with the answers.[1]

Notes

1 This paper is based on a presentation given at the Sixth TELRI European Seminar that was held in Bansko, Bulgaria from 8 to 11 November 2001. The research is being conducted in collaboration with Professor Paul Boucher, University of Nantes, and Professor Claude Sionis, University of La Rochelle, through the *Analyse Linguistique et Pratique Langagières* (ALPL) research group which is based at the University of Nantes, France.

References

Barber, C. L. (1962) 'Some Measurable Characteristics of Modern Scientific Prose', in Swales, John *Episodes in ESP.* Hemel Hempstead: Pergamon Press, 3–14.

Biber, Douglas (1986) 'Spoken and written textual dimensions in English: resolving the contradictory findings', *Language* 62: 384–414.

Ghadessy, Mohsen, Henry, Alex and Roseberry, Robert L. (2001) *Small corpus studies and ELT.* Amsterdam: John Benjamins.

Gledhill, Christopher J. (2000) *Collocations in science writing.* Tübingen: Gunter Narr Verlag.

Graddol, David (1999) 'The decline of the native speaker', in Graddol, David and Meinhof, Ulrich H. (eds) *English in a changing world. AILA Review* 13: 57–68.

Granger, Sylviane (ed.) (1998) *Learner English on Computer.* Harlow: Longman.

Nakamura, Junsaku (1993) 'Statistical Methods and Large Corpora – A new Tool for Describing Text Types', in Baker, Mona, Gill, Francis and Tognini-Bonelli, Elena (eds) *Text and Technology: in honour of John Sinclair.* Amsterdam: John Benjamins.

Quirk, Randolph, Greenbaum, Sidney, Leech, Geoffrey and Svartik, Jan (1985) *A Comprehensive Grammar of the English Language.* London: Longman.

Sperberg-McQueen, C. M. and Burnard, Lou (eds) (2002) *TEI P4: Guidelines for Electronic Text Encoding and Interchange.* Text Encoding Initiative Consortium. XML Version: Oxford/Providence, RI/Charlottesville, VN Bergen.

Swales, John (1990) *Genre Analysis: English in Academic and Research Settings.* Cambridge: Cambridge University Press.

Tognini-Bonelli, Elena (2001) *Corpus Linguistics at Work.* Amsterdam: John Benjamins.

Williams, Geoffrey (1998) 'Collocational Networks: Interlocking Patterns of Lexis in a Corpus of Plant Biology Research Articles', *International Journal of Corpus Linguistics* 3(1): 151–71.

Williams, Geoffrey (2001) *Les réseaux collocationnels dans la construction et l'exploitation d'un corpus dans le cadre d'une communauté de discours scientifique.* Lille: Presses Universitaires de Septentrion.

Part Two

Multilingual Corpora

13 Chinese-English translation database: extracting units of translation from parallel texts

Chang Baobao, Pernilla Danielsson and Wolfgang Teubert

Introduction

Machine translation has proved to be a very challenging task, much harder than originally imagined in the 1950s. More than 50 years of hard work has failed to change the field significantly. Many of the same problems that initially puzzled researchers are still present today.

Most of the Machine Translation (henceforth MT) systems that have become commercially available have adopted transfer-based strategies. These strategies are widely acknowledged to be the most practical approaches. In the transfer-based paradigm, translation is performed in three stages: 1. the source language is analysed into an intermediate source representation, such as syntactic parsed source language; 2. the source representation is then converted into target language dependent representation; 3. finally, the target translation is generated from the target representation.

However, a major problem with the transfer approach is its view of the translation unit as it assumes the single word is the unit of translation. Normally, an MT system begins by segmenting the source-language sentence into words, looking up the words in the MT source and transfer lexica. It then converts every source word into a target word. Finally, the MT system stitches all target words together into sentences, according to the rules stated in the syntactical component of the target language.

Using single source words as translation units causes several problems. First, it will make an unsuitable base for selecting proper target words since single-source words are usually polysemous. This is a problem that MT shares with all other computational linguistics applications as there currently exists no reliable way of disambiguating word senses. Another disadvantage when taking single words as translation units is that it leads to a word-by-word translation; good translations are done using a more holistic approach.

In this paper we propose that, instead of single words, the basic unit of meaning should be made up of one or more words in a meaningful unit. A group of source words should be treated as a whole, with the focus lying on the meaning of the unit. This is especially important in translation between unrelated language pairs, such as Chinese and English.

Following this observation, we believe translation units to be unambiguous words and word groups (multiword units). A collection of bilingual translation units, such as these multiword units, will then make a welcome contribution to any machine translation system.

The manual compilation of databases for translation units is particularly labour-intensive. However, following recent advances in Corpus Linguistics, especially in parallel corpus research (Gale 1991, Tufis 2001, Wu 1994), the automatic identification of translation units and their target equivalents, from existing authentic translations, may offer a feasible solution. At present, there is no method of obtaining the final results in the form of bilingual lexica from these parallel texts. Nevertheless, methods exist that can provide a useful candidate list of bilingual translation units. For further discussion of how parallel texts can contribute to bilingual lexicography, see Teubert (2001).

This paper will elaborate on current work towards the (semi-) automatic acquisition of translation databases; all consisting of Chinese–English translation units extracted from a parallel Chinese–English corpus. It describes work-in-progress and will offer examples from ongoing work. However, no final results will be given as yet.

The work is conducted at the Centre for Corpus Linguistics, Birmingham University. Thus far, a Chinese–English bilingual corpus has been compiled consisting of approximately 17 million words from each language. Comparing this parallel corpus to many present-day monolingual corpora (for example the Bank of English with its 450 million words) makes it appear small. One must bear in mind that parallel corpora are more labour-intensive in compilation when compared to their monolingual counterparts. Most often parallel corpora only reach a size of 2 million words (see for example ENPC: Johansson and Hofland 2001).

The texts in the corpus are mainly collected via the Internet, from sources covering all four Chinese-speaking regions, i.e. Mainland China, Hong Kong, Taiwan and Singapore. Initially, the Hong Kong Legal Documents subcorpus (HKLDC) with about 6 million words was selected and is used as a basis for our feasibility study.

Terminology definitions

In this section, we define the four terms that are frequently used in this paper.

Multi-Word Unit (MWU): a Multi-Word Unit is a group of words in a language. All words in a Multi-Word Unit tend to co-occur frequently and constitute a valid syntactic unit, for example, an adjective + noun combination.

Translation Unit (TU): a Translation Unit is a single or multiword unit in a language. Together with its context information, a Translation Unit is translated into another language unambiguously.

Translation Equivalent Pair (TEP): a Translation Equivalent Pair is composed of both a source-language Translation Unit and a target-language Translation Unit, which are mutual translations.

Context Profile: a Context Profile is an abstract description of the contexts of the source Translation Unit and the target Translation Unit in a Translation Equivalent Pair. This describes where the translation equivalence defined in a TEP holds.

Framework of automatic acquisition of bilingual Translation Units

The whole process of the identification of bilingual translation units may be further divided into 5 major steps as depicted in Figure 13.1. So far, the first three steps are completed, while the rest remain to be implemented.

1. For the purpose of extracting bilingual translation units, some prior processing of the corpus is necessary. These include alignment of the bilingual texts, at sentence level, and monolingual annotation of the source and target texts respectively.
2. As previously mentioned, our definition of the translation unit covers both single and multiword units. In this step, the source and target-language multiword units are identified and marked separately in the corpus.
3. After identification of the multiword units in both languages, the next step is to extract a list of bilingual Translation Equivalent Pairs. Every

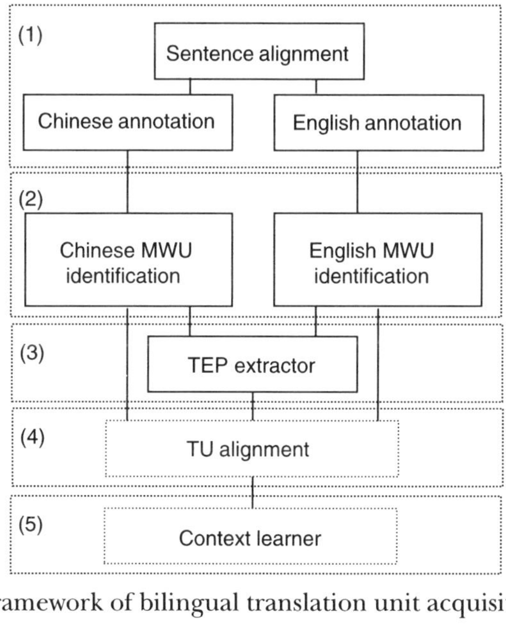

Figure 13.1 Framework of bilingual translation unit acquisition

TEP is composed of a Chinese Translation unit and an English Translation unit.

4. Step four will set the correspondences between the source Translation Unit and target Translation Unit in the corpus.
5. Lastly, a context learner is applied to the TU-aligned corpus (from step four) from which the context profiles are collected for each TEP.

Preprocessing the corpus

The Hong Kong Legal Documents Corpus is composed of laws and amendments issued by the Hong Kong Special Administration Region (HKSAR). All the texts are available in both Chinese and English and this corpus consists of approximately six million words per language.

The Chinese texts in the corpus are encoded with the Big-5 code. Due to the fact that our Chinese language tools only deal with Chinese GB code, all Chinese texts were initially converted from Big-5 code into GB code. After conversion, the corpus was aligned using a length-based sentence aligner (Danielsson and Ridings 1997). The legal documents are already well arranged, section-by-section, which enables an easy sentence alignment and the precision is therefore high. The Chinese texts were then segmented and Part of Speech (POS) tagged with a program developed by the Institute of Computational Linguistics, Peking University (see further specifications in Yu 2002). Subsequently, all English texts were tokenized, lemmatized and POS-tagged with a freely available tree-based tagger (Schmied 1994). Two tag sets were used for Chinese and English respectively: ICL/PKU tag set for Chinese texts and UPENN tag set for English texts. A comparison between the two tag sets can be found in the appendix. Figure 13.2 below is used to illustrate a sample of the corpus after preprocessing.

In Figure 13.2, both parts of the corpus are arranged into one token per line. The XML-like tag '<s>' marks the start of the sentence. The left-hand column gives the Chinese input while the right column is used for English. The single-letter tags on the right of the Chinese tokens are their POS tags. The two columns right of the English tokens are POS tags and lemmas.

Statistical measurement used

Four statistical measurements were used in the identification of monolingual multiword units and the correspondences of the bilingual translation units. All four statistical formulas measure the degree of association for two random events.

These two events, which are below denoted as *X* and *Y*, can be interpreted as two Chinese words appearing in the Chinese texts, or as two translation units appearing in an aligned region of the corpus. The distribution of the two events may be depicted by a two-by-two contingency table, see Figure 13.3.

Chinese texts		English Texts	
…		…	
<s id=5>		<s_id=5>	
本	r	This	DT this
条例	n	Ordinance	NN ordinance
可	d	may	MD may
…		…	
通则	n	General JJ	general
条例	n	Clauses NNS	clause
》	w	Ordinance	NN ordinance
。	w	. . .	
<s id=6>		<s_id=6>	
附注	n	Remarks	NNS
:	w	remark	
…		: : :	

Figure 13.2 Samples of the corpus after preprocessing

	Y	$\neg Y$
X	a	b
$\neg Y$	c	d

Figure 13.3 A 2 by 2 contingency table

The numbers in the four cells of the above table have the following meanings:

a: all counts of the cases where the two events *X* and *Y* co-occur
b: all counts of the cases where *X* occurs but *Y* does not
c: all counts of the cases where *X* does not occur but *Y* does
d: all counts of the cases where both *X* and *Y* do not occur

Based on this contingency table, different kinds of measurements may be used. We have tried four, namely the point-wise mutual information, the DICE coefficient, the χ^2 score and the Log-Likelihood score. One other measurement used by Gale (1991) is $ø^2$ score, which is equivalent to the χ^2 score. All four measurements have been calculated in our study using the following formula.

1. Point-wise mutual information

$$MI(st,tt) = \log_2 \frac{n \times a}{(a+b) \times (a+c)}$$

2. DICE coefficient

$$DICE(st,tt) = \frac{2a}{(a+b) \times (a+c)}$$

3. χ^2 score

$$\chi^2(st,tt) = \frac{n \times (a \times d - b \times c)^2}{(a+b) \times (a+c) \times (b+d) \times (c+d)}$$

4. Log-Likelihood score

$$LL(st,tt) = 2 \times (a \times \log \frac{a \times n}{(a+b) \times (a+c)} + b \times \log \frac{b \times n}{(a+b) \times (b+d)}$$

$$+ c \times \log \frac{c \times n}{(c+d) \times (a+c)} + d \times \log \frac{d \times n}{(c+d) \times (b+d)})$$

The results from our study, and a comparison between the four methods, will be presented in the results section.

Identification of multiword units

For this application, we have defined the multiword unit as having the following properties:

1. A multiword unit (MWU) is a unit where the words in the unit occur frequently together and where the whole MWU is recurrent. In the significance of statistics, multiword units should be word groups that co-occur more frequently than expected.
2. In this study, the MWUs will not be allowed to be arbitrary combinations of words and the MWUs must form valid syntactic structures, predefined in our project.

Based on the first property, an iterative algorithm has been developed using statistical means. This lists word groups, which show strong coherence.

The algorithm is based on the following specifications: if we assume that a text is a series of words, then a text T could be defined as:

$T = w_1, w_2 \ldots w_n$, n is the number of words in T.

Initially, the algorithm will try to find any multiword unit of length 2. All different consecutive word pairs are collected.

$WP = \{< w_i, w_{i+1} > | i = 1, \ldots, m\}$

The algorithm then calculates the degree of association using the statistical measurements listed in the section above. Word pairs, whose association values are greater than a predefined threshold, will be accepted as candidates of multiword units (of two words) and will be annotated as such in the corpus. In order to find word groups of more than two words, the algorithm needs to be run repeatedly and stopped when no word groups have a greater association value than the threshold. The algorithm is designed as a recursive structure; it identifies longer word groups by viewing the shorter word group marked in the previous run as one word.

Unfortunately, the results produced by this algorithm are not always meaningful units; they contain a substantial amount of so-called *statistical garbage*. Therefore, some kind of refinement is required. This is where the property of *valid syntactic structure* comes into use. By making use of a filter module all word groups are checked to see if they match a set of predefined syntactic patterns.

'a+n',	'NN+NN',
'b+n',	'NN+NNS',
'n+n',	......
...	'NN+IN<of>'
'MWU+n',	'JJ+NN',
'n+MWU',	...
'MWU+MWU'	'MWU+MWU'

Figure 13.4 Syntactic patterns

Figure 13.4 above shows some patterns used by the filter. The left-hand side patterns are used for the Chinese language while the right-hand side is for the English language.

Extracting bilingual translation units

We adopt the *hypothesis and testing* approach, used also in Tufis (2001) to extract translation equivalent pairs from a corpus. It follows the observation that words that are translations of each other are more likely to appear in aligned regions. In our study, both single and multiword units are taken into consideration.

The whole procedure could be divided logically into two phases. The first phase, 'the generative phase', lists all possible translation equivalent pairs from the aligned corpus. The second phase, 'the testing phase', selects Translation Equivalent correspondences that show an association measure higher than expected under the independence assumption as translation equivalence pairs. Again we use the same four statistical measurements, the DICE coefficient, the point-wise mutual information, the LL score and the χ^2 score, to measure the degree of association.

One problem of this approach is its inefficiency in processing large corpora. The generative phase, where all the translation equivalent pairs are listed, may lead to a huge search space. Therefore, to make the approach more efficient we adopted the following assumption from Tufis (2001): source translation units tend to be translated into translation units of the same syntactic category. For example, English nouns tend to be translated into Chinese nouns and the English pattern 'JJ+NN' tends to be translated into one of the Chinese patterns 'a+n' or 'b+n'. Obviously, this assumption is not always true for translation between Chinese and English. However, the gain in the efficiency of the algorithm is greatly improved, while the precision is not adversely affected.

Experiments and results

This section will show some results from our preliminary study where a small set of 500 sentences from the corpus was selected and used. We have performed preliminary experiments to test the performance of different statistical measurements and the performance changes when the category-based hypothesis is used.

The table below shows how many correct and partially correct correspondences there are in the first hundred translation equivalent pairs produced by the algorithm.

	MI	DICE	LL	χ^2
Correct	39	5	70	75
Partially correct	5	1	10	6
Accuracy	44%	6%	80%	81%

Figure 13.5 Performance variations of different statistical measurements

Figure 13.5 shows that the Log-Likelihood (LL) score and the χ^2 score achieve better accuracy over the mutual information and the DICE coefficient. The reason for this may be that the LL score and the χ^2 score take cell *d* of the contingency table into consideration, while the point-wise mutual information and the DICE coefficient do not.

Experiments also show that the category-based hypothesis might lead to a fall in accuracy. When we conducted tests on 500 sentence pairs, using this hypothesis, the precision fell by 4 per cent. However, the efficiency and recall improved by more than 200 per cent.

Figure 13.6 (opposite) illustrates a manually selected sample of extracted translation equivalent pairs from the test corpus. The sample contains a few errors (see for example number 2) while most of them are correct translation equivalent pairs.

1. 见 see /* CHI2 score=496.471 */

2. 追溯力_的 see /* CHI2 score=496.471 */

3. 款 subsection /* CHI2 score=496.237 */

4. 废除 repeal /* CHI2 score=495.814 */

5. 命令 order /* CHI2 score=493.195 */

7. 豁免 exemption /* CHI2 score=490.829 */

25. 附属_法例 subsidiary_legislation /* CHI2 score=477.173 */

26. 公共_机构 public_body /* CHI2 score=475.711 */

28. 财政司_司长 Financial_Secretary /* CHI2 score=475.711 */

31. 条例 ordinance /* CHI2 score=470.081 */

34. 基本_文书 primary_instrument /* CHI2 score=468.068 */

41. 卫生_主任 health_officer /* CHI2 score=468.068 */

42. 裁判官 magistrate /* CHI2 score=468.068 */

43. 担当 discharge /* CHI2 score=468.068 */

45. 合约 contract /* CHI2 score=468.068 */

46. 终审_法院_首席_法官 Chief_Justice_of_Final Appeal /* CHI2 score=468.068 */

53. 香港_特别_行政区 Hong_Kong_Special_Administrative_region /* CHI2 score=448.576 */

63. 审裁处 tribunal /* CHI2 score=420.579 */

64. 宣布 declare /* CHI2 score=420.579 */

Figure 13.6 Sample of results extracted from the corpus

Conclusion and further works to be done

Turning the focus towards multiword units rather than single words provides a better base for translation. It offers a solution, at least partially, to the ambiguities otherwise encountered by machine translation systems.

From the four statistical methods tested in our study, we found that the LL score and χ^2 score achieved better accuracy than the mutual information and DICE coefficient. The reason for this may be that the LL score and χ^2 score consider all cases where the keywords in questions do not occur at all, while the point-wise mutual information and DICE coefficient do not. However, none of the four statistical methods can be said to be perfect. While there is a link between frequency of occurrences in a corpus and meaningful units, it is not as straightforward as would be necessary to be picked up merely by statistical measures. The result lists will require further evaluation by lexicographers.

Acknowledgement

We would like to give our thanks to Professor Dan Tufis. His help and suggestions have been very important for our work. We also would like to give thanks to all our colleagues at the Centre of Corpus Linguistics: their help is greatly appreciated.

References

Danielsson, Pernilla and Ridings, Daniel (1997) 'Practical Presentation of a "Vanilla" aligner', presentation held at the *TELRI Workshop in Alignment and Exploitation of Texts*, Ljubljana, February, pp. 1–2.

Gale, William (1991) 'Identifying words correspondences in parallel Texts', *DARPA speech and natural language workshop.* Asilomar, CA.

Johansson, Stig and Hofland, Knut (2001) 'The English-Norwegian parallel corpus: current work and new directions', in Botley, S., McEnery, A. M. and Wilson, A. (eds) *Multilingual Corpora in Teaching and Research.* Amsterdam: Rodopi.

Manual of UPenn Tree Bank tag set, see: http://www.cis.upenn.edu/~treebank/

Schmied, Helmut (1994) 'Probabilistic Part-Of-Speech Tagging using decision trees', in *International Conference on New Methods in Language Processing.* Manchester, pp. 44–9.

Teubert, Wolfgang (2001) 'Corpus Linguistics and Lexicography', *International Journal of Corpus Linguistics* 6 (Special Issue): 125–53.

Tufis, Dan (2001) 'Computational bilingual lexicography: automatic extraction of translation dictionaries', in *Journal of Information Science and Technology, Romanian Academy* 4(3).

Wu, Dekai (1994) 'Learning an English-Chinese Lexicon from a Parallel Corpus', *AMTA-94, Association for MT in the Americas.* Columbia, MD, pp. 206–13.

Yu, Shiwen (2002). 'Specification of Chinese text segmentation and POS tagging', *The Journal of Chinese Information Processing* (5–6).

APPENDIX

We use Penn Tree Bank tag set for English and ICL/PKU tag set for Chinese. The following table shows the difference between the two tag sets.

The Penn Tree Bank English tag set		The ICL/PKU Chinese tag set	
CC	Coordinating conjunction	c	Conjunction
CD	Cardinal number	m	Cardinal number, Ordinal number
FW	Foreign word	x	Foreign word, Non-morpheme character
SYM	Symbol		
IN	Preposition, subordinating conjunction	p	Preposition
JJ	Adjective	a	Adjective
JJR	Adjective, comparative	b	Distinctive
JJS	Adjective, superlative	z	Status
NN	Noun, singular or mass	n	Noun
NNS	Noun, plural	s	Location
NP	Proper noun, singular		
NPS	Proper noun, plural		
PP	Personal pronoun	r	Pronoun
PP$	Possessive pronoun		
WP	Wh-pronoun		
WP$	Possessive wh-pronoun		
WRB	Wh-adverb		
RB	Adverb	d	Adverb
RBR	Adverb, comparative		
RBS	Adverb, superlative		
UH	Interjection	e	Interjection
VB	Verb, base form	v	Verb
VBD	Verb, past tense		
VBG	Verb, gerund or present participle		
VBN	Verb, past participle		

The Penn Tree Bank English tag set		The ICL/PKU Chinese tag set	
VBP	Verb, non-3rd person singular		
VBZ	present		
MD	Verb, 3rd person singular present		
	Modal		
,	Comma	w	Punctuation
.	Sentence-final punctuation		
:	Colon, semi-colon		
(	Left bracket character		
)	Right bracket character		
"	Straight double quote		
“	Left open double quote		
”	Right close double quote		
‘	Left open single quote		
’	Right close single quote		
EX	Existential *there*		
LS	List item marker		
RP	Particle		
TO	*to*		
DT	Determiner		
PDT	Predeterminer		
WDT	Wh-determiner		
POS	Possessive ending		
		f	Direction
		o	Onomatopoeia
		q	Classifier
		t	Time
		u	Auxiliary
		y	Final particle
		i	Idiom
		g	Morpheme
		h	Prefix
		j	Abbreviation
		k	Suffix
		l	Frequently used fixed expression

14 Abstract noun collocations: their nature in a parallel English–Czech corpus

František Čermák

Nouns: abstract versus concrete

On many occasions, the distinction *Abstract* versus *Concrete* noun is usually mentioned with the understanding that there is an obvious and familiar difference between both terms. Yet the distinction is hardly ever defined precisely, let alone investigated.

Briefly (and leaving aside border cases), abstract nouns are taken here to be defined semiotically, through their non-concrete, non-physical denotates, where no ostensive definition applies. Abstract nouns and notions are far from being derivable, in any straightforward way, from concrete nouns as cognitivists believe. As they are not anchored in the same reality as concrete nouns (where *rock, water* or *tree* is the same all around the world, basically), and as they are products of alternative cultural developments in various languages, one has to expect other types of differences here, both in their behaviour inside one language and across the language boundaries. Moreover, most languages differ between abstract nouns and their behaviour if these are 1. original nouns or 2. derivatives, mostly from verbs.

Thus, the corresponding Czech equivalent for the noun *love,* namely *láska,* is an instance of the former 1., where the corresponding verb *milovat* is, obviously, no cognate of *láska.* In English, *love,* being a case of the latter 2. type, is, due to a simple conversion, a case of the overlap type, where the noun and the verb are identical in form. It is not surprising, then, to observe a difference in the valency of the former case, too, e.g. *láska k někomu* (dative prepositional case) as against *milovat někoho* (accusative case, no preposition). The English retains here, in both cases, the same preposition, *love of* (or employs an alternative preposition *for*). Incidentally, the latter case, based on some kind of conversion (pure or supported by a morphological change), seems to be preferred by more languages, including, apart from English, also German, Dutch, Afrikaans, Finnish, Russian, Slovenian, Bulgarian, French, Italian, Romanian, Lithuanian, Greek, Swahili, Chinese and Turkish (and this might be the reason why this solution has been accepted for Esperanto, too). However, the former case, although in minority, is no exception including, apart from Czech, also Swedish, Danish, Polish, Serbian and Croatian obviously. Evidently, this might be an interesting research topic in itself, but it is hardly safe to expect here any comfortable uniformity (so much advocated for Esperanto).

A more subtle difference, along these lines, is to be seen between the Czech noun and verb as in *otázka* versus *zeptat se/otázat se* and the corresponding English noun *question* versus *ask (a) question*, where the verb *to question* is somewhat different. However, while the English phrase *ask a question* is perfectly normal, its literal counterpart in Czech **zeptat se/otázat se otázku* (both verbs corresponding to the English *ask*) is impossible, obviously due to its iterative character. On the other hand, while the cognate English noun and verb *speech–speak* seem to retain, at least, one of the same valencies (*about*), the similarly cognate Czech equivalents *řeč-říct* (derived, however, from 'say') are somewhat different, cf. *řeč o něčem* (preposition + locative case) versus *říct někomu něco* (dative + accusative case). It is just possible that the Czech noun prepositional valency *o něčem* has been influenced by *mluvit o něčem* 'to speak about something'.

Let us briefly have a look at the concrete–abstract noun distinction. Looking into textual and collocational behaviour of two less frequent and basically monosemous and randomly chosen nouns *pebble* and *purge* in the annotated British National Corpus (BNC), one can see other differences. The total frequency of the concrete noun *pebble* is 185, while the abstract noun *purge* frequency, from which the verb function has been taken, is similar, namely 123. The rest is not, however.

Due to the theory used in the BNC mark-up, there is no attempt to distinguish the attributive and hence modifying function of PEBBLE, such as in *pebble floor*, from the independent one, such as in *pebble (is) in the path.* This difference is rather crucial in comparing such languages as English and Czech, as it requires an adjectival equivalent for Czech (*oblázkový*) in the former case, while the latter has a noun. Taking this into account, one can safely say, that the (**A**) attributive function (or use, N–N) of this noun is dominant in English as most collocations and combinations belong here (*pebble floor*, etc.), the second prominent function (**B**) being that of the postverbal use (V–N), while the (**C**) subject use (N–V), i.e. the noun being subject of a sentence, is marginal (only 5 cases, such as *The pebble was resting in a hollow*). Other uses and functions have not been considered, being, basically, not relevant for the goal pursued.

It is, however, this (**B**) type of function which is highly interesting. Numerous V–N combinations, such as *clutch, dash, drop, flash, jet, kick, lift, move, roll, rub, throw, touch* PEBBLE, can hardly be said to show some stable pattern, system or even stable collocations. Apart from reflecting movements (locomotion) mostly, there seems to be a considerable freedom of combination of this concrete noun with verbs which finds its limit in semantic compatibility only. On a closer look, this conclusion seems to hold for many other concrete nouns.

The combinatorial and collocational life of the abstract noun PURGE seems to be rather different. Due to this form being used as a verb primarily, there is no attributive function to be found here (N–N -> V–N, e.g. *purge the party*), hence no (**A**) type, which is dominant with the concrete nouns (see above); the copious *of* construction is different, of course (*purge of the party*). The third (N-V) function is also quite limited, being represented by 9 cases only, e.g. *the purge continues.* It is, then, the second (**B**) type of function which is different. As the author does not subscribe to any of the numerous views as to what collocations are, it is much more useful first to try to pin down stable combinations, if any, and try to set them apart from those which are not stable. In doing this, quite a lot of grey zone of semi- or quasi-stable combinations has to be taken into account, too. Consider the combinations recorded, namely *build, call for, carry out, characterize, continue, delay, demand for, escape, force, have, launch, lead, make, press for, promise, require, trigger* PURGE, where some are undoubtedly more frequent than others. If any pattern seems to emerge here, at this stage, it is obviously one which has to do with time sequence. Thus, *launch/trigger purge* seems to suggest a beginning more often than, for example, *make/continue purge,* where the action seems to be in progress already.

A similar type of behaviour is to be observed for Czech and it can be checked on the basis of the Czech National Corpus (CNC) being of the same size, a possibility which will not be gone into now.

To sum up these findings, some of the basic tenets to be further explored here are these:

1. Concrete nouns do not have the same type of patterns in their behaviour; by patterns, both functional, syntactic and collocation types are meant.
2. Abstract nouns seem to follow few general patterns in their behaviour, which seem to be more structured, allowing for much less freedom than the concrete nouns. The patterns the abstract nouns enter are determined by their function and meaning.
3. Due to their different culture-bound origin, abstract nouns are cross-linguistically also more different in their behaviour.

One of the aims of this study is to show some tendencies in the behaviour of abstract nouns on a higher level, i.e. their stable and quasi-stable configurations or multiple patterns.

Contrastive analysis of abstract nouns in Orwell's *1984*

These suggestions will be examined on a rather small parallel corpus of Orwell's novel in Czech and English. Despite some disadvantages, obvious from comparison with very large corpora such as BNC or CNC, the small number of occurrences may show some very typical patterns more readily. Concordances of the items selected for further study have been made with the aid of the MonoConcPro program.

Distribution and choice of abstract nouns

To limit the selection, only the most frequent abstract nouns, down to the frequency of cca 30 occurrences, have been chosen in both languages. Because no lemmatization has been available, the summary frequencies had to be recalculated manually for both singular and plural cases. The functional type of the nouns chosen for scrutiny was the *postverbal V–N structure* (see p. 145). The frequency lists of the nouns found in the novel are qgiven below, where * marks concrete nouns and Czech is represented by contextual (case) forms of nouns:

English: *party (284), time (199), *face (195), thought (187), moment (152), way (127), words (123), war (120), *eyes (120), year (118), *thing (105), mind (98), voice (98), world (96), word (96), life (96), ?*room (90), *body (82), *hand (81), power (81), end (76), pain (69), feeling (68), work (66), *table (65), side (63), *head (63), love (47), memory (47), police (47), *heart (44), *paper (44), death (43), victory (43), *door (42), *street (42), matter (42), *book (40), meaning (37), truth (36), *arm (36), fear (32), sound (32), revolution (32), case (31), future (31), history (31)*

Czech: *strany (152), chvíli (78), strana (76), slova (69), slovo (67), pocit (62), straně (58), místo (53), slov (53), vědomí (52), *oči (51), *obrazovky (48), bolest (47), moc (46), *tělo (44), válka (44), vítězství (44), okamžiku (41), minulosti (41), věci (38), čas (37), *tváří (37), život (36), *rukou (36), okamžiku (35), života (35), minulost (34), *ruce (34), *stolu (34), *tváře (34), *vlasy (34), den (33), nenávisti (33), *očima (33), práce (31), význam (31), *ruku (31), oddělení (30), práci (30), století (30), způsobem (29), myšlení (28), stranu (28)*

There are at least 8 semantic areas where these abstract nouns belong. From these, only three obvious semantic classes (Action, Emotion, Language, see pp. 148 ff.) have been chosen, so that collocational behaviour of similar nouns could be observed and some suggestions, if any, made as to the emergence of a larger pattern of collocation types, linked with a certain type of the noun meaning (for Czech, mostly, see Čermák 1974, 1988 and *Slovník* . . . 1994).

Problems of equivalence

Although a simple equivalence study may not be the goal pursued here, it may be useful to sum up and briefly illustrate this. The obvious complex relationship of words across language boundaries is often quite surprising and no standard methodology is generally accepted here. Some of this has been a factor behind decisions taken in pursuing the proper aim of this study.

Major types of great and notable differences observed in this field may be best seen from 4 points of view, some of which may be considered to form scales, namely 1. *lexical*, 2. *functional*, 3. *fixed*, and 4. *occasional (not fixed).* However, a far greater factor contributing to the substance and shape of the differences is to be seen in typology, as, by contrasting Czech and English, representatives of the inflectional and isolating type of language are studied, etc.

Thus, the Czech noun VĚDOMÍ (frequency 54) corresponds to the English *mind* (24), but also, surprisingly, to *consciousness* (20), *knowledge* (5), *feeling* (1) and *sense* (1), none of the last 3 being given in dictionaries. It is of some surprise that also the most frequent *mind* is not found there, this being due to its frequent function in set phrases, obviously (numbers are those of their frequencies). In a single case, however, the noun *vědomí* corresponds to a verb in English, too. Reversing the direction and following the primary English equivalent *mind* back to Czech, a further ramification of equivalence options may be observed, where there is only a partial correspondence to be found with the initial Czech *vědomí*. The other options suggested by the Orwell corpus for MIND include the Czech *mysl, duch,* but also some idiomatic collocations such as *crossed his mind: napadlo ho, mind you: to se ví, he made up his mind: rozhodl se,* etc. It is evident that the last thing to expect from such a crosslinguistic comparison is a **one-to-one correspondence** which, with a possible exception of technical terms, does not seem to exist in general. This illustration covers problems of the *lexical* (1) functional (2) and, partly, fixed (3) and occasional (4) equivalents, invented by translators in this case. It must be pointed out, however, that the problem of how to decide what is fixed and stable on the one hand and what is not stable and fixed on the other hand is far from clear and it can hardly be simply matched with a difference in the corpus frequency only. Moreover, an equivalent being fixed and supported by frequency may not lead us to believe that it is to be automatically found in dictionaries, too (as in the case of *vědomí* versus *mind* above).

Dictionaries seem to be obsessed with recording the identity of function, within the scope of which most equivalents are found and treated. However, there are types of equivalents crossing this boundary of the identical *function* based on the tacit belief 'once a noun always a noun', etc. Let us illustrate this by the following case.

Thus, for the English noun VOICE (frequency 98), standard dictionaries suggest only such Czech equivalents which fall under the same function, namely that of noun in this case, offering the standard *hlas,* infrequent *mínění* (opinion), and *znělost* (in phonetics). Next to these, the Orwell parallel corpus has a number of other similar lexical equivalents (such as *tón, projev, slova*), but also equivalents which are either entirely or partly different in their function. Some of these are standard and fixed options which can hardly be left out of any decent dictionary. Compare some of these functionally different options (with resulting equivalents being verbs, mostly, where N=noun, V=verb, A=Adjective, Prep=preposition):

Noun (*voice*-V) -> V: *the voice paused: odmlčet se, the voice stopped: zmlknout*
Noun (in a A *-voice*) -> V: *in a huge voice: hulákat, in a loud booming voice: bědovat*

Noun (in idiom) -> Prep-A-N: *at the top of his voice: z plných plic* (the Czech noun used means 'lungs')

These are complemented by some odd cases where this noun is translated by a pronoun *někdo* ('somebody'), or is left out, or is semantically projected into a 'narrower' equivalent, such as *insect voice -> cvrlikání* 'twittering, chirping'. Due to the limited resources of the corpus, no adjectival equivalent is found here, which is a standard used for any such noun standing in front of another noun (*hlasový*), a fact commented on above.

The obvious question to ask is what functions offer at least some assurance that the same function may be expected in equivalents, too, and, conversely, which functions display a tendency for change. Here, for instance, it seems that the N–V (Noun–Verb) function safely preserves the identity of the noun.

ACTION, EMOTION and LANGUAGE abstract nouns and their patterns

For the three semantic noun classes denoting Action, Emotion and Language, which have been chosen for analysis, it is suggested that, due to their changing usage, a tripartite phase pattern may be used for characterizing V–N collocations and combinations. The three phases, reflecting different aspects or time slots in which these nouns are used, are those denoting, very broadly,

1. *beginning*, 2. *duration* or *continuation* and 3. *end* of effect (operation). Accordingly, these are called here *inchoative* (INCH), *durative* (DUR) and *terminative* (TERM) phases and their respective collocations **systematic collocations** in this sense.

To separate standard (fixed) collocations or combinations from those based on chance is not easy. Next to frequency, it was mostly the fact that a given combination fits into one of these phases that decided its inclusion in the body studied. Thus, the verb combinations offered for the English WAR by the Orwell text, made up of *be at, bring, declare, lose, mention, think about, transfer, wage, win (war)*, represent both a mixture of systematic and chance, ad hoc collocations or combinations, such as *mention* or *think about war*. The choice may become particularly difficult if the group of collocates, due to a limited size of the corpus, does not contain the most typical one at all, such as *say (a/the)* WORD, while a diversity of other, less typical or untypical ones is represented, such as *apply to, believe, clip, contain, consist of, destroy, distinguish, express, hear, invent, know, murmur, pronounce, read, replace, scribble, shout, write.*

An important goal, not pursued here, is the part played by the Noun Abstracts also in other functions. It is evident, for example, that there is a scale of functions to be found here, ranging from Abstracts which are quite common in the *subject function* (N–V), while others, such as *sleep*, do not enter this function here at all. This may be viewed as various manifestations of the *anthropocentric principle* in language, stating that the agent or doer of the active sentence is to be originally identified with the HUMAN agent in language (*John/man/he . . . brought/did/ . . . it*). It is only due to a long cultural development that some abstracts have gradually assumed this function as well. English, with its favoured use of the Passive voice, may not be the ideal language to illustrate what is much more prominent in other types of languages. Unfortunately, there is no sound study available to demonstrate any tendencies or directions here, its relations to types of meaning, etc. Yet it is surprising how often one comes, in contrast to *sleep* above, across cases like *war* (53 out of 132), *process* (13 out of 27 occurrences), or *change* (10 out of 13), in which the noun is used as the sentence subject, thus behaving like an animate thing, doer or agent.

It is important to note that without a prior semantic annotation no automatic computer treatment is possible at the moment. Likewise, no formalization has been considered outside the scope suggested in what follows. It is to be hoped that even ontology approaches such as WordNet might benefit from such an approach.

ACTION and PROCESS nouns

The structural **V–N** patterns for these nouns in English and Czech are the following (with total frequency of nouns in parentheses):

	INCH	**DUR**	**TERM**
WAR *(132):*	*declare*	*be at, wage*	*win, lose*
victory *(47):*	*win*	–	–
work *(51):*	*set to, go to*	*do, be at*	*leave, be back from*
revolution *(38):*	–	*make*	–
process *(27):*	*set in motion*	*be in*	–
movement *(45):*	*make*	–	–
change *(13):*	–	–	–
effort *(27):*	*make*	–	–
sleep *(16):*	*go to, sink into*	–	–
válka *(101):*	*vyhlásit*	*být ve, vést*	*vyhrát, prohrát*
vítězství *(49):*	*dovést k, skončit -ím*	–	–
práce *(63):*	*přijít do*	*být v, být zabrán do*	*vykonat*
revoluce *(34):*	–	*vést*	–
process *(29):*	*uvést do pohybu*	–	–
pohyb *(46):*	*uvést do, udělat*	*být v*	–
změna *(22):*	–	–	–
úsilí *(11):*	*vyvinout, vynaložit*	–	–
spánek *(11):*	*upadnout do*	–	–

It is tempting to go into a detailed analysis of individual correspondences of nouns, but that would hardly offer any systematic picture of their behaviour. Moving, then, to generalities, let us observe at least that the preponderance of the Inchoative Phase is obvious here, while the Terminative Phase suffers from lack of verbs, a fact which is general for the behaviour of the Abstract noun.

EMOTION and FEELING nouns

The **V–N** patterns for these nouns in English and Czech are the following:

	INCH	**DUR**	**TERM**
PAIN (69):	*-/ inflict*	*feel, be in*	*-/ stop*
***feeling** (68):*	*leave/bring*	*have*	–
***love** (47):*	*-/ give*	*have, feel*	–
***hatred** (26):*	*fill with*	–	–
***fear** (32):*	*produce*	*have*	*overcome*
BOLEST (76):	*ucítit/způsobit*	*cítit/trpět -í*	*-/zastavit*
***pocit** (84):*	*vyvolat, zanechat, přinášet*	*mít, zakoušet*	–
***láska** (36):*	*-/ dát*	*mít, cítit*	–
***nenávist** (56):*	*naplnit -í*	–	–
***strach** (39):*	*podlehnout -u/vyvolat*	*mít*	*přemoct*

There is no further attempt made here to further distinguish between various functional and meaning equivalents within the same phase, such as *feel pain* and *be in pain*; *polysemy* does often split the array of the collocations (see also next sub-section). It has to be pointed out, however, that, due to their semantic nature, some nouns are used in a double role, a *simple* and *causative* one (distinguished here by a slash). Thus, the Czech Inchoative use of *bolest* ('pain') suggests a simple use by *ucítit bolest* 'to start to feel pain' as against *způsobit bolest* 'to inflict, cause pain' which, clearly, includes an external doer or agent who caused it. The fact that this is not so clearly reflected in English, where only the Causative version is found, is due to a basic difference between Czech and English. Czech does always have to employ Verb Aspect, while this is, at best, only implicit in English. Thus, it is not clear whether the English *feel pain* is to be understood as Inchoative also, or Durative only (see above). More generally, English seems not to distinguish so sharply between these phases, too.

The obvious mismatches, such as the Czech *vědomí* (see 'Problems of equivalence' above), had to be left out, while great frequency differences, such as *hatred* (26) versus *nenávist* (56), suggest the cross-functional type of equivalence, discussed above. Here, English evidently prefers to use the verb *to hate* to the noun *hatred*, while Czech does not.

LANGUAGE nouns

The **V–N** patterns for these nouns in English and Czech are the following:

	INCH	DUR	TERM
***WORD** (219):*	*use, write*	–	–
***name** (48):*	*-/ give*	*bear/call by, know by*	–
***language** (26):*	*master*	–	–
***question** (34):*	*ask*	–	–
***expression** (22):*	–	–	–
***speech** (29):*	*make*	–	–
***sound** (31):*	*utter*	–	–
***slovo** (219):*	*použít, napsat*	–	–
***jméno** (53):*	–	*-/ znát, nazývat -em*	–
***jazyk** (37):*	*zvládnout*	–	–
***otázka** (29):*	*položit, klást si*	–	*odpovědět na*
***výraz** (42):*	–	–	–
***řeč** (12):*	–	*pronášet*	–
***projev** (17):*	*zaměřit*	–	–
***zvuk** (25):*	*vydat*	–	–

The gaps in the corresponding parts of the groups in the pair of languages suggest that the translator may have used a different functional solution. The case of one English noun, *expression* (22), represented by two in Czech, *výraz (42), projev (17),* suggests another type of *one to more equivalence,* which is in fact extremely common in general. It could be avoided here in most cases, but not quite.

A commentary and summary

It is obvious that, in general, it is the Inchoative Phase that is asymmetrically burdened with most collocations, while the Terminative displays the least, with the Durative Phase being in between. It is also clear that the three semantic classes behave differently in this, with the Language nouns avoiding the Terminative Phase, and so on. The following table shows this representation (i.e. use of at least one verb) in a synoptical way:

	INCH	DUR	TERM
Action Nouns:	EN=CZ 82%	EN=CZ 36%	EN=CZ 18%
Emotion Nouns:	EN=CZ 100%	EN=CZ 80%	EN=CZ 40%
Language Nouns:	EN 100%, CZ 80%	EN 14%, CZ 42%	EN 0%, CZ 14%

The tripartite division seems to be the prevailing one, with unequal representation of its phases, but it may not be the only one. In fact, some Abstracts seem to fit, to use the terminology adopted here, one phase only, such as the English *regard.* The dominant V–N collocation is *have regard,* a slightly less frequent is *hold in regard,* which, in turn, may easily be viewed as a kind of idiom, leaving thus the field for a single systematic verbal collocation, which is a rather unique situation here.

Since a number of questions which this limited attempt, based on a handful of Abstracts taken from a single novel, may not resolve, such as discrimination between stable and not stable collocations, further research on a broad scale is necessary. In doing this, a feasible conjecture may be confirmed, too, namely that narrower and semantically more compact classes within the three broad ones used here, as well as others lying beyond their scope, might show further regularities in their collocational behaviour. There is hardly any doubt about that, considering that one can easily use basically the same set of verbs, found here with *WORD*, for, say, *expression, name, slogan, label, message* and, perhaps, any other 'content language noun', etc., a fact which the limited data used here cannot reflect. However, even such a limited probe into the matter seems to suggest that what has been demonstrated on much broader data for one language (Čermák 1974) may hold more generally, for other languages. As it seems that there are very few Abstract Nouns that do not follow one or more such collocational patterns, shown above, the label *systematic* might be justified.

A final word of caution is necessary, however. Since most Abstracts used here are obvious *hyperonyms,* with hyponyms missing (*WORD* -> *table, water, dog . . .*), this fact should be taken into account in any further investigation. The hyperonyms seem to behave differently from their hyponyms.

An obvious application of these findings might call for a systematic inclusion of this systematic phenomenon in other approaches, including dictionaries, textbooks, etc.

References

British National Corpus, World edition (2000) Humanities Computing Unit of Oxford University (=BNC).

Čermák, František (1974) 'Víceslovné pojmenování typu verbum-substantivum v češtině. Příspěvek k syntagmatice tzv. abstrakt (The Verb-Noun Type of Multi-Word Nominations in Czech. A Contribution to the Syntagmatics of the so-called Abstracts)', in *Slovo a slovesnost* 34: 287–306.

Čermák, František (1998) 'Linguistic Units and Texts Entities: Theory and Practice', in Fontenelle, Thierry, Hiligsmann, Philippe *et al.* (eds) *Actes Euralex '98 Proceedings,* I–II. Université de Liège, Départ. d'anglais et néerlandais, pp. 281–90.

Čermák, František (2000) 'Combination, Collocation and Multi-Word Units', in Heid, Ulrich, Evert, Stefan, Lehmann, Egbert and Rohrer, Christian (eds) *Proceedings of The Ninth Euralex International Congress EURALEX 2000.* Stuttgart: Institut für Maschinelle Sprachverarbeitung, Universität Stuttgart, pp. 489–95.

Český národní korpus. SYN 2000 (Czech National Corpus. SYN2000). http:ucnk.ff.cuni.cz (=CNC).

Slovník české frazeologie a idiomatiky. Výrazy slovesné. A-P, R-Ž (1994) Praha: Academia. (ed. Čermák, František together with Hronek, Jiri and Machač, M. Dictionary of Czech Phraseology and Idiomatics).

East Meets West 1997 Erjavec, Tomaz, Lawson, Ann and Romary, Laurent Telri and Multext East (eds) (Orwell's *1984*).

15 Parallel corpora and translation studies: old questions, new perspectives? Reporting *that* in Gepcolt: a case study

Dorothy Kenny

Introduction

It has become something of a commonplace to say that in recent decades translation studies has undergone a shift away from a preoccupation with equivalence and fidelity to source texts and authors, and towards a rethinking of translations as texts in their own right, functioning in target-language environments, affecting the target community and, crucially from the current perspective, displaying characteristics that set them apart, not from their source texts, but from other native texts in the target culture. This new target-orientedness is evident in the corpus-based work of Baker (1993, 1996, 1999, 2000), Laviosa (1998a, 1998b), Olohan and Baker (2000) and Olohan (2001). All of these scholars have used the Translational English Corpus (TEC), which consists of texts translated into English from a variety of source languages, alongside a corpus of comparable native English texts, to compare patterns in translated and original English. This *comparable* corpus methodology has allowed them to pinpoint areas of difference between translated and non-translated English, thus highlighting the specificity of translated texts from the point of view of the target language. Such an approach sits comfortably with the target-oriented research agenda in translation studies alluded to at the start of this paragraph.

But what of *parallel* corpora in translation studies? Parallel corpora – that is, corpora of source texts aligned with their respective target texts in one or more languages – have been used extensively, although sometimes grudgingly (see Baker 1999: 282–3), by contrastive linguists in contrastive lexical and grammatical studies (see, for example, the volume edited by Johansson and Oksefjell 1998). Their usefulness in supplementing the methods of traditional bilingual and multilingual lexicography has been acknowledged (Teubert 2001; Váradi and Kiss 2001), as has their usefulness in other applied areas such as translator training and machine-aided translation (Baker 1995; Uzar and Walínski 2001; Zanettin 1998, 2000). But although researchers point to the advantages they offer in descriptive studies of 'what translators actually do with texts and how they transform them in the process of translation' (Zanettin 2000: 106), the deployment of parallel corpora in descriptive translation studies has been curiously limited to date. Kenny (2001: 62–5) lists just three small-scale descriptive studies based on computerized parallel corpora (Munday 1998; Opas and Kujamäki 1995; Øverås 1998), to which one could also add Kenny's own work (2001) and that of Bosseaux (2001).

One obstacle to the use of parallel corpora in descriptive translation studies has no doubt been the practical difficulty of amassing and aligning source and target texts in electronic form, but another, more subtle obstacle could be a reluctance among researchers to fall back into the kind of source text-oriented approach that dominated translation studies until the 1980s. In a recent spirited discussion of some of the more persistent dichotomies in translation studies, Dominic Stewart (2000: 208–9) describes what he sees as a contempt for source texts in current scholarship:

> The enthusiasm for the notion that translation should first and foremost respect TL conventions has given the source text . . . at best a subordinate role and at worst something of a raw deal. The SL, once the sovereign of translation theory and now little more than a tiresome interloper and a perennial nuisance, consistently eluding the clutches of tidy theories and neat taxonomies, has – at least for the present – been dethroned.

Stewart (ibid.: 210) goes on to associate the demotion of source texts in translation studies with the rise of comparable corpora like the TEC, mentioned above, and hence the prioritizing of translation products over process. It is, he says, an irony that:

> the TEC, to be admired as a commendable, outstanding enterprise destined to shed much light on how translated texts behave and the stuff they are made of, could at worst be interpreted as a condemnation of the translation process, a computerised monument to the irrelevance of the source text.

But Stewart might be overstating the case. Even the pioneers of comparable corpus studies have been careful to point out that when patterns are identified that appear to be indicative of translated as opposed to native texts, then, given a purely monolingual methodology, one (but not the only) source of explanations for such patterns is missing, namely the source texts (see Laviosa 1998b: 565; Baker 2000: 258; Puurtinen 1998: 529).[1] Comparable corpora may encourage a focus on target texts, but they also raise interesting questions which those with access to parallel corpora may wish to follow up. In particular, parallel corpus studies can take the findings of comparable corpus studies and attempt to seek explanations for these findings in source texts. In the second half of this paper I describe an exploratory study that does just this.

The question I wish to raise before moving on, however, and one that has already been broached in the title of this paper, is whether in going back to source texts, parallel corpus studies simply revert to old questions in translation studies, albeit old questions approached from new computer-enabled perspectives? The preceding paragraph has begun to answer this question in that it hints at how new questions can emerge from the kind of target-dominated studies conducted with comparable corpora. And studies of parallel corpora that take findings based on target texts as their starting points can hardly be accused of a reactionary return to a preoccupation with source texts.

A case study: optional *that* in translated English

We move now to an example of a study where a parallel corpus may be able to throw light on findings from research conducted using a comparable corpus. The parallel corpus in question is Gepcolt, a German–English Parallel Corpus of Literary Texts described in detail in Kenny (2001). Gepcolt consists of 17 works of narrative prose in German, plus their translations into English, amounting to approximately one million running words in each language. It includes work by twelve different authors and eleven different translators. All source texts date from the 1960s onwards, although most were written in the 1980s. Most of the translations date from the 1990s, although there are a number from the 1980s too. The research based on a comparable corpus is Olohan and Baker's (2000) investigation of reporting *that* in translated and original English.

Connective *that* is optional in constructions such as *He says that Mozart was a wonderful composer*,[2] and Olohan and Baker (ibid.) argue that its use signals a higher level of explicitness than would be the case if a *zero*-connective were used (as in the unattested *He says Mozart was a wonderful composer*). Using the TEC, and a comparable corpus of original English drawn from the British National Corpus, Olohan and Baker find that optional *that* is far more frequent in reporting structures in translated English than it is in texts originally written in English. This finding, based on an analysis of reporting structures built up around the verbs SAY and TELL, suggests that translated English is grammatically more explicit than original English, and adds weight to the idea that explicitation is an inherent part of the translation process (Blum-Kulka 1986).

Olohan and Baker draw on previous scholarship (see, especially, Elsness 1984) to outline the possible factors conditioning the inclusion or omission of optional *that* in original English, that is English whose production is not complicated by the fact of translation. These factors include:

- the level of formality of the text – formal styles are said to prefer inclusion of *that*
- the matrix verb – some verbs are said to favour use of *that* while others, especially high frequency verbs like SAY, can very easily do without
- potential ambiguity – *that* is preferred in cases where its absence would lead to ambiguity

- the intervention of adverbials between the matrix verb and the reported clause – longer adverbials trigger the use of *that*, and
- cognitive complexity – *that*, being a more explicit grammatical option than the alternative *zero*-connective, will tend to be favoured in cognitively more complex environments (see Rohdenburg 1996: 151)

Olohan and Baker (ibid.) are particularly interested in Rohdenburg's (ibid.) claim about cognitive complexity and go on to suggest that the high occurrence of the *that*-connective in translated English can be explained, at least in part, in terms of the cognitive complexity involved in translation. Olohan and Baker thus, quite rightly in my opinion, consider a wide range of formal and cognitive factors that influence the inclusion or exclusion of optional *that* in reporting structures in original and translated English. But, given their methodology, which is based on the use of monolingual comparable corpora, they are not in a position to consider what must be an important conditioning factor in the production of any translation: the source text.

In the study reported on below, I attempt to ascertain whether patterns of inclusion or exclusion of optional *that* in translated texts in Gepcolt can be linked to features of their respective source texts. This study, because of its limited scope, cannot be conclusive, but it is proffered here as an example of how parallel corpus studies can grow from and complement comparable corpus studies, in the same way as monolingual reference corpora have already been integrated into studies centred around parallel corpora (see Kenny 1998, 2001; Munday 1998). As has already been indicated, Gepcolt consists of original German texts and their translations into English. The German/English language pair offers considerable advantages in the kind of study envisaged here as German too has an optional connective *daß*, which can be used in reporting structures.[3] It is thus possible to investigate whether the inclusion or exclusion of *that* in the English texts follows patterns set for *daß* in the German texts. As in most cross-linguistic comparisons, however, things are not that simple.

German differs from English in that it can mark the reported nature of an assertion using the subjunctive mood. English generally indicates indirect speech by using a verb of saying and an optional *that* to introduce the reported clause. Where appropriate, English can also alter pronouns and shift tenses in the reported clause. The indirect speech equivalent of the hypothetical sentence *I want to buy newspapers and make a telephone call anyway* thus becomes the Gepcolt sentence: *Superficially satisfied, he said that he wanted to buy newspapers and make a telephone call anyway*. By way of contrast, the original German sentence in this case is: *Oberflächlich zufriedengestellt sagte er, daß er sowieso Zeitungen kaufen und telefonieren wolle*, where the indirect speech is signalled by the verb *sagte* (said), the connective *daß*, the third person pronoun *er* in the reported clause, and the third person singular subjunctive form *wolle* of the verb WOLLEN (to want).[4] Given the optional nature of *daß* in such structures, the following sentence is also possible: *Oberflächlich zufriedengestellt sagte er, er wolle sowieso Zeitungen kaufen und telefonieren.* Not only that, but the subjunctive mood is often enough to signal indirect speech in German, so it is even possible to omit the verb of saying, if the co-text has already set up some kind of speech exchange, as in example 1a from Gepcolt (the translation as it appears in the target text is given on the right in 1b):

1a . . . die Handgranaten pendelten. Der Deutsche trat etwas zurück. Er sei nur Tourist.	1b The handgrenades wobbled, the German recoiled slightly and said he was just a tourist.

Note here, how the subjunctive form *sei* is the principal indicator of reported speech in the German, whereas the English translator introduces a verb of saying (without an optional *that*) to do the same job.

A final complication in German is that, as in English, the indicative mood can be used to signal indirect speech. This is particularly the case in colloquial spoken German, or literary depictions thereof, as in 2a:[5]

2a Die Leute sagen, du liegst im Sterben.	2b Everyone says you're dying.

The discussion so far is in no way intended to be an exhaustive account of reporting structures or indirect speech in either German or English – the reader is referred to Durrell (1991) and Olohan and Baker (2000) for more in-depth analyses. It is intended, however, to demonstrate the factors that may influence patterns of inclusion or exclusion of *that* in English translations from German: alongside issues of formality, lexis, and structural and cognitive complexity in English, other factors come into play, including no doubt the formality, lexis, and structural and cognitive complexity of the German source texts, as well as the systemic differences between German and English, and the shifts translators make partly, at least, in response to these differences.

Methodology

Before presenting the results of the small-scale study outlined here, it is advisable to make some brief points about the methodology adopted. The point of departure for this study is the translated text, more specifically a concordance of the node SAY as it appears in the English texts in Gepcolt. In this way, an attempt is made to replicate the conditions under which Olohan and Baker (2000) conducted their research, which starts with the identification of reporting structures in translated English and then goes on to compare these with reporting structures in texts originally written in English. The aim in the current study is not to account for every reporting structure built up around a particular German verb in the source texts, but rather to seek out explanations in source texts for phenomena identified initially in target texts. In this way, the methodology adopted here broadly follows that advocated by Gideon Toury (1995: 36). The software used to create the monolingual concordance of SAY is WordSmith Tools (Scott 1997). Bilingual concordances were later created for selected instances of SAY using Multiconcord (Woolls 1997).

Results

There are just over 5000 instances of SAY in Gepcolt. Given that we are interested only in those uses of SAY that occur in reporting structures where use of the *that*-connective is possible, although not obligatory, we exclude from our analysis concordance lines where, for example, SAY is used to indicate direct speech, as in *Oh well, our Edgar says,* or takes a nominal complement, as in *No one says a word.* Nominal complements include endophoric uses of demonstrative *that,* as in *Doesn't one say that anymore?* This leaves a total of 376 relevant instances of SAY in Gepcolt. Their distribution across the different forms of SAY, and according to whether or not they are followed by optional *that,* is given in Table 15.1.[6]

Table 15.1 Optional *that* v *zero*-connective with SAY in English reporting structures in Gepcolt

	number of instances in reporting structures where optional *that*		
form of SAY	**is possible**	**is used**	**is not used, though possible**
said	101	36	65
says	152	61	91
say	97	41	56
saying	26	19	7
total	**376**	**157**	**219**
	100%	**42%**	**58%**

Table 15.1 shows that optional *that* is used 42 per cent of the time in relevant reporting structures using SAY in Gepcolt, and is omitted 58 per cent of the time. These findings are broadly consistent with those of Olohan and Baker (2000), whose data suggest that the *that* and *zero*-connectives are equiprobable in such structures in translated English, although the *zero*-connective is three times more common in the same structures in comparable texts originally written in English. The translated texts in Gepcolt thus appear to be nearer the norm for translated English than for original English.[7]

Table 15.2 shows how many of the 157 instances of SAY+*that* can be linked to an instance of *daß* in the source language.

Table 15.2 shows that when *that* is used in a reporting structure with SAY in the English texts in Gepcolt, roughly half the time there is a corresponding *daß* in the original German; half the time there is not. The presence of

Table 15.2 Link between optional *that* in English and optional *daß* and *zero*-connective in German

form of SAY + *that*	no. of occurrences	*daß* in original	*zero*-connective in original
said	36	11	25
says	61	35	26
say	41	23	18
saying	19	9	10
total	**157**	**78**	**79**
	100%	**49%**	**51%**

optional *that* in the translations does not, therefore, reflect in any predictable way, the presence of *daß* in the source texts.[8]

Table 15.3, on the other hand, shows that in cases where the English text uses a *zero*-connective, the great likelihood is that the German source text did too (this is true in roughly eight out of ten cases).

Thus patterns of omission of optional *that* in English tend to reflect patterns of omission of optional *daß* in German, whereas patterns of inclusion of optional *that* do not reflect patterns of inclusion of *daß*.

Discussion

At this point it is useful to ask whether the preliminary study presented above has told us anything new about translation, and specifically whether the study does complement Olohan and Baker's (2000) work as intended.

First, we have seen that the English texts in Gepcolt tend to include optional *that* more often than the original English texts investigated by Olohan and Baker (ibid.), and have argued that this finding is consistent

Table 15.3 Link between *zero*-connective in English and optional *daß* and *zero*-connective in German

form of SAY+*zero*-connective	no. of occurrences	*daß* in original	*zero*-connective in original
said	65	7	58
says	91	22	69
say	56	15	41
saying	7	2	5
total	**219**	**46**	**173**
	100%	**21%**	**79%**

with Olohan and Baker's finding for translated English in general. Bringing source texts into the picture, we have seen that half the time that English-language translators in Gepcolt use optional *that* in reporting structures with SAY, the motivation for this inclusion is something other than the presence of *daß* in German. At first glance one could propose that translators are making target texts grammatically more explicit than their respective source texts, but one would first have to ascertain whether translators insert *that* in places where the German did not use *daß*, but did use a subjunctive form to make the reported nature of a clause explicit. If this were the case, it might be difficult to argue that the English structure including *that* was actually more explicit than the German structure with no *daß*. It is clear here that more qualitative analysis of the data gleaned from Gepcolt is required. Looking at patterns of omission of *that* in the English texts, it appears to be the case that these broadly follow patterns of omission of *daß* in German. It is interesting, however, that in 46, or one in five, cases, translators have replaced a *daß* with a *zero*-connective. Given the higher number (79, or one in two cases) of *zero*-connectives to *that* shifts and, notwithstanding the comments made above about the interpretation of *that* insertions, the overall tendency seems to be one of explicitation rather than implicitation (see Klaudy 1998). This finding is consistent with those from Øverås's (1998) related study of implicitating and explicitating shifts in translation.

Another finding from the current study suggests ways in which the influence of source languages can be isolated in comparable corpus studies. For reporting structures using SAY, the use of the *zero*-connective appears to be relatively more frequent in translated texts in Gepcolt than it is in the multi-source language TEC investigated by Olohan and Baker (2000). Given that the use of a *zero*-connective is an option in German, whereas it may not be in other source languages, the influence of source texts might be felt more strongly in studies of *that* v *zero*-connectives in Gepcolt than in TEC in general. In other words, the influence that the make-up of German source texts exerts on the overall findings for TEC is much more constrained than the influence German source texts have on Gepcolt. This is how it should be. TEC is designed, after all, to limit the influence of any single source language on overall findings, while simultaneously allowing the influence of individual source languages to be monitored with the help of meticulous documentation (in file headers) of source languages, authors, etc. To my knowledge, no published studies have yet attempted to seek out source-text influences in TEC texts. The present study may mark a start in this regard.

Conclusion

The case study reported on here is not intended to be an exhaustive account of patterns of inclusion or exclusion of reporting *that* in Gepcolt. One reason for this is that the study concentrates on just one verb, SAY, to the exclusion of others like TELL, or CLAIM, not to mention more subjective verbs like THINK and BELIEVE (see Olohan and Baker 2000). A second reason is that the focus here is on global patterns of distribution of the *that* vs the *zero*-connective, and only tentative conclusions can be drawn from the kind of quantitative results presented here. A more qualitative analysis of the data gleaned from Gepcolt is underway. Given the current interest in translation studies in translators' style (see, for example, Baker 2000, and a number of ongoing projects at Dublin City University), and the role the depiction of speech (as direct, indirect, etc.) is assigned in studies of style, it is envisaged that studies like the one broached here will become more common, and more sophisticated, in the very near future. Finally, it is hoped that this study has shown that source texts can indeed be integrated into research programmes more normally associated with target-oriented comparable corpora, and that one of Stewart's (2000) 'black sheep' of translation studies may be on its way back to the fold.

Notes

1 Note here that I am not attempting to suggest that target texts are *determined* by source texts. Translators and translation theorists know that this is simply not the case, and corpus based studies of translation have themselves shown how the same source-text phenomenon (creative coinages, non-standard syntax, etc.) will be approached in different ways by different translators (Kenny 2001), or the same stretch of source text will be translated in almost as many different ways as there are translators (Malmkjær 1998).

2 Unless otherwise indicated, all examples in this paper come from Gepcolt.

3 I use the 'old' German spelling *daß* (the reformed version is *dass*) to maintain consistency with the concordance examples given in this paper. As all the German texts contained in Gepcolt were published before German spelling reform happened in the mid-1990s, they use this older spelling.

4 The subjunctive form in question is actually a *Konjunktiv I* form. A second subjunctive, *Konjunktiv II*, is also used in reporting structures in German. For details, see Durrell (1991: 306–26).

5 In colloquial German either the indicative or the *Konjunktiv II* is used to indicate indirect speech (Durrell 1991: 315).

6 I do not elaborate here on the association between different forms of SAY and the use of optional *that* in Gepcolt. It was considered useful to break down these results by form of the lemma, however, as this ensures a level of comparability with results presented by Olohan and Baker (2000).

7 Olohan and Baker do not claim to have established norms for the distribution of optional *that* in translated and original English, but given that their sample of translated English is, at 3.5 milllion words, over three times larger than mine, and also contains texts translated from

more than one source language, one can assume it to be a more representative sample of translated English than the English translation in Gepcolt. It should also be pointed out that there is some overlap between the English subcorpus of Gepcolt and the Translational English Corpus used by Olohan and Baker (see Kenny 2001: 119–20).

8 Note here that no claims are being made about the verbs that accompany *daß* in the original. Indeed there may not be an accompanying verb, as in example 3a, where the *daß* clause follows the noun *Plakat* (poster):

3a Auch an dem Tor von Herrn Direktor Schüssl, dessen jüngster Sohn nun auch gefallen ist, klebt so ein Plakat: Daß wir nachts nicht aus den Häusern dürfen und zu gehorchen haben und daß eine Zuwiderhandlung nicht geduldet, sondern mit dem Tod bestraft wird.	3b There's even a poster on the gate to Herr Direktor Schüssl's house – his youngest son has also been recently killed in action. It says that we aren't allowed to leave our houses at night and that we have to obey and that no infraction will be allowed but punished with death.

References

Baker, Mona (1993) 'Corpus Linguistics and Translation Studies. Implications and Applications', in Baker, Mona, Francis, Gill and Tognini-Bonelli, Elena (eds) *Text and Technology: In Honour of John Sinclair*. Amsterdam and Philadelphia: John Benjamins, pp. 233–50.

Baker, Mona (1995) 'Corpora in Translation Studies: An Overview and Some Suggestions for Future Research', *Target* 7(2): 223–43.

Baker, Mona (1996) 'Corpus-based Translation Studies: The Challenges that Lie Ahead', in Somers, Harold (ed.) *Terminology, LSP and Translation: Studies in Language Engineering, in Honour of Juan C. Sager*. Amsterdam and Philadelphia: John Benjamins, pp. 175–86.

Baker, Mona (1999) 'The Role of Corpora in Investigating the Linguistic Behaviour of Professional Translators', *International Journal of Corpus Linguistics* 4(2): 281–98.

Baker, Mona (2000) 'Towards a Methodology for Investigating the Style of a Literary Translator', *Target* 12(2): 241–66.

Blum-Kulka, Shoshana (1986) 'Shifts of cohesion and coherence in translation', in House, Juliane and Blum-Kulka, Shoshana (eds) *Interlingual and Intercultural Communication: Discourse and Cognition in Translation and Second Language Acquisition Studies*. Tübingen: Gunter Narr, pp. 17–35.

Bosseaux, Charlotte (2001) 'A Study of the Translator's Voice and Style in the French Translations of Virginia Woolf's *The Waves*', in Olohan, Maeve (ed.) *CTIS Occasional Papers* 1: 55–75.

Durrell, Martin (1991) *Hammer's German Grammar and Usage*, revised 2nd edn. London, Sydney and Auckland: Edward Arnold.

Elsness, Johan (1984) '*That* or Zero? A Look at the Choice of Object Clause Connective in a Corpus of American English', *English Studies* 65: 519–33.

Johansson, Stig and Oksefjell, Signe (eds) (1998) *Corpora and Cross-linguistic Research*. Amsterdam and Atlanta, GA: Rodopi.

Kenny, Dorothy (1998) 'Creatures of Habit? What translators usually do with words', in Laviosa, Sara (ed.) Special issue of *Meta* 43(4): 515–23.

Kenny, Dorothy (2001) *Lexis and Creativity in Translation: a corpus-based study*. Manchester: St Jerome.

Klaudy, Kinga (1998) 'Explicitation', in Baker, Mona (ed.) *Routledge Encyclopedia of Translation Studies*. London: Routledge, pp. 80–4.

Laviosa, Sara (1998a) 'The English Comparable Corpus: A Resource and a Methodology', in Bowker, Lynne, Cronin, Michael, Kenny, Dorothy and Pearson, Jennifer (eds) *Unity in Diversity? Current Trends in Translation Studies*. Manchester: St Jerome, pp. 101–12.

Laviosa, Sara (1998b) 'Core patterns of lexical use in a comparable corpus of English narrative prose', in Laviosa, Sara (ed.) Special issue of *Meta* 43(4): 557–70.

Malmkjær, Kirsten (1998) 'Love thy neighbour: Will parallel corpora endear linguists to translators?', in Laviosa, Sara (ed.) Special issue of *Meta* 43(4): 532–41.

Munday, Jeremy (1998) 'A computer assisted approach to the analysis of translation shifts', in Laviosa, Sara (ed.) Special issue of *Meta* 43(4): 542–56.

Olohan, Maeve (2001) 'Spelling out the optionals in translation: a corpus study', in Rayson, Paul, Wilson, Andrew, McEnery, Tony, Hardie, Andrew and Khoja, Shereen (eds) *Proceedings of the Corpus Linguistics 2001 Conference*. Lancaster: UCREL, pp. 423–32.

Olohan, Maeve and Baker, Mona (2000) 'Reporting *that* in Translated English: Evidence for Subconscious Processes of Explicitation?', *Across Languages and Cultures* 1(2): 141–58.

Opas, Lisa Lena and Kujamäki, Pekka (1995) 'A Cross-linguistic Study of Stream-of-consciousness Techniques', *Literary and Linguistic Computing* 10(4): 287–91.

Øverås, Linn (1998) 'In search of the third code: an investigation of norms in literary translation', in Laviosa, Sara (ed.) Special issue of *Meta* 43(4): 571–88.

Puurtinen, Tiina (1998) 'Syntax, readability and ideology in children's literature', in Laviosa, Sara (ed.) Special issue of *Meta* 43(4): 524–33.

Rohdenburg, Günter (1996) 'Cognitive Complexity and Increased Grammatical Explicitness in English', *Cognitive Linguistics* 7(2): 149–82.

Scott, Mike (1997) *WordSmith Tools version 2.0*. Oxford: Oxford University Press.

Stewart, Dominic (2000) 'Poor Relations and Black Sheep in Translation Studies', *Target* 12(2): 205–28.

Teubert, Wolfgang (2001) 'Corpus Linguistics and Lexicography', *International Journal of Corpus Linguistics* 6 (special issue): 125–53.

Toury, Gideon (1995) *Descriptive Translation Studies and Beyond.* Amsterdam and Philadelphia: John Benjamins.

Uzar, Rafal and Waliński, Jacek (2001) 'Analysing the Fluency of Translators', *International Journal of Corpus Linguistics* 6 (special issue): 155–66.

Váradi, Tamás and Kiss, Gábor (2001) 'Equivalence and Non-equivalence in Parallel Corpora', *International Journal of Corpus Linguistics* 6 (special issue): 167–77.

Woolls, David (1997) *Multiconcord version 1.5.* Birmingham: CFL Software Development.

Zanettin, Frederico (1998) 'Bilingual comparable corpora and the training of translators', in Laviosa, Sara (ed.) Special issue of *Meta* 43(4): 616–30.

Zanettin, Frederico (2000) 'Parallel Corpora in Translation Studies. Issues in Corpus Design and Analysis', In Olohan, Maeve (ed.) *Intercultural Faultlines. Research Models in Translation Studies I. Textual and Cognitive Aspects.* Manchester: St Jerome, pp. 105–18.

16 Structural derivation and meaning extraction: a comparative study of French/Serbo-Croatian parallel texts

Cvetana Krstev and Duško Vitas

Serbian v Serbo-Croatian

Serbian literary language is the national language of Serbs and Montenegrins that originated from the language reform of Vuk Stefanović Karadžić in the first half of the nineteenth century. At the base of this reform is the reform of the alphabet and the adoption, in principle, of the phonetic orthography. The Cyrillic alphabet was the main alphabet of the reformed language, but today Serbian language equally uses the Latin alphabet.[1] Its counterpart is Croatian literary language as a national language of Croats that originated from the reform conducted by the Illyrian Movement also in the first half of the nineteenth century. This reform was partly modified at the middle of the nineteenth century by acceptance of Vuk's principles. Croatian literary language uses the Latin alphabet exclusively. There are three main dialects in the vernacular language: shtokavian, kajkavian, and chakavian named upon the different pronunciation of the pronoun *šta* (Engl. what). Both literary languages were, however, developed on the basis of the new-shtokavian dialect. The name Serbo-Croatian appeared with the establishment of the Kingdom of Yugoslavia in 1918 and existed as a diasystem of Serbian and Croatian literary languages. Until the 1960s, Serbo-Croatian was seen as a single language with two alphabets. From that time on, it is rather seen as a language with two variants – Serbian and Croatian. After the breakdown of Yugoslavia, the Croatian variant of Serbo-Croatian is called Croatian literary language, and the Serbian variant Serbian literary language. The overlapping in the framework of this diasystem is, however, still present. Ljubomir Popović (1996, 2000) gives a more detailed description of the development of the Serbian language.

Structural derivation

The phenomenon of structural derivation in Serbo-Croatian consists of those derivational processes that induce change to the lexeme meaning in a predictable way. Traditional Serbo-Croatian lexicography determines the form of an entry according to its inflective features while the systematic character of structural derivation is not taken into consideration. For those entries that were derived through the process of structural derivation, the lexicographic description usually consists of the indication of the derivational process and the reference to the basic entry. However, this is not done in a systematic way. It could be said that the border between inflection and structural derivation is especially vague in the cases in which the structural derivation does not change the part of speech, such as derivation of diminutive and augmentative. But even in the cases in which the change of the part of speech occurs, such as derivation of possessive adjectives from nouns or gerunds from verbs, the semantic links between the basic entry and the derived entries remain stable.

As an example, we present in Table 16.1 the derivational forms of the nouns *glumac* (Engl. actor) and *baron* (Engl. baron), according to RMS-MH (1967). This phenomenon enables the derivation from the basic entry of the forms for feminine gender, and respective diminutives, augmentatives and possessive adjectives. Traditional lexicography records only some of them – the shaded boxes in Table 16.1 are not described in RMS-MH (1967). The lexicographic description for these missing forms, if produced by analogy, is given in the column 4 of Table 16.1.

Analysis that included several dictionaries of Serbo-Croatian showed that at least 20–25% of all dictionary entries is produced by this sort of derivation. As a consequence, the inconsistent treatment of structural derivation phenomena implies at least one of the following problems: a) redundant entries, b) missing entries.

Table 16.1 Structural derivation for nouns *glumac, baron*

glum+ac (*actor,* [RMS-MH]: *the artist that acts in a drama*)
baron+ε ([RMS-MH]: *noble title of lower degree*)

type of process	base	suffix	definition
Gender motion	glum; baron	ica	*woman actor* – (*actress*)
Augmentative	glum	cyina	augmentative of *actor*
Augmentative	baron	cyina	?augmentative of *baron*
Diminutive	glum; baron	cyicx	diminutive of *actor, baron*
Diminutive	glum; baron	icyica	? diminutive of *actress, baroness*
Adjective Poss.	glum; baron	cyev; ov	belonging to *actor, baron*
Adjective Poss.	glum; baron	icyin	belonging to *actress, baroness*
Adjective Poss.	glum; baron	cyicxev	? belonging to dim. of *actor, baron*
Adjective Poss.	glum; baron	icyicin	? belonging to dim. of *actress, baroness*
Adjective Rel.	glum; baron	acyki; ski	relating to *actor, baron*
Adverb	glum; baron	acyki; ski	in the way of *actor, baron*

Electronic dictionary and structural derivation

The system of electronic morphological dictionaries was originally constructed for French by Blandine Courtois. Its production has been explained in full detail in Courtois and Silberztein (1990), Courtois (1992), and Gross and Perrin (1989). The basic part of this system consists of morphological dictionaries of simple words. The notion of simple word is here formally introduced as a character string between two consecutive separators, such as blanks, punctuation marks, etc. There are two different morphological dictionaries of simple words, known as DELAS and DELAF. The DELAS dictionary consists of simple lexical words represented in the form of the entries in traditional dictionaries: their infinitive form represents verbs, while nouns are represented by their nominative singular form. To each lexical word a code is attached that uniquely describes its inflectional paradigm. Entries in DELAF are all inflectional forms of the lexical words presented in the corresponding DELAS. To each entry its corresponding uniquely coded lemma from DELAS is attached together with the sequence of codes representing its possible grammatical realization. The entries for *baron* (Engl. baron) in DELAS and DELAF are represented in Table 16.2.

The interpretation of the code N1 attached to lemma *baron* is that it is a noun that belongs to the morphological class 1 (Vitas 1993). The interpretation of the information *baron.N1:msv:mpa* attached to the textual word *barone* is that it can be either the vocative singular or accusative plural of the masculine noun *baron* from the morphological class 1.

In the context of the construction of an electronic dictionary of Serbo-Croatian according to this model, the phenomenon of structural derivation raises several problems. The first problem arises from the way traditional lexicography determines the entries. If the results of structural derivation are considered as separate entries, then relations with derived entries having the predictable meaning are lost on the dictionary level. Also, automatic text indexing does not enable the identification of synonymous

Table 16.2 The entries for the noun *baron* in Serbian morphological dictionaries DELAS and DELAF

DELAS	baron.N1
DELAF	baron, .N1:msn barona,baron.N1:msg:msa:mpg barone,baron.N1:msv:mpa baroni,baron.N1:mpn:mpv baronima,baron.N1:mpd:mpi:mpl baronom,baron.N1:msi baronu,baron.N1:msd:msl

compounds, such as Adj. N and N N_{gen} – *baronov sin* (Engl. baron's son) and *sin baron* (Engl. son of the baron). Second, if the processes of structural derivation are not described as exhaustively as the inflective processes, then automatic indexing by e-dictionaries identifies as unknown all those words that are not separate entries in a dictionary of DELAS type, but have origins in structural derivation. Contributions to the solving of problems that occur due to derivational morphology in the application of the system of electronic dictionaries were given by Clemanceau (1993) and Mota (1998/1999), while the possible solutions of problems limited to the structural derivation were discussed in Vitas et al (2001). Third, the results of tagging by e-dictionaries of texts in different languages are difficult to compare if the phenomenon of structural derivation is not treated in the e-dictionaries of respective languages in the same or comparable way. Finally, the problem of maintenance of the system of the e-dictionary becomes a very complex task if the phenomenon of structural derivation is not solved in a systematic way.

One experiment

The investigation of the frequency of the phenomenon of structural derivation started with the following experiment. The texts belonging to French classical literature have been chosen for which multiple translations into Serbo-Croatian exist. From these texts the bilingual parallel corpus has been produced. Using the language of the original (French in this case) as a meta-language, it has been observed how the entries of the original text have been mapped to the target language in respect of the phenomenon of structural derivation.

As a first text for this experiment Voltaire's *Candide* was chosen, for which two independent translations in Serbo-Croatian exist.[2] Both translations were produced during the existence of Serbo-Croatian as a language, but they both belong to the Serbian variant. The first one was published before the Second World War, and was done by the eminent translator Milan S. Nedić, who has translated many classical works from English and French, such as Flaubert's *Madam Bovary* and Melville's *Moby Dick*. The other translation was done approximately thirty years later by Milan Predić who is less known for the translation of classical novels, but his translation conforms with the contemporary language more than Nedić's.

Electronic versions of both texts were obtained in different ways. The French untagged text was obtained from *Association de Bibliophiles Universels* (http://abu.cnam.fr/), while both translations were retyped. All three texts were tagged according to TEI guidelines to the sentence level, with many phrase-level elements tagged as well.

These texts have been aligned using the Vanilla aligner (Danielsson and Ridings 1997), forming three pairs: French/Serbian (34), French/Serbian (63), and Serbian (63)/Serbian (34). The obtained results had to be manually corrected, as the sentence boundaries vary considerably from one text to another. The most prominent example is one French sentence aligned with eight sentences in Serbian translation. The example of the alignment for the pair French/Serbian (63) is given in Table 16.3.

Table 16.3 An example of the French/Serbian (63) alignment[3]

*** Link: 1–2 ***
<seg id='KanFr.1.13.2.10'>Candide dans l'instant tire la sienne et l'enfonce jusqu'à la garde dans le ventre du baron jésuite; mais, en la retirant toute fumante, il se mit à pleurer: </seg>.EOS

<seg id='Kan63.1.13.2.12'> U tren oka Kandid izvu&cy;e svoj ma&cy; i zari ga baronu jezuiti do korica u trbuh. </seg ><seg id='Kan63.1.13.2.13'> Ali kad je izvla&cy;io o&sx;tricu koja se jo&sx; pu&sx;ila od tople krvi, on zaplaka: </seg>. EOS

*** Link: 1–3 ***
<seg id='KanFr.1.13.2.11'>«Hélas! mon Dieu, dit-il, j'ai tué mon ancien maître, mon ami, mon beau-frère; je suis le meilleur homme du monde, et voilà déjà trois hommes que je tue; et dans ces trois il y a deux prêtres. » </seg> .EOS

<seg id='Kan63.1.13.2.14'> «Ah, bo&zx;e moj! – uzviknu. </seg> <seg id='Kan63.1.13.2.15'> – Ubio sam svog biv&sx;eg gospodara, svog prijate&lx;a, svog &sx;uraka. </seg><seg id='Kan63.1.13.2.16'>Nema bo&lx;eg &cy;oveka na svetu od mene, a evo ubio sam ve&cx; tri &cy;oveka i me&dx;u tom trojicom dvojica su sve&sx;tenici.» </seg> .EOS
.EOP

Candide in an instant drew his rapier and plunged it up to the hilt in the Jesuit's body; but in pulling it out reeking hot, he burst into tears. 'Good God!' cried he, 'I have killed my old master, my friend, my brother-in-law. I am the best man in the world, and yet I have already killed three men, and of these three, two were priests.'

Concordances

The lemmatized concordances of French text have been produced by system Intex (Silberztein 1993). For instance, the entry <baron>, which corresponds to the inflective class N/A41 according to the LADL enumeration and representing the regular expression (n/ms +nne/fs+ns/ms+nnes/fs), has 56 occurrences in text. The short extract from these concordances is given in Table 16.4.

If the lemmatization of one of the translated texts is done according to the traditional Serbo-Croatian lexicographic practice, then the entry <baron> will encompass only the inflective forms of the noun *baron* listed in Table 16.2.

Table 16.4 Keyword: <baron>, frequency=56, class: N/A41

<seg id='KanFr.1.1.3.3'>	grasse, appétissante. Le fils du	**baron** paraissait en tout digne de son père.
<seg id='KanFr.1.27.9.1'>	Candide embrassa cent fois le	**baron** et Pangloss. « Et comment ne vous
<seg id='KanFr.1.4.1.19'>	qui voulait la défendre; madame la	**baronne** a été coupée en morceaux; mon
<seg id='KanFr.1.10.3.10'>	sur moi; ajoutez que je suis née	**baronne** avec soixante et douze quartiers,
<seg id='KanFr.1.1.4.2'>	châteaux et madame la meilleure des	**baronnes** possibles. « Il est démontré,
<seg id='KanFr.1.11.1.3'>	à lequel tous les châteaux de vos	**barons** allemands ne auraient pas servi de
<seg id='KanFr.1.27.8.3'>	Thunder-ten-tronckh, un des premiers	**barons** de l'Empire, et de M. Pangloss, le

Table 16.5 Serbian keyword: <baron>, frequency=45, class: N1

<seg id='Kan63.1.27.9.1'>	vazduh proseca. Kandid zagrli	**barona** i Panglosa po stotinu puta.
<seg id='KanFr.1.11.1.3'>	zamci va&sx;ih snova nema&cy;kih	**barona** ne bi mogli biti ni ko&nx;u&sx;ni
<seg id='KanFr.1.27.8.5'>	Tunder-ten-tronka, jednog od prvih	**barona** carstva, i za gospodina Panglosa,

In lemmatized concordances of both translations, the entry <baron> that corresponds to the above extract from the e-dictionary has 44 in the 1934 translation and 45 in the 1963 translation. The differences between frequencies in French and Serbian texts are due to the phenomenon of structural derivation. The French class <baron> is mapped to the Serbo-Croatian entries <baron>:Nm; <baronica>:Nf; <baronov>:Adj(Nm). The French form <baronette> which is not included in the class N/A41 is translated in both Serbian texts by <baroni~ica>:Dem(Nf) (diminutive of *baronica*). The excerpt from the lemmatized concordances of the Serbian translation from 1963 is given in Table 16.5.

The following three examples illustrate this phenomenon. To the French entry *baron,* which appears in the original text in the sentence identified by KanFr.1.1.3.3, in both translations corresponds the possessive adjective *baronov: le fils du baron* is either *baronov sin* or *sin baronov,* as can be seen in Table 16.6.

Table 16.6 Mapping of a French noun *baron* to the Serbian possessive adjective *baronov*

French/Serbian (63)
*** Link: 1–1 ***
Le fils du **baron** paraissait en tout digne de son père. .EOS
Sin **baronov** izgledao je u svemu dostojan svog roditelja. .EOS

Serbian(34)/Serbian (63)
*** Link: 1–1 ***
Baronov je sin izgledao u svemu dostojan svoga oca. .EOS
Sin **baronov** izgledao je u svemu dostojan svog roditelja. .EOS

The Baron's son seemed to be a youth in every respect worthy of the father he sprung from.

In contrast to the previous example, to the occurrence of the French entry *baron,* which appears in the original text in the sentence identified by KanFr.1.27.7.1, corresponds the noun *baron* in one translation and the possessive adjective *baronov* in the other, as shown in Table 16.7.

Similarly, the French compound <le roi des Bulgares> appears in the sentence KanFr.1.2.2.10. It is mapped in the 1934 text to <kralj bugarski>, where *bugarski* is a relative adjective, and in the 1963 text to <kralj Bugara>, where *Bugarin* is a noun (Table 16.8).

The given examples show that in order to improve the extraction of meaning it is necessary to expand the inflective class so that it encompasses the cases of structural derivation too. This approach means that one textual word (word form) can be reduced to more lemma forms, depending to what level structural derivation has been included. Thus, the Serbo-Croatian entry <baron> can be considered in different ways:

Table 16.7 Mapping of a French noun *baron* to the Serbian noun *baron* and to the Serbian possessive adjective *baronov*

French/Serbian (63)
*** Link: 1–1 ***
Au nom du **baron** et de Pangloss les deux forçats poussèrent un grand cri, s'arrêtèrent sur leur banc et laissèrent tomber leurs rames. .EOS
Pri pomenu **baronova** i Panglosova imena, oba roba uzviknu&sx;e iz sveg glasa, zasta&sx;e nepomi&cy;ni na klupama i ispusti&sx;e vesla. . EOS

Serbian(34)/Serbian (63)
*** Link: 1–1 ***
Pri pomenu **barona** i Panglosa, ova dva roba vrisnu&sx;e, prestado&sx;e veslati sa svoje klupe i upusti&sx;e vesla. .EOS
Pri pomenu **baronova** i Panglosova imena, oba roba uzviknu&sx;e iz sveg glasa, zasta&sx;e nepomi&cy;ni na klupama i ispusti&sx;e vesla. .EOS

No sooner had Candide uttered the names of the Baron and Pangloss, than the two slaves gave a great cry, ceased rowing, and let fall their oars out of their hands.

Table 16.8 Mapping of a French compound *le roi des Bulgares* to the Serbian compound *kralj Bugara* and *bugarski kralj*

French/Serbian (63)
*** Link: 1–1 ***
Il avait déjà un peu de peau et pouvait marcher, quand le **roi des Bulgares** livra bataille au roi des Abares. .EOS
Ve&cx; be&sx;e dobio malo ko&zx;e i mogao je hodati, kad **kralj Bugara** zametnu boj sa kraljem Abara. .EOS

Serbian(34)/Serbian (63)
*** Link: 1–1 ***
Ve&cx; je imao pomalo ko&zx;e i mogao je i&cx;i, kad se **kralj bugarski** upusti u bitku s kraljem Abara. .EOS
Ve&cx; be&sx;e dobio malo ko&zx;e i mogao je hodati, kad **kralj Bugara** zametnu boj sa kraljem Abara. .EOS

His sores were now skimmed over and he was able to march, when the King of the Bulgarians gave battle to the King of the Abares.

a) <baron> which corresponds to Serbo-Croatian DELAS entry baron.N01.01;
b) <baron> which assembles Serbo-Croatian DELAS entries baron.N01.01 and baronica,N71.01, as in French;
c) <baron> which assembles, besides (b) the corresponding forms of diminutives, augmentatives, possessive adjectives, etc.

The improvement of Serbian concordances

The lemmatization with the entries augmented in the described way can be implemented in the system Intex by finite automata whose every node corresponds to the appropriate e-dictionary segment. Such an automaton for the Serbian entry <baron> is presented in Figure 16.1.

This automaton covers the inflective paradigms of separate entries, as seen in traditional lexicography, into one entry named BaronPlus.grf. This new entry neutralizes the effects of structural derivation. In Serbo-Croatian DELAF dictionary 56 different word forms correspond to the elements of the inflective paradigms of five separate entries from this automaton. Some of these word forms are:

barona,baron.N1:msg:msa:mpg
baroncyicxe,baroncyicx.N21:mpa
baronicama,baronica.N71:fpd:fpi:fpl
baronicyice,baronicyica.N71:fsg:fsv:fpn:fpa:fpv
baronicyine,baronicyin.A2:qnmpa:qnfsg:qnfpn:qnfpa:qnfpv
baronove,baronov.A2:qnmpa:qnfsg:qnfpn:qnfpa:qnfpv
baronskim,baronski.A3:qomsi:qonsi:qompd:qompi:qompl:qonpd:qonpi:qonpl:
qofpd:qofpi:qofpl

When the lemmatized concordances of translated text are produced using the given automaton, then the frequencies of the entry <baron> in the source and target texts become approximately equal. Lemmatization of translations by Intex using the automaton BaronPlus.grf instead of <baron> yields 56 occurrences in the 1934 text and 57 occurrences in the 1963 text. The excerpt from concordances produced in this way is given in Table 16.9.

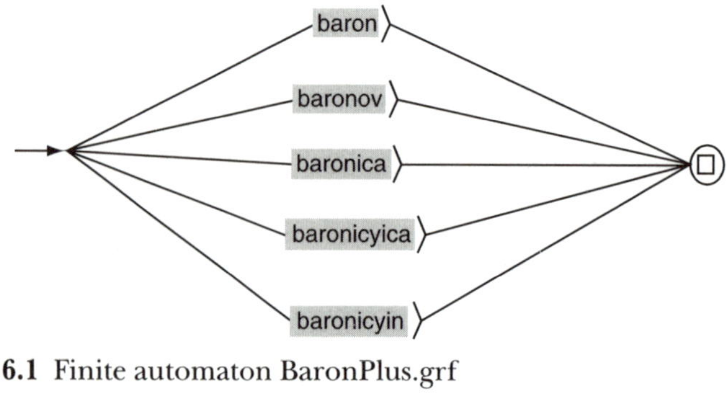

Figure 16.1 Finite automaton BaronPlus.grf

Table 16.9 Serbian keyword: BaronPlus.grf (FS graph), frequency=57

<seg id='Kan63.1.27.9.1'>	vazduh proseca. Kandid zagrli	**barona** i Panglosa po stotinu puta.
<seg id='KanFr.1.11.1.3'>	zamci va&sx;ih snova nema&cy;kih	**barona** ne bi mogli biti ni ko&nx;u&sx;ni
<seg id='KanFr.1.27.8.5'>	Tunder-ten-tronka, jednog od prvih	**barona** carstva, i za gospodina Panglosa,
<seg id='KanFr.1.4.1.23'>	kad je hteo da je brani; gospo&dx;a	**baronica** je ise&cy;ena na komade; moj
<seg id='KanFr.1.10.3.14'>	Dodajte jo&sx; da sam se rodila	**baronica** sa sedamdeset dva pretka, a da
<seg id='KanFr.1.1.4.2'>	najbo&lx;a od svih mogu&cx;ih	**baronica.** 'Dokazano je,' govorio je on
<seg id='Kan63.1.1.3.3'>	i naoko primam&lx;iva. Sin	**baronov** izgledao je u svemu dostojan
<seg id='Kan63.1.2.1.1'>	skrivao u sebi najlep&sx;u od svih	**baroni&cy;ica**. Le&zx;e da spava, bez

The exhibited procedure has been applied to some other entries of source and target texts and appropriate lemmatized concordances have been produced. Their respective frequencies in the original text and the 1963 translation are presented in Table 16.10. In the column *SC class* the frequency of traditionally conceived Serbo-Croatian entries is given, in the column *Serbian FSA* the frequency of the entry described by the appropriate local grammar, and in the column *French Class* the frequency of the corresponding entry in the source text. The insignificant differences in frequencies between French lemma and Serbo-Croatian lemma defined by local grammar can have different sources. Some are not the consequences of the structural derivation at all (for instance, the French *actrice* is once translated by *pevacyica* instead of the direct translation *glumica*), and some are the results of different levels of involvement of this phenomenon in applied classes (for instance, the French diminutive *baronnette* is not in the class <baron>, while the Serbian counterpart *baronicyica* is in BaronPlus.grf).

Table 16.10 Frequencies of some French entries and respective Serbian traditional and new entries

English	SC class	F	Serbian FSA	F	French class	F
(*baron*)	<baron> Nm	45	BaronPlus.grf	57	<baron> N/A	56*
(*Bulgarian*)	<Bugarin> Nm	17	BugarinPlus.grf	30	<bulgaire> N/A	30
(*Christian*)	<hrisxcxanin> Nm	4	HristPlus.grf	7	<chrétien> N/A	7
(*actor*)	<glumac> Nm	4	GlumacPlus.grf	7	<acteur> N	8*
(*canon*)	<top> Nm	2	TopPlus.grf	6	<canon> Nm	6
(*Pope*)	<papa> Nm	4	PapaPlus.grf	6	<pape> Nm	6
(*lover*)	<lxubavnik> Nm	3	LxubavnikPlus.grf	5	<amant> N	6*

The further improvement in neutralizing the influence of structural derivation on the results of lemmatization can be achieved if the automaton in Figure 16.1 is replaced by the finite transducer given in Figure 16.2 (Gross 1997). If a transducer is used in the process of lexical recognition to the textual words, the string attached to the graph node is associated instead of a dummy entry BaronPlus. For instance, to the form *baronice*, which in Serbo-Croatian DELAS can represent genitive singular of class <baronica>, lemma *baron* is associated with a semantic mark of feminine gender by gender motion.

Conclusion

The traditional definition of the inflective classes in lexicography of Serbo-Croatian cannot link the entries between which there exists a close structural derivation relationship. This relationship is on the dictionary level usually expressed by a stereotype definition that is based on the meaning of

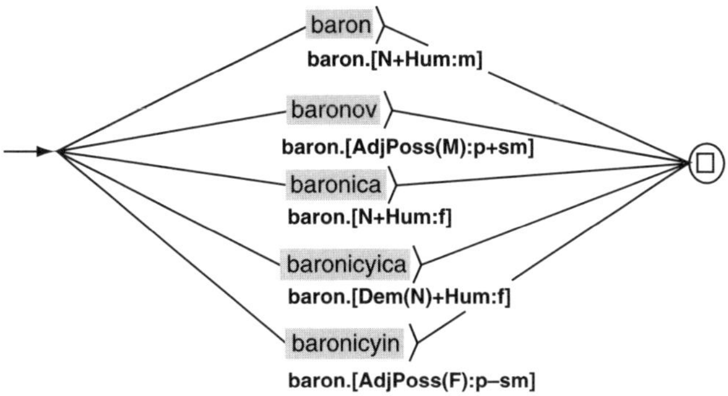

Figure 16.2 Transducer BaronPlus

the basic entry. Several types of nominal modifiers of this kind are discussed in this paper: modifiers for the gender motion, modifiers for amplification (formation of diminutives and augmentatives), and modifiers for derivation of adjectives from nouns. It is shown that both modifiers form the new noun from the initial one according to the same model and in a similar way that the inflective classes are described. The extension of the traditional nominal class can thus be seen as a tuple of the elementary classes that describe the derivatives of the basic entry.

Notes

1 The codes cx, cy, dx, dy, sx, zx, nx, lx, dy for Latin letters and digraphs ć, č, đ, š, ž, nj, lj, dž are used to neutralize in text processing the usage of two different alphabets.

2 The first translation is by Milan S. Nedić, published by Izdavačka knjižarnica Rajković, in Belgrade in 1934, and second translation is by Milan Predić, published by Izdavačko preduzeće 'Rad' in Beograd in 1963.

3 In this and the following examples the English text is given only to provide the translation. It has been obtained from the address http://www.literature.org/

References

Clemanceau, David (1993) 'Structuration du lexique et reconnaissance de mots dérivés', thèse de doctorat d'informatique fondamentale, Université Paris 7, LADL, CERIL.

Courtois, Blandine (1992) *Dictionnaire électronique des mots simples du français* DELAS V07-E1. Paris: LADL.

Courtois, Blandine and Silberztein, Max (eds) (1990) 'Dictionnaires électroniques du français', *Langue française* 87. Paris: Larousse.

Danielsson, Pernilla and Ridings, Daniel (1997) *Practical Presentation of a 'Vanilla' Aligner*, presentation held at the TELRI Workshop in Alignment and Exploitation of Texts, Ljubljana, 1–2 February.

Gross, Maurice and Perrin, Dominique (eds) (1989) *Electronic Dictionaries and Automata in Computational Linguistics*, Lecture Notes in Computer Science. Berlin: Springer Verlag.

Gross, Maurice (1997) 'The Construction of Local Grammars', in Roche, Emmanuel and Schabes, Yves (eds) *Finite State Language Processing*, Cambridge, MA: MIT Press.

Mota, Cristina (1998/1999) 'Enhancing the INTEX Morphological Parser with Lexical Constraints', in Shevalier, Jean-Claude, Gross, Maurice and Leclere, Christiane (eds) *Lingvisticae Investigationes*. Amsterdam: John Benjamins, pp. 413–23.

Popović, Ljubomir (1996) 'Deux approches idéologiques de la vernacularisation de la langue littéraire chez les Serbs à la fin du 18e et dans la première moitié du 19e siècle', in *Langues et nations en Europe Centrale et Oriental du 19e siècle à nos jours*. Lausanne: Cahiers de l'ILSL 8: 209–40.

Popović, Ljubomir (2000) 'From Standard Serbian to Standard Serbo-Croatian to Standard Serbian', in *Proceedings of the Conference 'Languages in the Former Yugoslav Lands'* (London SSEES, 8–9 September 2000) (forthcoming)

RMS-MH (1967) *Rečnik srpskohrvatskoga književnog jezika*, vols 1–6, Beograd-Zagreb: Matica Srpska, Matica Hrvatska.

Silberztein, Max D. (1993) *Le dictionnaire électronique et analyse automatique de textes: Le systeme INTEX*. Paris: Masson.

Vitas, Duško (1993) *Matematički model morfologije srpskohrvatskog jezika (imenska fleksija)*. Beograd: Matematički fakultet, Univerzitet u Beogradu.

Vitas, Duško, Krstev, Cvetana and Pavlović-Lažetić, Gordana (2001) 'Flexible Dictionary Entry', in Zybatow, Gerhild (ed.) *Current Issues in Formal Slavic Linguistics*. Frankfurt am Main: Peter Lang, pp. 461–8.

17 Noun collocations from a multilingual perspective

Rūta Marcinkevičienė

Introduction

The notion of multilingualism usually implies diversity of linguistic expression. Specific linguistic features manifest themselves in all the levels of a language, but the most peculiar seem to be those that are related to meaning and semantics and reveal the different ways of structuring and verbalizing reality. A good example of linguistic diversity is the collocability of abstract nouns that denote the phenomena of mentality and conceptualizing the non-physical in terms of the physical world, i.e. the so-called mentalese. The best way to investigate language-specific phenomena is to compare a selected item in several languages. Thus, the aim of our analysis is to find out to what extent verbal collocates of *memory* are universal or language specific, i.e. whether the meanings of collocating verbs and collocational patterns are preserved in translations or not.

I have chosen the noun *memory* as it is used in Orwell's novel *1984* and its six translations into five languages for a pilot study of collocability. Due to the topic of the novel, *memory* is a frequently used noun, predominantly in the singular (47 times out of 62), but also in the plural (15 times out of 62) in one of its meanings, i.e. either a) as the ability to remember, or the metonymical extension of the first meaning, b) as something that we remember about the past. Due to these two meanings, the English noun *memory* has two different noun equivalents in the languages of translation, i.e. in Lithuanian, Czech, Polish, German and Russian (further shortened as Lt, Cz, Pl, De and Ru respectively). The existence of two translations into the Russian language allows us to determine the degree of subjective, translator-dependent, versus objective, language-dependent choices; the first translation as presented in the list of examples is performed by Golyshev, the second by Ivanov and Nedoshyvin.

Out of the considerable variety of usages of the lexeme *memory*, I have chosen verbal collocations since they prove to be the most interesting from a multilingual perspective, i.e. they present a varicty of metaphorical patterns and figurative meanings of verbs used with the noun under investigation. It is obvious that the meanings of nouns are much better preserved in the languages of translation than the meanings of their verbal collocates which are selected according to the laws of the target language and the judgement of the translator. Verbal collocates are more language-dependent and culture-specific.

Basic assumptions

The analysis is based on three basic assumptions that shape the methodology of comparison. The first assumption postulates the semantic relationship of all the senses of the same lexeme, the principal of relatedness of a polysemic lexeme (Leech 1981: 229, Lyons 1981: 147, Palmer 1981: 101) and thus of the relatedness of collocates of the same verb in one language (no matter whether different collocates are presented lexicographically as forming different meanings or not), e.g. if you *stir* a liquid with a spoon in a container, or if you *stir* with your body because you feel uncomfortable, or if the wind *stirs* an object, i.e. moves it gently, or if something beautiful or moving *stirs* you and you react with a strong emotion, or if you *stir up* a feeling (meaning that you cause people to have it) – all those usages have common semantic components. This assumption allows us to claim the presence of semantic relationship between the noun under investigation and other collocates used with the same verb, i.e. it allows us to conceive *memory* as a moving entity of some (hard or liquid) consistency (cf. the notion of *metalinguistic slot sharing* by Montemagni *et al.* 1996, Dufour 1998).

Another assumption related to the first one is as follows: the prototypical or basic or central senses of a verb are those where the verb collocates with nouns denoting concrete, tangible objects of the physical world (cf. Taylor 1990: 99–121, Ungerer *et al.* 1996: 99–109), e.g. in the case of stirring, it is the idea of mixing some liquid (no matter whether these nominal collocates are used more or less often than the rest). Mentalese, as abstract nouns used with common verbs are conceived, is conceptually based on these prototypical verbal usages, semantically derived from them. Languages differ from the point of view of verbal collocability, thus presenting different prototypes for the same abstract noun – cf. in Lithuanian, for example, *enthusiasm goes out* like a *fire* and does not *wane* like the *moon* in English. This approach is based on the idea of collocational networks that influence description and comprehension of non-physical reality.

The third assumption has to do with the existence of context-independent or so-called dictionary equivalents that, if presented in isolation of their syntagmatic context, have identical or very close meanings in several languages (Jarošova 1997: 73, Marcinkevičienė 2001: 60–4), e.g. *stir* – De *umrühren,* Ru *мешать переметивать,* Lt *maišyti, plakti.* If we admit that such equivalents exist and that in most cases they correspond to prototypical usages of a verb translated into similar prototypical usages of other languages, we can talk about the possibility of preserving similar collocational patterns in different languages. In other words, if we take *memory* and its closest dictionary equivalent in Lithuanian *prisiminimas* to denote something that we remember, and look for their verbal collocates denoting repetitive obtaining of *memory/prisiminimas,* we find the verb *stir* in English and *pa(su)žadinti* in Lithuanian. The latter in its prototypical usage can be translated by the dictionary equivalent *wake up* or *revive* or *call up.* Since the two verbal collocates performing the same lexicogrammatical function of the same noun in two languages differ in their prototypical usages (one has to do with causing some substance to move and another with causing a living being to change its state of mind), we can claim that they are language-specific. This approach gives us the possibility to talk about universal and language-specific features of the collocability of *memory.*

Analysis of the collocations of *memory*

Out of the multiple cases of verbal collocations of *memory* only those were selected which formed certain lexicogrammatical groups. In Orwell's novel there were four such groups: verbs denoting 'appearance' (*to come, to clarify, to float, to swim*) and 'motion' (*to move around*) of a *memory* in its role as the subject of a sentence, as well as 'retrieval' (*drag out, dig out, awaken, stir up*), and 'rejection' (*to black out*) of a *memory* in its role as the object. These groups roughly coincide with inchoative, durative and terminative verbs: 'appearance' and 'retrieval' verbs representing inchoative action, 'motion' verbs representing durative process and 'rejection' verbs coinciding with terminative action (cf. Čermák present volume, Chapter 14). In the languages of translation only those equivalents were taken into consideration that preserved the same verb–noun structure of a collocation (translated by the verb alone nominal collocations do not retain their original collocational pattern, e.g. *the memory came back to him – he remembered.*) Verbal collocations forming the groups mentioned above in one source and five target languages were analysed from the point of view of preservation of their original collocational pattern.

The first group of verbal collocations shares the same lexicogrammatical meaning of 'appearance' of memory. It comprises the following verbs in English *clarify, float, come back, swim* which convey the common inchoative meaning of appearance with the help of different, more or less specific verbs in the original version and its translations (fragments of translations are supplied by prototypical dictionary equivalents of the verbs from the languages of translations back to English in order to demonstrate the similarity or difference of the collocational pattern), cf.:

Eng	a totally different memory had clarified itself in his mind
Lt	jam atbudo (wake up) visai kitokio pobūdžio prisiminimas
Cz	že se mu přitom v mysli vynořila (pop out, emerge) vzpomínka na úplně jinou událost
Pl	Zupełne inne wydarzenie stanęło (rise) mu w pamięci

De daß in ihm währenddessen eine völlig andere Erinnerung aufgestiegen war (rise, go up)
Ru[1] в памяти у него отстоялось (settle) совсем другое происшедствие
Ru[2] совершенно иное воспоминание возникло (arise, appear) в его голове

As it can be seen from the reverse translations of the verbal collocates of *memory* from the languages of translation back into English, none of them preserve the original notion of the memory as getting *clear* while appearing in a person's mind. Most of the verbal translation equivalents denote the more abstract notion of appearance as arising (as in Pl, De, Ru[2]) or the more specific notion of awakening, popping out or settling (as in Lt, Cz, Ru[1] translations respectively). Thus it can be stated that *to clarify* as verbal collocate is quite specific for English.

Other verbal collocates denoting appearance of *memory* are rendered into the target languages in a similar way, i.e. by changing instead of retaining their original collocational patterns. In the case of translation of the verb *float* only Ru[2] translation preserves the prototypical image of *float*, i.e. to move slowly onto the surface of a liquid, cf.:

Eng Uncalled, a memory floated into his mind
Lt Jo sąmonęje savaime iškilo (rise, emerge, come to the surface) prisiminimas
Cz Bezděky se mu v mysli vynořila (pop out, emerge) vzpomínka
Pl Nagle bez powodu stanał (rise) przed oczami pewien obraz
De Ungerufen stieg eine Erinnerung in ihm auf (rise, go up)
Ru[1] Незванное явилось (appear, present oneself) воспоминание
Ru[2] Незванно в памяти всплыла (come to the surface) картинка из детства

The synonymical verb *to swim* as used with *memory* has also lost its prototypical meaning in some of the translations except for the Lt and Ru[1]. The existence of a different Russian translation exhibits the systemic possibilities for a translation closer to the original chosen by one and neglected by another translator:

Eng There was the dream itself, and there was a memory connected with it that had swum into his mind in the few seconds after waking
Lt ir pats sapnas, ir su juo susiję prisiminimai, atplaukę (swim) sąmonėn per keletą sekundžių
Cz V několika vteřinách po probuzení mu sen i vzpomínka, kterou v něm vyvolal, splynuly v jedno (blend together)
Pl Chodziło nie tule o sam sen, ile o związane z nim wspomnienie, które nawiedziły (call on) Winstona kilka sekund po przebudzeniu
De Da war zum einen der Traum selbst; hinzu kam eine mit ihm verknüpfte Erinnerung, die in den ersten Sekunden nach dem Erwachen in ihm aufgestiegen war (rise, go up)

Ru[1] Тут был и сам по себе сон, и воспоминание, с ним связанное, – оно всплыло (come to the surface) через несколко секунд после провуждения

Ru[2] Был сон, были воспоминания, возникшие (arise, appear) сразу же после ровуждения

In the case of a more abstract English verbal collocation *to come back*, translations show the tendency to preserve its meaning more easily than the previous specific verbs up to the omission of verb+noun pattern altogether and replacing it with one verb *to remember*.

Eng Then the memory of her face came back

Lt Paskui jis vėl prisiminė ją, (remember)

Cz Potom se mu však vrátila (come back) podoba její tváře a přepadla ho zběsilá

Pl Ale potem jej twarz znów stanęła (rise) mu przed oczyma

De Dann kehrte die Erinnerung an ihr Gesicht zurück (come back)

Ru[1] Но потом ее лицо снова возникло (arise, appear) перед газами

Ru[2] Но потом опять вспомнилось (remember) ее лицо.

In general, the lexicogrammatical group of verbs of 'appearance', as used with the noun *memory*, tends to manifest specific collocational patterns in six languages and only in the case of the abstract verb *to come back* the prototypical meaning of the verb is preserved in the target languages. Thus it can be inferred that collocations with abstract verbs are less diverse than those with specific concrete verbs.

The objective usage of *memory* with verbs of 'retrieval', i.e. *drag out, dig out, awaken, stir up*, also manifests a range of translation equivalents ranging from language-specific in the case of the collocation *to stir up some memory* to the universal in the case of *to awaken some memory*. Intermediate cases consist of the specific verbs *dig out* and *drag out* that are translated with the help of concrete metaphorical verbs more often changing than preserving the specific prototypical meaning of the English verb:

Eng He would drag the rest of that poem out of Mr Charrington's memory

Lt Pamėgins iš misterio Čaringtono atminties ištraukti (pull out) tą eilėraštį, visą iš eilės

Cz Vydoluje (dig/mine out) paměti pana Charringtona zbytek té říkánky

Pl Wyciągnie (pull out) resztę strof wiersza z pamieci pana Charringtona

De Er würde Mr Charrington den Rest dieses Gedichts aus dem Gedächtnis reißen (tear, pull)

Ru[1] Заставит мистера Чаррингтона вспомнить (remember) стишок до конца

Ru[2] Я выужу (fish out) из памяти мистера Чаррингтона недостающие строчки стихов

Since the original collocation contains a verb with a well-expressed metaphorical meaning, its translations also retain metaphoricity with the help of more abstract (*pull out* in Lt, Pl and De) or more specific (*dig out, fish out* in Cz and Ru[2]) verbs. The combination of *memory* with *dig out* and *drag out* can be called unusual, occasional, typical of a literary style and therefore unsuitable for more general, style-independent systemic considerations concerning the ways of expressing the notion of remembering with the help of verb+noun collocations. Nevertheless, translation equivalents of both verbs *drag* and *dig* show the general tendency to use systemic, usual and language-specific collocations instead of the occasional English metaphor (cf. literal translations of the verbs back into English):

Eng Perhaps it could be dug out of Mr Charrington's memory
Lt Gal ją galima iškapstyti (scratch up, dig up) iš misterio Čaringtono atminties
Cz Možná že by ho pan Charrington vyhrabal (rake out) z paměti
Pl Może uda się jakoś ożywić (revive) pamięć pana Charringtona
De Vielleicht konnte man ihn aus Mr Charringtons Erinnerung hervorholen (get something out of)
Ru[1] Может быть, удастся узвлечь (extract) из памяти Чаррингтона
Ru[2] Быть может, ее удастся выудить (fish out) из памяти мистера Чаррингтона

It is only in the case of Lt translation of *dig out* that the collocational pattern and the prototypical meaning of the original verb are retained. In De and Ru[1] translations the more abstract verbs are used. Ru[1], Cz, Pl translations contain specific verbs with different prototypical meanings. The two different Ru translations show a variety of systemic means to express the given lexicogrammatical meaning (*remember, fish out, extract*) which are differently employed by the translators.

The following collocation is translated using the same collocational pattern in all the target languages and it is only in the Ru[2] case that the prototypical meaning is not preserved. Thus *awaken* is another verb after *to come* which forms a preservable collocational pattern:

Eng but the room had awakened in him a sort of nostalgia, a sort of ancestral memory
Lt bet šitas kambarys sužadino (awaken, arouse) jam savotišką nostalgiją, savotišką protėvių atmintį
Cz Ale ten pokoj v něm probudil (wake up) nostalgii, vzpomínku zděděnou po předcích
Pl Lecz pokój obudził (wake up) w Winstonie jakąś tęsknotę, jakieś wspomnienie genetycznie zakodowane w pamięci

De doch das Zimmer hatte so etwas wie Nostalgie in ihm geweckt (wake up), eine Art Urerinnerung
Ru[1] Но комната пробудила (wake up) в нем какую-то ностальгию, какую-то память, дремавшую в крови
Ru[2] но комната вызвала (call out) в нем какую-то ностальгию, какуюто древную, родовую память

The collocation *to stir up one's memory*, on the contrary, seems to be English language-specific since none of the translations retain the original prototypical meaning of the verb which is rendered with the help of previous anthropomorphic metaphors of reviving (Lt translation) or waking (Pl, De, Ru[2] translations) used because of the absence of analogous means:

Eng The first whiff of its scent had stirred up some memory
Lt Pirmas to kvapo dvelktelėjimas atgaivino (revive, revitalize) kažkokį atsiminimą
Cz Když ji ucítil, vyvolala (call up) v něm vzpomínku
Pl Sam zapach zbudził (wake up) w nim silne, niepokojące, lecz całkiem zatarte wspomnienia
De Gleich der erste Duft hatte eine Erinnerung in ihm geweckt (wake up)
Ru[1] Запах сразу напомнил (remind) о чем-то
Ru[2] Его запах разбудил (wake up) в нем какие-то воспоминания

The verb of 'rejection' of memory as used in Orwell's novel is also language-specific from the point of view of its translations. Every target language uses its own verb to render the original collocation *to black out the memory* in a metaphorical and language-specific way. It is only the common lexicogrammatical meaning of 'rejection' that is preserved in all the translations but not the prototypical meaning of the original verb implying the visual image of blacking out some memory, e.g. the verbs *to drive away, to wipe off/efface, to erase, to put out/wipe out, to muffle, to switch/turn off* are used in Lithuanian, Czech, Polish, German and Russian translations respectively:

Eng that might *black out* the memory that was tormenting him
Lt kad nuvytų šalin (drive away) tą kankinantį prisiminimą
Cz co by mu z mysli vymazalo (wipe off, efface) trýznivou vzpomínku
Pl Zrobić coś gwałtownego . . . byleby tylko zatrzeć (erase) dręczące wspomnienie
De das die Erinnerung auslöschen (put out, wipe out) könnte, die ihn marterte
Ru[1] заглушить (muffle) рвущее душу воспоминание
Ru[2] чтобы отключить (turn/switch off) мучающую память

The last group of verbal collocates of the noun under consideration can be exemplified by the abstract verb of motion which is also translated by verbs of motion of a varied specificity. Translation equivalents differ from the point of view of prototypical nominal collocates, nevertheless they preserve the idea of a circular motion in Czech, Polish and Russian[2] and convey the idea of a slight motion in Lithuanian, German and Russian[1]:

Eng But there was still that memory moving round the edges of his consciousness
Lt Bet jo sąmonės gilumoje tebekirbėjo (move, stir) tas prisiminimas
Cz Ale v paměti neustále něco kroužilo (twirl, curl, twist) kolem nejasných obrysů vzpomínky
Pl Tuź na skraju jego świadomości kołotał sie (turn, go round) jakiś zapomniany obraz
De Aber immer noch trieb (drive) dicht unter seiner Bewußtseinsschwelle diese Erinnerung
Ru[1] Но что-то все шевелилось (stir, move) в глубинах памяти
Ru[2] А давнее воспоминание все крутилось (twist, twirl) у него в голове

Conclusions

Memory collocations with a verb viewed from a multilingual perspective, using the translation of one novel into five languages as the basis for the pilot study, demonstrated a variety of ways to render collocational patterns and lexicogrammatical meanings. It can be stated that the original collocational patterns are preserved to a different extent in translations, which reveal systemic means to verbalize the notion of memory. The general meaning of initiation (as in the case of inchoative verbs of 'appearance' and 'retrieval'), duration (verbs of motion) and termination (verbs of 'rejection') of actions and processes of memory combined with the syntactic function of the noun *memory* is preserved in the translation. Lexical meanings of specific verbs collocating with *memory*, as rendered in the translations, range from the more universal (as in the case of both abstract and concrete verbs *to come back, to awaken, to swim*) to language-specific (*to stir up, to black out*) and comprise intermediate cases within the scale.

In general, each language has its own set of verb–noun collocations expressing certain lexicogrammatical meanings. Since the choice of the specific verb is mostly predetermined by this general or aspectual meaning, lexical meaning seems to be secondary and therefore is seldom/rarely preserved in translation no matter whether the particular language has or does not have TE of the same or similar metaphor. It is only the occasional, innovative word combinations (cf. *drag out, dig out*) that are followed in the translation to a certain extent.

The parallel corpora used for the analyses have the disadvantage of being small though they present the usage of the selected lexical item in identical contexts. Objective reasons, such as the influence of context for the choice of translation equivalents, as well as subjective ones, especially the translator's approach, do not allow us to draw reliable conclusions. Therefore it is necessary to resort to general corpora for the information about the collocates of the item under investigation that perform specific lexical functions and have the same general meaning. This is the way to get more numerous and possibly more frequent collocates.

References

Čermák, František. 'Abstract Noun Collocations: Their Nature in a Parallel Czech-English Corpus'. Present volume.

Dufour, Nicolas (1998) 'Recognizing Collocational Constraints for Translation Selection: DEFI's Combined Approach', in Fontenelle, Thierry *et al.* (eds) *Euralex'98 Proceedings.* Liège: University of Liège, pp. 109–18.

Jarošová, Aleksandra (1997) 'Parallel Corpora and Equivalents not Found in Bilingual Dictionaries', in Marcinkevičienė, Rūta and Volz, Norbert (eds) *Proceedings of the Second European Seminar 'Language Applications for a Multilingual Europe'.* Mannheim/Kaunas: IDS/VDU, pp. 69–76.

Leech, Geoffrey (1981) *Semantics.* London: Penguin.

Lyons, John (1981) *Language and Linguistics.* Cambridge: Cambridge University Press.

Marcinkevičienė, Rūta (2001) 'The Importance of the Syntagmatic Dimension in the Multilingual Lexical Database'. *International Journal of Corpus Linguistics,* Special Issue: 55–65.

Montemagni, Simonetta, Federici, Stefano and Pirrelli, Vito (1996) 'Example-based Word Sense Disambiguation: a Paradigm-driven Approach', in Gellerstam, Martin *et al.* (eds) *Euralex '96 Proceedings.* Göteborg: Göteborg University, pp. 151–60.

Palmer, Frank R. (1981) *Semantics.* Cambridge: Cambridge University Press.

Taylor, R. John (1990) *Linguistic Categorization.* Oxford: Clarendon Press.

Ungerer, Friedrich and Schmid, Hans-Jörg (1996) *An Introduction to Cognitive Linguistics.* New York: Addison-Wesley Longman.

Sources

Orwell, George (1954) *Nineteen Eighty-Four.* London: Penguin.

Orvelas, Džordžas (1991) *1984-ieji.* Vilnius: Vyturys.

Orwell, George (2000) *Rok 1984.* Przełożył Tomasz Mirkowicz. Warszawa: Muza Sa.

Orwell, George (2000) *1984* Übersetzt von Michael Walter. München: Ullstein.

Оруэль, Джордж (1989) *1984.* Перевод В. Голышева. Москва: Новый мир.

Оруэль, Джордж (1991) *1984.* Перевод В. Иванова, В. Недошивина. Свердловск: Средне-Урадьское издатльсво.

18 Studies of English–Latvian legal texts for Machine Translation

Inguna Skadiņa

Introduction

Since 1993 the Artificial Intelligence Laboratory of the Institute of Mathematics and Computer Science, University of Latvia has been working on automatic translation tools for the Latvian language. This work is supported by the Latvian Science Council through several projects: Limited Model of Automated Machine Translation (MT) System for Latvian (1993–6), Development of Probabilistic Methods for Automated Disambiguation of Natural Language Texts and Applications for Machine Translation (1997–9) and Automatic synthesis of language independent text representation (2000–).

During the first years the machine translation system model LATRA (Greitāne 1997) for translation of weather reports and stock market texts was developed. The system uses an interlingua approach from the SWETRA system (Sigurd: 1994). SWETRA is a multilingual interlingua MT system for an automated translation of stock market texts between English, Swedish, Russian, Polish and German. The interlingua approach allows us to include the Latvian model LATRA into the system and supports translation from Latvian into English as well as translation from Swedish, Russian and English into Latvian.

The first results of LATRA were promising so therefore the work was continued with the aim of widening the domain of application. The Translation Centre of the European Commission is using machine translation for draft translations. Since translation of EC legislation is an important task for pre-accession states, in the further studies the role of MT in translation of the EC documents is evaluated.

The quality of automated translation is closely related to the understanding of the meaning of text, sentences and words. The aim of this study was to find out how the parallel texts could help to improve the quality of MT and to find meaning. We concentrated on the following tasks:

- to study ambiguous words and their translations in parallel texts

- to find out how syntactic patterns limit a meaning of ambiguous word forms

The data

The White Paper, *Preparation of the Associated Countries of Central and Eastern Europe for Integration into the Internal Market of the Union*, in English and Latvian provided by the Translation and Terminological Centre was used for the studies. It was the first EC document translated into Latvian by a group of translators.

The Latvian text contains approximately 158,600 running words and the English text contains approximately 186,500 running words. So the huge differences in numbers of words is caused by diverse syntactic structures of source and target languages:

- in English, articles are used, while in the Latvian language there are no articles
- in English auxiliaries are used to express the debitive, while in Latvian the debitive is marked by the prefix *jā–*
  priority should be given – prioritāte jāpiešķir
  these measures should be complemented – šie pasākumi jāpapildina
  eggs must also meet – arī olām jāatbilst
- in English negation for verbs is formed with *not*, while in Latvian negation is often formed with the prefix *ne–*
  regulators do not regard – regulētāji neuzskatītu
  the system would not operate properly – sistēma pienācīgi nedarbosies
  do not cover phytosanitary aspects – neietver fitosanitāros aspektus

As in ordinary texts the most frequent words are *un (and)* 3998, *ir (is)* 2076, *par (about)* 2041, immediately followed by domain-specific words – *EEC* 1869, *Padome* (*Council*) 1316, *OJ* 1295, *direktīva* (*directive*) 1175.

Development of the dictionary

Since the aim of study was to find out how parallel texts could help in the development of an automated translation system, a dictionary was developed from the parallel text. The work on the dictionary was divided into the following steps:

- extraction of words
- word-list generation
- finding translations in the parallel texts

Extraction of words

At first all words from the texts were automatically counted and sorted alphabetically. For English words obtained, the list served as a final word-list, while for Latvian, the base forms from this list were obtained.

Word-list generation

Because of the rich morphology of the Latvian language, the morphological analyser was used to obtain base forms of the words extracted from the text.

Latvian is a highly inflected language with rich morphology. Latvian nouns are divided into six declensions. Latvian nouns and pronouns have six cases in both singular and plural. Adjectives, numerals and participles have six cases in singular and plural, two genders and definite and indefinite form. The rules of case generation are different for each group.

In the Latvian conjugation system there are two numbers, three persons and three tenses (present, future and past tenses), both simple and compound and five moods.

Latvian is quite regular in the sense of forming inflected forms, but the form endings in Latvian are highly ambiguous. Nouns in Latvian have 29 graphically different endings and only 13 of them are unambiguous, adjectives have 24 graphically different endings and half of them are ambiguous, verbs have 28 graphically different endings and only 17 of them are unambiguous. For instance, the word form *ceļu* could be present singular, first person of verb *celt* (*to build*), singular accusative or plural genitive of noun *ceļš* (*road*) and plural genitive of noun *celis* (*knee*).

With the morphological analyser the base forms of the words were obtained. Since the analyser is lexicon-based the base forms were obtained for common words, while specific words, for instance abbreviations (*PRAQ, PT, PVN*) and foreign names (*Heylens, Shift, Comité*), were kept as they were in the text.

Finding translations in the parallel texts

The next and most time-consuming task was to create a dictionary based on parallel texts and word-lists. Translations from the texts were extracted manually. To speed up the development of the dictionary and to facilitate inclusion of all the translations from the text, several tools were used.

To find occurrences and usage of the wordforms in the text, QWICK was used. With QWICK different meanings and syntactic patterns were determined.

Another tool used for dictionary building was Trados Winalign Demo, which was useful for sentence alignment. Afterwards for detailed analysis ParaConc Beta was used.

Although the parallel texts contain more than 150,000 words in each language the dictionary is rather small. There are 6117 translation pairs formed by 4638 Latvian words and 5414 English words.

The dictionary is created for machine translation and has the following form: [*Latvian stem*] '*translation into English*' (*grammatical and syntactic information about Latvian word*)

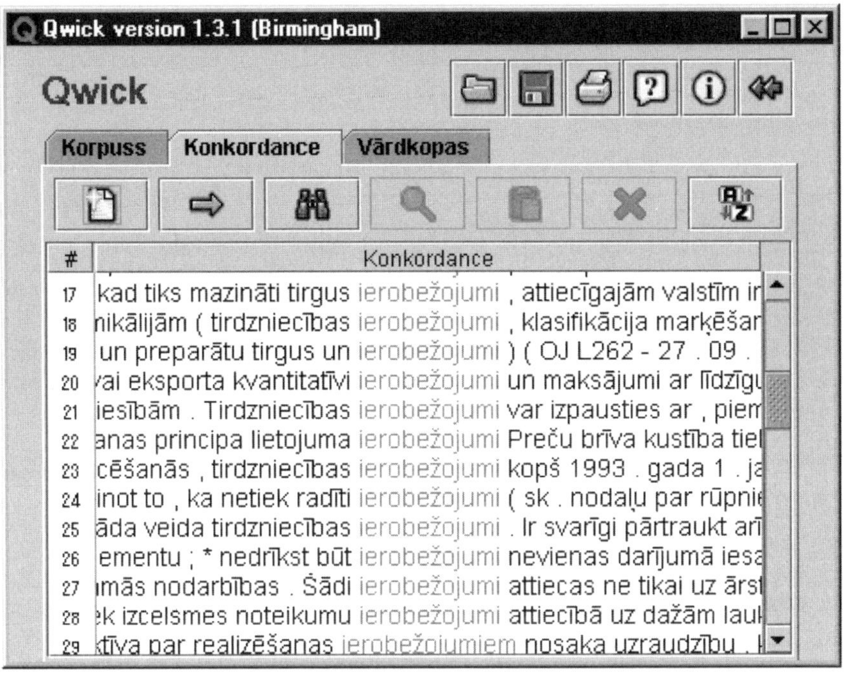

Figure 18.1 Screenshot from QWICK, concordances of *ierobežojums*

The example below shows dictionary entries of the noun *ierobežojums*:

[ierobežojum] 'restriction' (N,MASC,1DECL)
[ierobežojum] 'constraint' (N,MASC,1DECL)
[ierobežojum] 'restraint' (N,MASC,1DECL)
[ierobežojum] 'barrier' (N,MASC,1DECL)
[ierobežojum] 'limit' (N,MASC,1DECL)
[ierobežojum] 'regulatory barrier' (N,MASC,1DECL)

Studies of meanings

The dictionary developed from parallel texts was used for tests of LATRA. In this study the dictionary was necessary to find out how parallel texts and dictionaries obtained from these texts could help to understand meaning.

As was mentioned before, the dictionary is quite small. As envisaged, the language of legal texts is precise – most of the words have only one or two translations. However, in 4 cases the Latvian word has 6 translations, 11 words have 5 translations, 21 words have 4 translations, 83 have 3 translations and 405 have 2 translations.

Our interest was to find out why some words have many translations. Is it inconsistency of translation, or, are different words used for different meanings, or, does difference in context determine usage of distinct words?

The rest of the paper will describe four cases where the Latvian words have six translations.

Participle atbilstošs

The participle *atbilstošs* is frequently used in translation. It occurs 86 times. The following seven translations are fixed in our dictionary: *appropriate, adequate, suitable, comparable, proportionate, fulfil the conditions.*

In comparison the printed dictionary (Veisbergs 2001) gives the following translations: *corresponding, conformable; (piemērots) suitable, adequate; proper, appropriate.*

The dictionary entries were also compared with Tilde's electronic dictionary (Vasiljevs and Greitāne: 2001), which is a compilation of a general dictionary and terminological dictionaries. The following translations of the word *atbilstošs* were not found in any of them: *comparable, proportionate, fulfil the conditions.* Therefore occurrences of translation pairs in the texts and their frequencies were studied:

- *comparable* – total frequency 10, frequency of translation pair – 2
  atbilstoša sistēma – comparable system
  atbilstoša finansu informācija – comparable financial information
- *proportionate* total frequency 2, frequency of translation pair – 2
  atbilstošam izvirzītajam mērķim – proportionate to the purpose (2)
- *fulfil the conditions* total frequency 1, frequency of translation pair –1
  nosacījumiem atbilstošs auditors – auditor fulfilling the conditions

Words *proportionate* and *fulfil the conditions* are always translated as *atbilstošs.* What are the other translations for *comparable?*

comparable to – kāds ir
comparable between companies – līdzīga organizācija
equivalent and comparable – ekvivalenta un salīdzināmas
comparable system – salīdzināma sistēma
comparable advantages – ievērojamas priekšrocības
a comparable entity – līdzīga organizācija

It is possible to conclude that *atbilstošs* forms rare but different meanings from those recorded in any printed or electronic dictionary.

Noun ierobežojums

The previous sample shows that in parallel texts for words with low frequency new consistent translations can be found. In this section the case of frequent words with different translations will be discussed.

The noun *ierobežojums* is used 70 times in the text as a translation for *barrier, limit, restriction, restraint, constraint* and *regulatory barrier.* In the printed dictionary the following translations occur: *limit, restriction, confinement, restraint; jur. abridgement. Ierobežojums* as translation of *barrier* and *regulatory barrier* occurs only in the text. Occurrence of *regulatory barrier* in the text is 1, while *barrier* occurs 58 times and in 24 cases (41 per cent) is translated as *ierobežojums:*

> *tirdzniecības ierobežojumi(10) – barriers to trade*
> *tirdzniecības ierobežojumi(6) – trade barriers*
> *ierobežojumu novēršanai tirdzniecībā(2) – barriers to trade*
> *ierobežojumu atcelšana (2) – abolition of barriers*
> *tehniskie ierobežojumi tirdzniecībā – technical barriers to trade*
> *neformāli ierobežojumi – informal barriers*
> *novērst ierobežojumus – remove barriers*
> *preču kustības ierobežojumi – barriers to the movement of goods*

Since *barrier* is translated as *ierobežojums* in 24 cases, in order to find objectives for this translation the concordances of *barrier* and their translations were examined. The texts showed that *trade barriers* is also often translated as *tirdzniecības šķersļi*. Similarly *barriers to trade* is translated as *šķēršļi tidzniecībai.*

Verb noteikt, *participle and adjective* noteikts

The last two words with six translations are the verb *noteikt*, corresponding participle and adjective *noteikts.*

The verb *noteikt* occurs 43 times in the text. In the developed dictionary the verb *noteikt* is a translation for *lay down, set up, determine, put in place, stipulate, prescribe.* The translation pair *put in place – noteikt* is not mentioned in any dictionary.

Noteikts occurs in the text 236 times and is translation for *certain, specific, defined, required by, imposed, enshrined.* Translations *required by, imposed, enshrined* are found in parallel texts.

The mentioned translation pairs are rare in text, while the occurrence of the corresponding English word is high:

- *put in place* – occurs in text 16 times, translated as *noteikt* –2
  noteikt alternatīvus administratīvos pasākumus – put in place alternative administrative arrangements
  noteikti trīs speciāli nodokļu aplikšanas gadījumi galapunktā – special arrangements for taxation at destination were put in place
- *required by* – occurs in text 14 times, translated as *noteikts* –2
  direktīvu noteiktā atklātības un reklamēšanas efektivitāte – effectiveness of the transparency and advertising required by the directives
  Kopienas likumdošanā noteiktie auditi – audits required by Community law
- *imposed* – occurs in text 10 times, translated as *noteikts* –1
  uzņēmumam noteiktie ierobežojumi par pašam savu akciju pirkšanu – restrictions imposed on the acquisition of a company's own shares
- *enshrined* – occurs in text 4 times, translated as *noteikts* –1
  Līgumā noteiktās četras brīvības – four freedoms enshrined in the Treaty

This allows us to conclude that the parallel texts also contain 'unstable' translations. In such cases only detailed analysis can help to determine whether the translation is relevant.

Conclusions

This study allows us to make the following conclusions:

- even in small parallel texts there are meanings which are not in general and even terminological dictionaries

All four cases discussed above demonstrated that in parallel texts not only rare translations, but also frequent translations, which are never mentioned in dictionaries before, can be found.

- the corpus-based approach is useful for printed dictionaries as well as for computer-readable dictionaries

For both types of dictionaries the parallel text is useful. In translation tools, mainly frequent translations and domain-specific translations will be included. In printed dictionaries all possible translations need to be included.

- quality of translation needs to be evaluated when the texts are used for dictionary building

The study also shows that parallel texts may contain inconsistencies in translation, especially if they are translated by several translators. This is mainly important for legal texts, not literary works. Therefore the quality of translation needs to be evaluated before the text is used for dictionary development.

- data from the corpus needs to be included not only in the dictionary, but also in language-processing systems

This relates mainly to syntactic patterns and cases when context determines the usage of synonymies.

Acknowledgements

I would like to thank Baiba Krūze-Krauze and Everita Milčonoka for their accurate work on the dictionary development.

I would also like to thank the developers of the tools mentioned, which helped a lot in this study.

References

Greitāne, Inguna (1997) 'Mašīntulkošanas sistēma LATRA', *LZA Vēstis* 3(4): 1–6.

Greitāne, Inguna (1998) 'Machine Translation and Multilingual Resources for Latvian', *Proceedings of the Third European Seminar 'Translation Equivalence'*, pp. 79–86.

Sigurd, Bengt (1994) 'Swetra Referent Grammar', in *Computerized Grammars for Analysis and Machine Translation.* Lund: Lund University Press, pp. 7–56.

Vasiļjevs, Andrejs and Greitāne, Inguna (2001) 'Baltic challenges on the IT frontier: language and culture', Proceedings of Baltic IT&T 2001 forum: eBaltics, pp. 195–9.

Veisbergs, Andrejs (2001) *Jaunā latviešu – angļu vārdnīca.* Rīga: SIA Eknomikas attiecību institūts.

19 The applicability of lemmatization in translation equivalents detection

Marko Tadić, Sanja Fulgosi and Krešimir Šojat

Introduction

In contemporary lexicography computer corpora have become the dominant source of material needed for evidence of language units and their usage. As opposed to monolingual corpora, important mostly for monolingual lexicography, parallel corpora (consisting of two or more languages) are taking on special significance in bilingual lexicography. Such corpora provide a corpus-linguistic insight into multilingual language material. Methods of data-exploring resulting in alphabetic and frequency lists, concordances, detection of collocations, phrases, idioms, multiword units, etc. can be applied in a multilingual environment. The data and relations within one corpus can be comparatively observed through their translations, i.e. the same text coded in units of other language(s). Aligned parallel corpora offer explicit possibilities for such comparisons. If a corpus is aligned to the sentence level, it is easy to identify translations of sentences and to determine in what relation they stand to each other. The main intention of this paper is to test the practicability of statistical measures in translation equivalents' detection at the level of the word in the parallel corpus consisting of typologically relatively different languages: Croatian and English.

Corpus

The Croatian–English parallel corpus was compiled at the Institute of Linguistics, Faculty of Philosophy, University of Zagreb in 2000 and 2001. The corpus consists of Croatian texts and their translations in English, all from the same source – *Croatia Weekly*, the newspaper published in Zagreb from January 1998 to April 2000. 111 issues out of the total of 118 were available for the compilation of this corpus (Tadić 2000 for other details about the corpus).

The corpus is aligned at the level of sentence with the DOS version of the *Vanilla aligner* (Danielsson and Ridings 1999).

Table 19.1 Corpus parameters

	Croatian	English
articles	4748	4748
sentences	74,638	82,898
tokens	1,636,246	1,968,874

Table 19.2 shows that more than 83 per cent of Croatian sentences were translated into a single English sentence. This is particularly important for the research work presented further in the paper.

Table 19.2 The alignment statistics

0:1	250	0.35 %
1:0	19	0.03 %
1:1	58,788	83.52 %
1:2	9374	13.32 %
2:1	1529	2.17 %
2:2	432	0.61 %
total	70,392	100.00 %

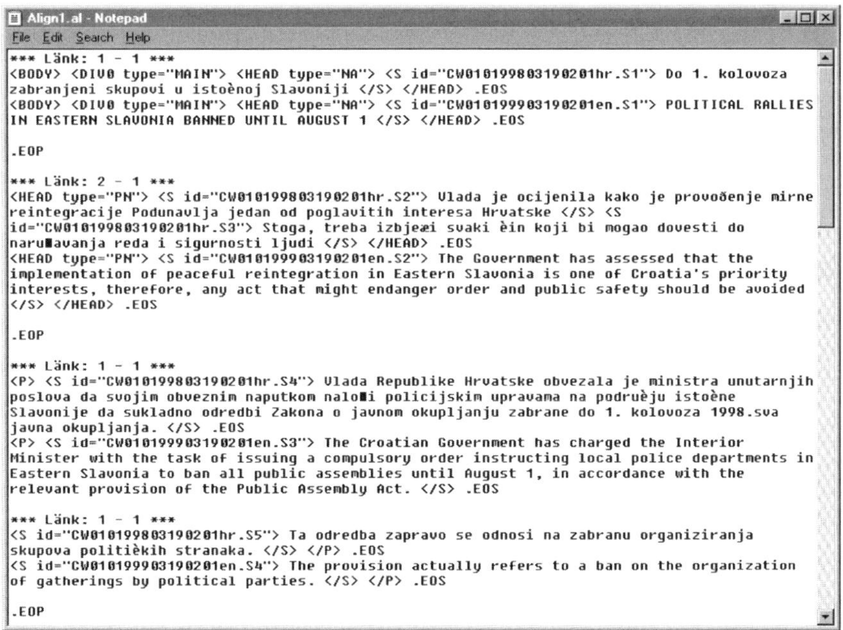

```
Align1.al - Notepad
File Edit Search Help
*** Länk: 1 - 1 ***
<BODY> <DIV0 type="MAIN"> <HEAD type="NA"> <S id="CW010199803190201hr.S1"> Do 1. kolovoza
zabranjeni skupovi u istoènoj Slavoniji </S> </HEAD> .EOS
<BODY> <DIV0 type="MAIN"> <HEAD type="NA"> <S id="CW010199903190201en.S1"> POLITICAL RALLIES
IN EASTERN SLAVONIA BANNED UNTIL AUGUST 1 </S> </HEAD> .EOS

.EOP

*** Länk: 2 - 1 ***
<HEAD type="PN"> <S id="CW010199803190201hr.S2"> Vlada je ocijenila kako je provoðenje mirne
reintegracije Podunavlja jedan od poglavitih interesa Hrvatske </S> <S
id="CW010199803190201hr.S3"> Stoga, treba izbjeæi svaki èin koji bi mogao dovesti do
naru■avanja reda i sigurnosti ljudi </S> </HEAD> .EOS
<HEAD type="PN"> <S id="CW010199903190201en.S2"> The Government has assessed that the
implementation of peaceful reintegration in Eastern Slavonia is one of Croatia's priority
interests, therefore, any act that might endanger order and public safety should be avoided
</S> </HEAD> .EOS

.EOP

*** Länk: 1 - 1 ***
<P> <S id="CW010199803190201hr.S4"> Vlada Republike Hrvatske obvezala je ministra unutarnjih
poslova da svojim obveznim naputkom nalo■i policijskim upravama na podruèju istoène
Slavonije da sukladno odredbi Zakona o javnom okupljanju zabrane do 1. kolovoza 1998.sva
javna okupljanja. </S> .EOS
<P> <S id="CW010199903190201en.S3"> The Croatian Government has charged the Interior
Minister with the task of issuing a compulsory order instructing local police departments in
Eastern Slavonia to ban all public assemblies until August 1, in accordance with the
relevant provision of the Public Assembly Act. </S> .EOS

*** Länk: 1 - 1 ***
<S id="CW010199803190201hr.S5"> Ta odredba zapravo se odnosi na zabranu organiziranja
skupova politièkih stranaka. </S> </P> .EOS
<S id="CW010199903190201en.S4"> The provision actually refers to a ban on the organization
of gatherings by political parties. </S> </P> .EOS

.EOP
```

Figure 19.1 Example of alignment

Subcorpus

The processing of the whole corpus through the method described in TE_{11} detection (see below) would result in an extremely vast amount of data and eventually lead to 'combinatory explosion'. Therefore, it was decided to limit the research to a part of the corpus. The seventh page of all magazine issues was chosen as a subcorpus (the page gives the news of the economy, banking, stock exchange, etc.). Such a subcorpus was selected in order to ensure the consistency of terminology used in translations and to investigate the applicability of statistical measures to real text, i.e. the text comprising digits and proper names highly characteristic of topics from that field.

The total number of alignments in the subcorpus is 8187. 6786 sentences were aligned in the 1:1 form consisting of 202,081 Croatian and 241,376 English tokens. The research was based on this sample.

Aim

The aim of the research is to identify translation equivalents (TE) appearing in 1:1 aligned sentences. The research procedure can be divided into several steps:

- detection of TE_{11}, i.e. translation equivalents consisting of 1 Croatian word : 1 English word
- detection of TE_{22}, i.e. translation equivalents consisting of 2 Croatian words : 2 English words

In general the TE detection between two languages (L_1 and L_2) can be formulated as detection of TExy, i.e. translation equivalents consisting of x words from L_1 : y words from L_2 (where $x <=> y$)

In this paper we concentrated on the first case only, i.e. the possibility of detection of TE_{11} and with both non-lemmatized and lemmatized material.

Theoretical background

The constantly increasing amount of electronically stored multilingual texts provides an exceptional basis for the research of parallel corpora. The identification of TEs is one of the areas where the investigation of parallel

Table 19.3 Parameters of the subcorpus

	Croatian	English
articles	404	404
sentences	8420	9373
tokens	195,510	234,365

corpora proved to be extremely useful. Contemporary research work in this area focuses on word alignment (e.g. Tiedemann 1999; Ahrenberg *et al.* 1998), i.e. identifying TEs below the sentence level and feeding the corpus with information about these units and their links. Identification of such TEs can be performed on two levels:

1. level of single-word units = detecting W_{L1}:W_{L2} relations
2. level of multiword units = detecting W_{1L1}–W_{2L1} and W_{1L2}–W_{2L2} relations in each language separately and after that also W_{1L1}–W_{2L1} : W_{1L2}–W_{2L2} relations

Systems for TE identification aim at finding either the highest possible number of pairs (e.g. Ahrenberg *et al.* 1998, Melamed 1999) or concentrate on the accuracy of pairs, which should usually provide the basis for the creation of bilingual lexicons (e.g. Tiedemann 1998, 1999). Investigated units are either specific types of pairs – e.g. terms (Dagan and Church 1994) or collocations (Smadja *et al.* 1996).

Melamed (2000: 227) claims that 'almost all known systems functioning through [statistic] similarity are based on some model of co-occurrences with application of some linguistically determined filter'. Consequently, linguistic filters are being applied simultaneously with statistical processing (mostly at the level of morphology or simple syntactical constructions) restricting the input and output of data. Such filters can be applied to collocation extraction in a monolingual corpus as well as to the identification of translation equivalents.

Besides strictly statistically based methods (e.g. Gale and Church 1991, Smadja *et al.* 1996, Dagan *et al.* 1999) there are systems with some linguistic knowledge integrated in collecting and processing the data from corpora (e.g. Daille 1996, Hatzivassiloglou 1996, Jacquemin 2001).

The method described in this paper is based entirely on a statistical approach. No linguistic filter was applied before or after the processing. Possible applications of filters will be examined in future research.

TE_{11} detection

Method

The method for detection of translation equivalents developed and applied in this research can be divided into several steps:

1. generation of all possible pairs of tokens in 1:1 aligned sentences (simple Carthesius product of two sentences at the word level):
   The following pairs of possible TE_{11} are generated from the aligned sentences *Ivan jede jabuku* and *John eats an apple: Ivan:John, Ivan:eats, Ivan:an, Ivan:apple, jede:John, jede:eats, jede:an, jede:apple, jabuku:John, jabuku:eats, jabuku:an, jabuku:apple*
2. application of a statistical measure to generated pairs in order to detect pairs that are statistically relevant candidates for real TE

Table 19.4 The scheme of possible TE_{11} pairs generation

	hr sentence	en sentence	hr-en pairs
1. word	*a*	*w*	*aw, ax, ay, az*
2. word	*b*	*x*	*bw, bx, by, bz*
3. word	*c*	*y*	*cw, cx, cy, cz*
4. word		*z*	

3. sorting the pairs according to calculated results and choosing real TE for further lexicographic use

In this research the statistical measure of mutual information (MI) was chosen (precisely *pointwise mutual information* as defined in Manning and Schütze 1999: 178) with the formula $MI = \log_2 \frac{P(x,y)}{P(x)\,P(y)}$. With some caution in applications,[1] mostly with low-frequency linguistic units, it yields rather useful results.

Results

The processing of the subcorpus described above using the method defined above produced the following results:

- 202,081 Croatian and 241,376 English tokens from 6786 sentences made 26,166 Croatian and 13,234 English types
- generating pairs resulted in 4,819,953 pairs of tokens out of which 1,944,377 were different pairs of types
- however, out of almost 2 million different pairs of types 262,625 had a frequency higher than 2. The threshold was set at this level and only the pairs of types with frequency higher than 2 were used for further analysis
- the pairs were sorted according to descending MI value for these 262,625 pairs of types. The threshold of MI value for evaluation was set at =>9. For the evaluation of results the frequencies of pairs as well as of single words were taken into consideration.

Until now we were dealing with non-lemmatized words. Since Croatian is a morphologically complex language we expected to gain better results after lemmatization. We also expected that the lemmatization would be more significant for Croatian than for English but we still applied it to both languages. The lemmatization was performed semi-automatically with the use of lists of lemmas and wordforms from the *Croatian frequency dictionary* (Moguš *et al.* 1999) and the test version of the noun part of *Croatian morphological lexicon*, which is being compiled at the Institute of Linguistics. For English lemmatization a list of lemmas with wordforms from TELRI

Table 19.5 The results of evaluation of pairs of types as candidates for TE_{11}

frequency	pairs detected	correct TE	%
>9	9	9	100.0
>8	15	15	100.0
>7	30	30	100.0
>6	51	45	88.2
>5	110	84	76.3
>4	210	157	74.7
>3	394	280	71.0
>2	976	645	67.0

CD-ROM (Erjavec *et al.* 1998) was used. After automatic replacement of types with lemmas, the whole list was manually checked. The results for lemmatized material are as follows:

- from the same number of tokens and sentences as above, 26,166 Croatian and 13,234 English types after lemmatization gave 13,222 Croatian and 10,403 English lemmas
- out of the same amount of generated pairs of tokens as above, the 1,944,377 different pairs of types resulted in 1,407,727 pairs of lemmas
- out of almost a million and a half of different pairs of lemmas only 262,858 had a frequency higher than 2. The threshold was also set at this level and pairs of lemmas with frequency higher than 2 were used for further analysis
- the pairs were sorted according to descending MI value for these 262,858 pairs of lemmas and the threshold of MI value as well as frequencies were treated as above

Tables 19.5 and 19.6 show that the precision of real TE pairs decreases with pairs with lower frequency, but there is also an increase of the number recall of possible pairs. The comparison of results between the two tables shows that pairings of lemmas gave the results which are 4.5 per cent better than pairings of types. This leads to the conclusion that lemmatization should be done for morphologically complex languages in order to get better precision and recall in TE candidates detection.

Problems

The chosen method of investigation confronts us with several questions.

Do all the pairs make real TEs? The evaluation criterion is based on foreign language knowledge. Strictly methodologically taken, as there was no additional verification of results, it could be claimed that they are dependent on the evaluator's knowledge of the English language. It seems

Table 19.6 The results of evaluation of pairs of lemmas as candidates for TE_{11}

frequency	pairs detected	correct TE	%
>9	18	18	100.0
>8	32	32	100.0
>7	53	53	100.0
>6	99	91	91.9
>5	169	146	86.3
>4	293	235	80.2
>3	534	413	77.3
>2	1081	825	77.0

L1	L1_	L2	L2_	L12	L12	MI_L
željezara	9	željezara	9	željezara željezara	8	9,3884957118
lokomotiva	13	locomotive	9	lokomotiva locomotive	11	9,3174126138
seminar	9	seminar	12	seminar seminar	10	9,2953863074
kaznen	12	criminal	9	kaznen criminal	10	9,2953863074
vegeta	11	vegeta	11	vegeta vegeta	11	9,2689140961
crnogorski	11	montenegrin	8	crnogorski montenegrin	8	9,2689140961
ivo	10	ivo	11	ivo ivo	10	9,2689140961
bedekov&#269,ina	10	bedekovčina	10	bedekovčina bedekovčina	9	9,2544145264
kw	10	kw	9	kw kw	8	9,2364926184
17,5	10	17.5	9	17,5 17.5	8	9,2364926184
1,9	12	1.9	12	1,9 1.9	12	9,143383214
benetton	10	benetton	12	benetton benetton	10	9,143383214
2,9	12	2.9	12	2,9 2.9	12	9,143383214
2,4	12	2.4	10	2,4 2.4	10	9,143383214
hektar	12	hectare	8	hektar hectare	8	9,143383214
MW	11	mw	11	MW mw	10	9,1314105723
kulturan	11	cultural	10	kulturan cultural	9	9,1169110026
55	11	55	10	55 55	9	9,1169110026
7,5	11	7.5	10	7,5 7.5	9	9,1169110026
libor	11	libor	10	libor libor	9	9,1169110026
španjolski	17	spanish	8	španjolski spanish	11	9,1003144921
disciplina	9	discipline	11	disciplina discipline	8	9,0989890946
lužavac	9	lužavec	11	lužavac lužavec	8	9,0989890946
kalogjera	10	kalogjera	10	kalogjera kalogjera	8	9,0844895249
anketa	10	survey	13	anketa survey	10	9,0279059966
billa	9	billa	13	billa billa	9	9,0279059966
2,7	13	2.7	12	2,7 2.7	12	9,0279059966
produktivnost	8	productivity	13	produktivnost productivity	8	9,0279059966
0,8	13	0.8	13	0,8 0.8	13	9,0279059966
recesija	13	recession	13	recesija recession	13	9,0279059966
cigareta	11	cigarette	13	cigareta cigarette	11	9,0279059966
bouygues	12	bouygues	11	bouygues bouygues	10	9,0058796902

Record: 1 of 53 (Filtered)

Figure 19.2 an example of pairs of lemmas as candidates for TE_{11}, sorted according to descending MI value

that there is no other method for checking the correctness of TEs but to use human evaluators and their knowledge of both languages.

The second question concerns the presence of digits and proper names in the list of pairs. Are digits and proper names being translated from one language to the other real TEs at all? Arguments for inclusion of digits, beside our intention to check the method on the real (not filtered) language material, can be found in spelling differences of Croatian and English (e.g. digits in Croatian are written with a decimal comma, while in English with a decimal point). As far as the digits are concerned, the results were 100 per cent accurate and no further analysis was necessary. On the other hand, proper names in Croatian are subject to morphological variation (the issue solved through lemmatization). The problem of morphological variation is found also in language-specific lexical units, e.g. toponyms *Beč:Vienna, Bruxelles:Brussels,* etc. In this case the method yields the same results as for any other pair of real TEs. Therefore, our decision was to treat digits and proper names the same way as other tokens.

The third question is about ruining the 'collocational strength' by lemmatization. The collocation can be seen as characteristic combination, a pattern of, e.g., two nouns where one is in the nominative and other in the genitive. If we apply lemmatization to both of them, the second will turn to the nominative as well. That combination of words will gain better statistical results but we will also lose the characteristic collocational pattern. Even more, the statistical processing of lemmatized combinations of words can include in the processing the combinations (e.g. nominative + dative) which are not a result of collocation and its characteristic pattern, but are there because of chance. The exact relationship between characteristic collocational patterns and lemmatization in Croatian remains to be investigated in the future and it surely represents a vast field for further research.

The next disadvantage of such a method based on the generation of possible TE pairs is a certain 'overgeneration of pairs' as a consequence of the multiple occurrence of particular words either in the source-language sentence or in the target-language sentence. The characteristic example is the situation when the frequency of a particular pair exceeds individual frequencies of elements involved in a pair. Schematically, this can be illustrated with the following table:

Table 19.8 The scheme of 'overgeneration' of possible TE_{11} pairs

	hr sentence	en sentence	hr-en pairs
1. word	*a*	*w*	*aw, ax, ay, ax, az*
2. word	*b*	*x*	*bw, bx, by, bx, bz*
3. word	*a*	*y*	*aw, ax, ay, ax, az*
4. word	*c*	*x*	*cw, cx, cy, cx, cz*
5. word		*z*	

Table 19.8 reveals that the pair *ax* was generated twice, although there are only 2 occurrences in different sentences of *a* and *x* respectively. In this research we put this problem aside because it would make the generation of pairs too complex. Besides, most of the overgenerated pairs were exact

TEs with high frequencies so they did not influence the precision. The solution of this problem could be a frequency check of all tokens within a sentence where in the case of multiple occurrence of a particular token the overgeneration of pairs should be revisited.

Further, there are noticeable characteristic errors produced through 'indirect pairs'. The problem concerns the generation of pairs consisting of frequent collocation elements either in the source language or in the target language e.g. *Plitvička:Plitvice, Plitvička:lakes, jezera:Plitvice, jezera:lakes* (see also in Melamed 2000: 227). It can be illustrated through the following figure:

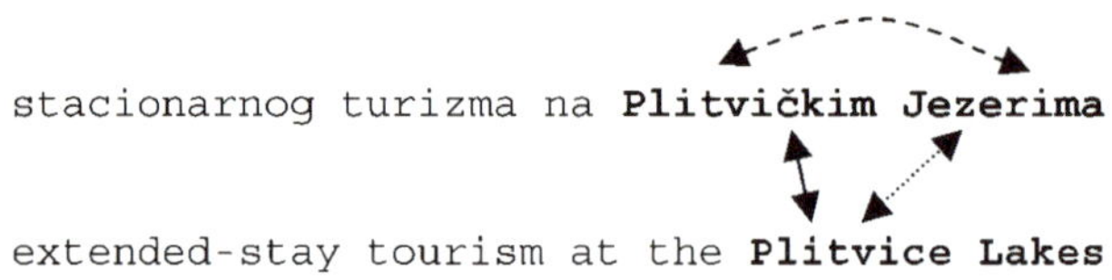

Figure 19.3 An example of direct (full line) and indirect (dotted line) pairs and collocations (dashed line)

Is there a way to avoid indirect pairs? Can we achieve it through the generation of pairs of collocations from the source language and the target language? The procedure of detecting the pairs of collocations, i.e. the pairs of pairs (TE_{22}), could be seen as an expansion of the method used for detection of TE_{11}:

Table 19.9 The scheme of possible TE_{22} pairs

	hr sentence	en sentence	hr-en pairs of pairs
1. word	*a*	*v*	*abvw, abwx, abxy, abyz*
2. word	*b*	*w*	*bcvw, bcwx, bcxy, bcyz*
3. word	*c*	*x*	*cdvw, cdwx, cdxy, cdyz*
4. word	*d*	*y*	
5. word		*z*	

This expansion of the above presented method unfortunately runs beyond the scope of this paper and represents the topic of another paper (see Tadić and Šojat 2003).

Further research directions

The method described above, for the time being based on pure statistics, could be further enhanced and applied to different areas:

- generation of other possible pairs: TE_{12}, TE_{21}, TE_{22}, TE_{23}, TE_{32}, TE_{33}, TE_{34}, TE_{43}, TE_{44} . . .

- experiments with other frequency and MI-value thresholds
- application of other statistical measures: e.g. Dice coefficient, χ^2-test, log-likelihood
- reiteration of TE_{11} with already detected TE_{12}, TE_{21}, TE_{22} included, which would lead to the avoidance of 'indirect pairs'
- use of linguistic filters (e.g. adding the POS or MSD information) before or after the application of statistical measures in order to limit their scope to, e.g., only combinations of *adjective* + *noun* etc.

Conclusion

The paper illustrates the application of one of the statistical measures for detection of translation equivalents based on the sentence-aligned Croatian–English parallel corpus, namely mutual information. Translation equivalents were sought and detected at the level of single words (TE_{11}). The efficiency of MI-value calculation was demonstrated for the identification of TE_{11}, on both non-lemmatized and lemmatized material. The lemmatized TE Croatian–English pairs performed better on average 4.5 per cent in precision and recall. The conclusion was that the lemmatization could be performed before applying statistical measures in TE detection in order to get better results, particularly for morphologically complex languages.

Notes

1 See in McEnery *et al.* (1997: 222) in note 6, about the variant of MI called MI3. Also see in Smadja *et al.* (1996: 8–14) about other definitions of MI and about possible problems of its application. About problems of applying MI see also in Manning and Schütze (1999: 181) as well as in Gale and Church (1991).

References

Ahrenberg, Lars, Andersson, Mikael and Merkel, Magnus (1998) 'A Simple Hybrid Aligner for Generating Lexical Correspondences in Parallel Texts', *Proceedings of COLING-ACL '98*, Montreal: ACL, pp. 29–35.

Ahrenberg, Lars, Merkel, Magnus, Hein, Anna Sågvall and Tiedemann, Jörg (2000) 'Evaluation of Word Alignment Systems', *LREC2000 Proceedings: Second International Conference on Language Resources and Evaluation,* eds Gavrilidou, M., Carayannis, G., Markantonatou, S., Piperidis, S. and Stainhaouer, G. Atena-Paris: ELRA, pp. 1255–61.

Armstrong, Susan, Church, Kenneth W., Isabelle, Pierre, Manzi, Sandra, Tzoukermann, Evelyne and Yarowsky, David (eds) (1999) *Natural Language Processing Using Very Large Corpora.* Dordrecht: Kluwer.

Choueka, Yaacov, Conley, Ehud S. and Dagan, Ido (1998) 'A Comprehensive

Bilingual Word Alignment System – Application to Disparate Languages', *Parallel Text Processing: Alignment and Use of Translation Corpora*, ed. Veronis, J. Dordrecht: Kluwer, 69–96.

Dagan, Ido and Church, Kenneth W. (1994) 'Termight: Identifying and Translating Technical Terminology', *Proceedings of the 4th Conference on Applied Natural Language Processing ANLP-94*, ACL: Stuttgart, pp. 34–40.

Dagan, Ido, Church, Kenneth W. and Gale, William A. (1999) 'Robust Bilingual Word Alignment for Machine Aided Translation', *Natural Language Processing Using Very Large Corpora*, eds Armstrong, S., Church, K., Isabelle, P., Manzi, S., Tzoukermann, E. and Yarowsky, D. Dordrecht: Kluwer, pp. 209–24.

Daille, Béatrice (1996) 'Study and Implementation of Combined Techniques for Automatic Extraction of Terminology', *The Balancing Act*, ed. Klavans, Judith L. and Resnik, Philip. Cambridge, MA/London: MIT Press, pp. 49–66.

Danielsson, Pernilla and Ridings, Daniel (1999) *Practical Presentation of a »Vanilla« Aligner*, 1999–10–11, URL:http://nl.ijs.si/telri/Vanilla/doc/ljubljana.html.

Erjavec, Tomaž, Lawson, Ann and Romary, Laurent (1998) *East Meets West – A Compendium of Multilingual Resources*, 2 CD-ROMs. Mannheim: TELRI-IDS.

Frantzi, Katerina T., Ananiadou, Sophia and Tssujii, Junichi (1999) 'Automatic Classification of Technical Terms using the NC-value Method for Term Recognition', *Papers in Computational Lexicography: COMPLEX '99*, eds. Kiefer, Ferenc, Kiss, Gábor and Pajzs, Júlia. Budapest: Linguistic Institute of Hungarian Academy of Sciences, pp. 57–66.

Gale, William A. and Church, Kenneth W. (1991) 'Identifying Word Correspondences in Parallel Texts', *Proceedings DARPA Speech and Natural Language Workshop*, San Mateo: Morgan Kaufmann, pp. 152–7.

Hatzivassiloglou, Vasileios (1996) 'Do We Need Linguistics When We Have Statistics?: A Comparative Analysis of the Contributions of Linguistic Cues to a Statistical Word Grouping System', *The Balancing Act*, eds Klavans, Judith L. and Resnik, Philip. Cambridge, MA/London: MIT Press, pp. 67–94.

Jacquemin, Christian (2001) *Spotting and Discovering Terms through Natural Language Processing*. Cambridge, MA/London: MIT Press.

Klavans, Judith K. and Resnik, Philip (eds) (1996) *The Balancing Act: Combining Symbolic and Statistical Approaches to Language*. Cambridge, MA/London: MIT Press.

Manning, Christopher and Schütze, Hinrich (1999) *Foundations of Statistic Natural Language Processing*. Cambridge, MA/London: MIT Press.

McEnery, A. M., Wilson A., Sanchez-Leon, F. and Nieto-Serano, A. (1997) 'Multilingual resources for European languages: Contributions of the Crater Project', *Literary and Linguistic Computing*, Volume 12, Issue 4, Oxford: OUP, pp. 219–26.

Melamed, I. Dan (1996) 'Automatic construction of clean broad-coverage translation lexicons', *Proceedings of the 2nd Conference of the Association of Machine Translation in the Americas.* Montreal, pp. 125–34.

Melamed, I. Dan (1999) 'Bitext Maps and Alignment via Pattern Recognition', *Computational Linguistics* 25(1): 107–30.

Melamed, I. Dan (2000) 'Models of Translational Equivalence among Words', *Computational Linguistics* 26(2): 221–49.

Moguš, Milan, Bratanić, Maja and Tadić, Marko (1999) *Hrvatski čestotni rječnik.* Zagreb: Školska knjiga, Zavod za lingvistiku Filozofskoga fakulteta Sveučilišta u Zagrebu.

Resnik, Philip and Melamed, I. Dan (1997) 'Semi-Automatic Acquisition of Domain-Specific Translation Lexicons', *Proceedings of the 7th ACL Conference on Applied Natural Language Processing.* Washington DC.

Smadja, Frank (1993) 'Retrieving Collocations from Text : XTRACT', *Computational Linguistics* 19(1): 143–77.

Smadja, Frank, McKeown, Kathleen R. and Hatzivassiloglou, Vasileios (1996) 'Translating Collocations for Bilingual Lexicons: A Statistical Approach', *Computational Linguistics* 22(1): 1–38.

Tadić, Marko (2000) 'Building the Croatian–English Parallel Corpus', *LREC2000 Proceedings: Second International Conference on Language Resources and Evaluation,* eds Gavrilidou, M., Carayannis, G., Markantonatou, S., Piperidis, S. and Stainhaouer, G. Atena-Paris: ELRA, pp. 523–30.

Tadić, Marko (2001) 'Procedures in Building the Croatian-English Parallel Corpus'. *International Journal of Corpus Linguistics: Special issue.* 2001, 1–17.

Tadić, Marko and Šojat, Krešo (2003) 'Identifikacija prijevodnih ekvivalenata u Hrvatsko-engleskom paralelnom korpusu', *Filologija* 36–37.

Tiedemann, Jörg (1998) 'Extraction of translation equivalents from parallel corpora', *Proceedings of the 11th Nordic Conference on Computational Linguistics NODALI98,* Kopenhagen: Centre for Human Language Technologies and Department for General and Applied Linguistics, University of Copenhagen.

Tiedemann, Jörg (1999) 'Word Alignment Step by Step', *Proceedings of the 12th Nordic Conference on Computational Linguistics NODALIDA99,* Trondheim: University of Trondheim.

Tiedemann, Jörg (2000) 'Exatracting Phrasal Terms using Bitexts', *Proceedings of the Workshop on Terminology Resources and Computation within the LREC2000,* ed. Choi, Key-Sun. Atena-Paris: ELRA, pp. 57–63.

Vintar, Špela (1999) 'A Lexical Analysis of the IJS-ELAN Slovene–English Parallel Corpus', *Language technologies – multilingual aspects: proceedings of the workshop within the framework of the 32nd Annual Meeting of the Societas Linguistica Europaea,* ed. Vintar, Špela. Ljubljana: Faculty of philosophy, Department of translation and interpretation, pp. 63–70.

20 Cognates: free rides, false friends or stylistic devices? A corpus-based comparative study

Špela Vintar and Silvia Hansen-Schirra

Introduction and motivation

Cognates, words that exhibit formal similarity across languages due to common etymology, have been studied and exploited in the past from various linguistic perspectives ranging from historical linguistics and contrastive lexicology to computational and corpus linguistics. As words that appear in similar or identical orthographical form in two or more languages they are immediately recognized as being related, either because the languages themselves share a common ancestor, as in the case of English *father* and German *Vater*, or the word was borrowed. Borrowings from classical languages, e.g. English *information*, German *Information* and Slovene *informacija*, typically appear in cognate forms across many languages and are usually well integrated into the lexicon, so that they might not even be perceived as foreign anymore. Other lexical items spread more recently from modern languages and gained international and interlingual use for cultural, economic or political reasons. Though similar in form, cognates may not be as transparent in their semantics. Depending both on the type of concept they designate and the level of integration into the lexicon, their meaning might be relatively fixed and unambiguous across many languages (e.g. *taxi, hotel*), while others undergo considerable semantic shifts and the similarity stays merely formal (e.g. English *local* and German (noun) *Lokal*).

In computational linguistics, particularly in parallel text processing, formal similarity can be identified automatically using string-based comparison and items found to match in parallel texts can be seen as anchors or indicators of correspondence between parallel segments. The use of cognates in text alignment is described in more detail in the next section.

The experiment we describe in this paper explores cognates from a different perspective, combining both the contrastive-lexicological and computational points of view but focusing on the aspect of translation. We chose cognates and a corpus-based methodology to explore the strategies of translators in dealing with foreign or non-native lexical material. We are aware of the fact that cognates and borrowings cannot be used interchangeably, however cognates – using the working definition of cognates as formally similar words – due to their retrievability can serve as a comparative measure of the presence of non-native elements in a corpus setting. Taking English as the source language, for many general language words of Greek/Latin origin (e.g. *process, structure, criterion*) there exist cognate translation equivalents in most European languages. For a number of these words the target language also provides a partly or entirely synonymous native alternative. In such cases, the translator is given the choice between one or the other, and our hypothesis is that this decision is by no means arbitrary but is made on the basis of a translation strategy which is biased either towards choosing cognate equivalents or against them.

This strategy is rarely consistently employed, indeed our study shows that it is extremely difficult to draw generalizations because so many different factors come into play. Sometimes the cognate and its native counterpart are used in alternation within a text for stylistic reasons, or other foreign words within the same context would influence the choice in the sense of maintaining a consistent ratio between foreign and native elements within the text.

The research was performed for two language pairs: English–German and English–Slovene. The aim was first to determine whether there were any observable and statistically significant differences in the use of cognates in translated and original texts within the same language, which would indicate that translators indeed employ specific translation strategies in dealing with non-native word material. Secondly, our goal was to compare the results obtained for German and Slovene and thus draw conclusions about the language specificity of translation strategies, especially in view of suspected differences in the overall attitude towards borrowings in the two languages. More specifically, German is generally considered to be very open to linguistic influences from abroad, particularly from the English-speaking world, so that new borrowings often appear even in conservative media and are readily adapted to German by taking on native affixes and entering mixed compounds (*einscannen, Topangebot*). On the other hand, Slovene as a language of only two million speakers tends to be much more cautious and reluctant to accept borrowings, perhaps due to a lack of linguistic confidence or as a result of the very protective attitude of its speakers towards the language as a major element of the still evolving national identity.

The chapter is structured as follows: the next two sections briefly describe the theoretical background of our study: the semantic characteristics of cognates and the types of shifts that may be observed across languages, a review of cognate-related research within traditional and computational linguistics as well as the position of our research with regard to contemporary corpus-based translation studies. The fourth section presents the research itself and is divided into two parts: the first part represents the quantitative analysis: we describe the methodology, the corpora and the computational tools that were used and finally discuss the results for each language pair, English–German and English–Slovene. The second part is a qualitative description and exemplification of translation strategies that were observed, where we focus on selected lexical items to demonstrate and interpret the results obtained for Slovene and German. We end by summarizing our conclusions in view of the initial hypothesis and suggesting possible expansions and improvements of the methodology.

Theoretical background

Characteristics of cognates from a contrastive semantics point of view

Continuing from our working definition of cognates as formally similar lexical items appearing accross different languages we may identify several common groups:

- named entities *(Clinton)*
- citations (*status quo*)
- internationalisms *(taxi, UNICEF)*
- 'classical' borrowings (EN *institution*/GE *Institution*/SL *inštitucija*)

The characteristic that makes those items interesting from a contrastive or translatological perspective is their proneness to semantic shifting, i.e. despite their orthographical, in most cases etymologically based, similarity these items are likely to differ as regards their meaning, usage and phrasal patterning. An example of such a shift would be the English word *modern* as opposed to *moderno* in Slovene. In most contexts the English cognate roughly corresponds to *contemporary*, while the Slovene parallel word rather means *fashionable.* In translated texts however the Slovene *moderno* is often used in the English sense, probably due to translational interference or the so-called 'shining-through' effect.

Another type of lexical shift that may occur is conversion or transposition of part of speech, as in English *local* (adjective), German *Lokal* (noun) or *lokal* (adjective) and Slovene *lokal* (noun) or *lokalno* (adjective), also with considerable differences in meaning.

Cognates are usually elements that exhibit a certain level of foreignness in a language and they often coexist with parallel 'native' lexemes, that is, words that existed in the language prior to the borrowing (e.g. GE *komplex* [EN *complex*] v *schwierig* [EN *difficult*]). In some cases these seemingly parallel or synonymous forms can indeed be used interchangeably, but more often it turns out that each of the two forms has a preferred register- or style-specific pattern of usage (e.g. GE *System* [EN *system*] v *Installation* [EN *installation*]).

Cognates as anchors in NLP

The study of cognates in corpus linguistics is a well-known topic, finding applications mainly in the development of tools for multilingual corpus processing where cognates can be used as anchor points facilitating, for example, sentence alignment. Simard *et al.* (1992) used cognates to improve length-based alignment methods. They based their research on the notion of 'cognateness', i.e. the assumption that cognates are likely to be mutual translations. They extended this notion to include proper names, numerical expressions and punctuation as well. The alignment program computes and recognizes cognateness according to the following criteria:

a) Cognate candidates include at least one digit.
b) Cognate candidates include a punctuation character.
c) Cognate candidates are exclusively composed of letters. They contain at least four letters. Their first four characters are identical.

On the basis of condition a), numerical expression can be detected. With condition b), punctuation is covered. Condition c) tries to exclude function words, which are often composed of less than four characters, but matches identical proper names and 'real' cognates.

Since alignment programs based on sentence length function fairly well, Simard *et al.* (1992) use the notion of cognateness only if the length-based programs run into trouble. For such cases, a scoring list is produced using the length-based algorithm. Additionally, another scoring list is computed according to the cognateness of the possible translations. The best alignment candidate can be found by matching both lists on the basis of a heuristic. This approach thus focuses on cognates as formal entities that can – on account of their easy retrievability – support the computational processing of bilingual texts.

Original v translated language

Sager (1984) was one of the first researchers who saw the need to examine translations as a special kind of text production and to discover their special characteristics. Nevertheless, he thought that the value of the translation is dependent on that of its original text (cf. Sager 1994). In contrast to Sager, Baker (1995) goes a step further by trying to exclude the influence which the source language has on a translation in order to analyse characteristic patterns of translation which are independent of the source language. For this purpose, the Department of Language Engineering, University of Manchester Institute of Science and Technology (UMIST) built up a monolingual corpus of English translations (TEC: Translational English Corpus). If this corpus is compared with English originals, it is possible to analyse the universal features of translation which include *explicitation, simplification, normalization* and *levelling out* (cf. Baker 1996).

By contrast, Toury (1995) identifies two laws of translational behaviour: he explains that there is a law of growing standardization, i.e. that 'in translation, textual relations obtaining in the original are often modified, sometimes to the point of being totally ignored, in favour of [more] habitual options offered by a target repertoire' (Toury 1995: 268). This law can also be found in Baker's universal feature of normalization. However, Toury also suggests that translators tend to produce a translated utterance not by retrieving the target language via their own linguistic knowledge, but directly from the source utterance itself. The universality of discourse transfer is expressed through another translational law, the *law of interference*: 'in translation, phenomena pertaining to the make-up of the source text tend to be transferred to the target text' (Toury 1995: 275). According to Toury, discourse transfer, both negative and positive, is inherent in the mental processes involved in translation. From a psycholinguistic perspective, the operation of this law depends on the particular manner in which the source text is processed, so that 'the more the make-up of a text is taken as a factor in the formulation of its translation, the more the target text can be expected to show traces of interference' (Toury 1995: 276).

For the purposes of our analyses we focus particularly on Baker's universal features of translation (cf. Baker 1996), which are described in the following:

- **Explicitation**: explicitation means that translators tend to explain implicit contents of the source text in their translations. According to Baker (1996), translations should be longer than originally produced texts in the target language or in the source language. The evidence for this tendency may, for example, be found in the text length (number of words of the individual texts).
- **Simplification**: simplification means that translators tend (consciously or unconsciously) to simplify texts in order to improve the readability of their translations. The evidence for this tendency may, for example, be found in the average sentence length, because translators often break up long and complex sentences into two or more sentences in their translations. Laviosa-Braithwaite (1996) found that the average sentence length of translated texts in the *Guardian* is significantly lower than the average sentence length of English originals in the same newspaper. By using a lower mean sentence length, the translators wanted to make the texts easier for the readers. Some linguistic features indicating simplification (e.g. the use of finite structures in English originals as opposed to non-finite structures in English translations) may also indicate explicitation at the same time.

Another piece of evidence for simplification is the lexical density of a corpus. According to Baker (1996), the lexical density of English translations should be lower than the lexical density of English originals. This means that translations contain more function words and fewer lexical words than originals and are thus easier to read. Laviosa-Braithwaite (1996) was able to confirm this hypothesis, discovering that the lexical density of translated texts in the *Guardian* is significantly lower than the lexical density of originals in the same newspaper.

A further method to test simplification is the type-token ratio. Baker (1996) assumes that translators tend to use fewer types in their English translations than authors do in English originals. According to her, the type-token ratio of translations should be lower than the type-token ratio of originals. Again, Laviosa-Braithwaite (1996) investigated this hypothesis and found that the type-token ratio of translated texts in the *Guardian* is lower than the type-token ratio of originals in the same newspaper. But this difference is not statistically significant. Thus, the translated texts in the *Guardian* appear simplified in terms of their mean sentence length and their lexical density, but not simplified in terms of type-token ratio.

- **Normalization**: normalization (or conservatism) means that translators tend to conform to the typical patterns of the target language or even to exaggerate their use. But if the status of the source language is significantly higher than the status of the target language (for example, English compared with other languages in the area of software), normalization in translations is weakened or there is even the contrary tendency. If this is the case, the typical patterns of the source language are still visible in the translations. This universal feature also includes the tendency to normalize marked and ungrammatical structures.
- **Levelling out**: in a corpus which consists of a subcorpus of translations, a subcorpus of source language texts and a subcorpus of texts produced in the target language, the translations are more like each other in terms of features such as lexical density, type-token ratio and average sentence length than the individual texts in the comparable corpus or the individual texts in the corpus of source language texts. This means that translators tend to 'pull various linguistic features towards the centre', moving them away from extremes. Laviosa-Braithwaite (1996) found that the translated texts in the *Guardian* are more similar to each other than the originals in terms of lexical density, type-token ratio and mean sentence length. But mean sentence length was the only feature which had a highly significant variance.

Cognates in translation: hypotheses

As a transfer between languages, cultures and communicative settings, translation is an activity continuously crossing, or rather dissolving, the border between what is foreign and what is native in a language. In a bluntly trivialized definition of translation into the mother tongue, the translator is replacing foreign language words in the source text with native words of the target language. However, since the lexicons of all languages contain a certain amount of words of foreign origin and since every text to be translated opens up lexical gaps to be filled by the translator using either native or foreign word material, the resulting translation will always exhibit a certain level of 'foreignness'.

Naturally, the same can be said of any text originally written in a language, but in the case of translation the issue of a foreign language forcing itself upon the target language is much more apparent. In addition to this, each language community has a certain attitude towards foreign elements in its language, which may run the gamut from aggressively puristic combat against borrowings to very permissive and liberal approaches to using foreign words. These attitudes may be more or less explicitly expressed and practised – in some countries publishing houses employ proofreaders who systematically replace foreign words with native ones – and they may vary across registers – scientific and technical texts generally contain more non-native words.

Within this context, the following two contrasting hypotheses can be formulated which reflect the usage of cognates and native words in translations and originally produced texts:

- **Shining-through hypothesis**: this hypothesis is based on Teich's notion of shining through, i.e. translations reflect the typical use of lexico-grammatical features of the source language rather than of the target language such that the source language 'shines through' (cf. Teich 2001). This means for the comparison of cognates and native words in translations that translators tend to choose cognates more often than native words. This tendency may be due to the translator's laziness or a 'register-based overdose' exhibited in the source-language text.
- **Aversion hypothesis**: the basis for this hypothesis is Baker's notion of normalization, i.e. translations conform to the norms of the target language such that untypical usage is 'normalized' (cf. Baker 1996). This means for the investigation of the usage of cognates and native words in translations compared to that in originally produced texts in the target language that translators tend to choose native words more often than cognates. This tendency may be due to the 'foreignness' of the cognate word which is inappropriate in the given context or to semantic or register-dependent non-equivalence.

In order to test both hypotheses, shining-through can be investigated on the basis of a parallel corpus, whereas for the aversion hypothesis a comparable target-language corpus is additionally necessary.

Corpus-based study

Structure of the experiment

The corpus-based study was performed in a comparative bilingual framework using English–German and English–Slovene translations as well as German and Slovene original comparable texts.

For the quantitative experiment, the cognate pairs were extracted fully automatically from parallel English–German and English–Slovene texts using an implementation of the Levenstein's edit distance algorithm in the Perl String::Approx module[1]. The frequency of cognates in German or Slovene translations was compared to the usage of cognates in original German or Slovene texts.

The qualitative analysis focused on selected cognates which conform to the following criteria: the occurrence of the cognate word should be sufficiently frequent; a highly synonymous native word should exist, whereby neither should be pragmatically marked; the cognate word should not be part of a technical term or a fixed expression.

Corpora

Different kinds of language resources were used to perform the corpus-based experiment. For the automatic extraction of cognates, and thus for the qualitative analysis, a parallel English–German and English–Slovene corpus of popular scientific texts was collected. For the comparison of the cognate frequencies, a parallel English–German and English–Slovene subcorpus and a comparable German and Slovene subcorpus were built up which should be as comparable as possible in terms of corpus size and register. For this reason, all subcorpora comprised 10,000 tokens and consisted of popular scientific texts. In order to level out personal preferences of translators or authors, each subcorpus was composed of 10 text extracts consisting of 1000 tokens respectively. As monolingual reference corpora the COSMAS corpus was used for German[2] and the FIDA was used for Slovene[3].

Quantitative analysis

The number of cognates extracted from the English–Slovene and English–German parallel corpora are displayed in Table 20.1. As can be seen, the difference between the English–Slovene and English–German ratio of extracted cognates is surprisingly small. Without a closer look at the examples and a comparison with originally produced texts in the target language, one could conclude that the tendency to use cognates in Slovene is similar to that in German.

But the comparison of the cognate frequencies in Slovene (SL-trans) and German (GE-trans) translations and Slovene (SL-orig) and German (GE-orig) originals shows that the German translations exhibit significantly more cognates than the German originals, whereas the use of cognates in the Slovene translations is slightly lower than in the Slovene originals (see Table 20.2).

Table 20.1 Number of cognates extracted

	EN-SL	EN-GE
Corpus size	53,908	56,718
Cognates extracted	1026	1173
Ratio	19.03	20.68

Table 20.2 Original v translation – cognates frequency

	SL-orig	SL-trans	GE-orig	GE-trans
Tokens	10,798	11,428	14,807	14,990
Types	4,231	4,850	4,781	4,204
T/T ratio	39.18	42.44	32.15	28.03
Cog.-tokens	274	216	527	977
Cog.-ratio	0.025	0.019	0.036	0.065

These results illustrate that there is a slight aversion against the use of cognates in Slovene translations, whereas translations into German seem to be rather receptive to the use of cognates.

Qualitative analysis

In the following the examples chosen for the English–Slovene and the English–German cognate pairs and their frequencies (in brackets) are displayed. Furthermore, their usage is compared to the use of these cognates in the Slovene and German reference corpora.

20.1. Example : **action** (English–Slovene)

translation	*FIDA*
delovanje (4)	21,839
akcija (2)	17,819
tehnika (2)	
ukrepanje (2)	
aktivnost	
izvedba	
operacija	
udejstvovanje	

Example 20.1 illustrates that the English–Slovene translators tend to use the native word *delovanje* more frequently than the cognate word *akcija*. Thus, Example 20.1 supports the assumption gained through the quantitative analysis that the Slovene exhibits an aversion against the use of cognate words in translations. This result is also supported through the frequencies of the cognate word and the native word found in the Slovene reference corpus: the native word occurs more often than the cognate. This leads to the conclusion that Slovene originals show the same aversion against the cognate word *akcija* that Slovene translations do.

20.2. Example : **modern** (English–Slovene)

translation	*FIDA*
moderen (7)	1227
sodoben (3)	17,692
današnji	

In Example 20.2, the cognate word *moderen* is more frequently used than the native word *sodoben.* However, as can be seen in Examples 20.2a and 20.2b, a slight shift in meaning can be observed between the Slovene cognate word *moderen* and the Slovene native word *sodoben.*

20.2a Modern machines are quintessentially microelectronic devices: they are everywhere and they are invisible.

20.2b Moderni stroji so v osnovi mikroelektronske naprave: so vsepovsod, a so nevidni.

These examples show that the Slovene cognate word *moderen* adopts the meaning of the English cognate word *modern,* i.e. *contemporary,* whereas the word *moderen* in original Slovene texts usually means *fashionable.* Thus, the cognate word features shining-through because the typical usage of the source language is adopted, which causes a semantic shift between the Slovene cognate used in translated and in original text.

Nevertheless, this usage of the cognate word *moderen* which can be found in the English–Slovene translations is not reflected in the Slovene reference corpus. Thus, the English–Slovene translations are more receptive to the cognate word *moderen* than the Slovene originals are, which again exhibit an aversion against the use of the cognate word.

20.3. Example: **aspect** (English-Slovene)

translation	*FIDA*
vidik (13)	7321
aspekt (3)	1109
del	
element	
način	
narava	
položaj	
značilnost	

Example 20.3 again clearly supports the assumption that Slovene translated as well as original texts show an aversion against the use of cognates

such that the native word *vidik* is used more often in the translations as well as in the originals than the cognate word *aspekt.*

20.4. Example : **process** (English–German)

translation	*IDS*
Prozess (15)	10,003
Vorgang (2)	4341
Verfahren	10,059
Verlauf	9905

Example 20.4 shows that the German cognate word *Prozess* is more often used than the German native words *Vorgang, Verfahren* or *Verlauf.* However, this tendency cannot be found in the German reference corpus, where the native words occur more frequently than the cognate word. Thus, German translations seem to be more receptive to the cognate word *Prozess* than German originals are.

20.5. Example: **materials** (English–German)

translation	*IDS*
Material (15)	10,056
Rohstoffe (5)	1532
Stoffe (8)	5154

In Example 20.5, the German cognate word *Material* occurs slightly more frequently than the German native words *Rohstoffe* or *Stoffe.* This usage is reflected in the German reference corpus as well. However, in the German translations, the native words are only used in cases in which the English compound demands it (e.g. English *raw material,* German *Rohstoffe*). In all other cases, the German language (translated as well as original) seems to be more receptive to the German cognate word *Material.*

20.6. Example: **system** (English–German)

translation	*IDS*
System (11)	9977
Versuch	
Formation	
Geräte	

Example 20.6 clearly illustrates that the German language is very receptive to the cognate word *System.* The native words *Versuch, Formation* and *Geräte* are only rarely used. Their usage depends on the English compound as can be seen in Examples 6a to 6c.

20.6a English *cloud systems,* German *Wolkenformationen*
20.6b English *engineering systems,* German *technische Geräte*
20.6c English *experimental systems,* German *Laborversuche*

These examples show that the English compounds trigger the use of the German native words avoiding the German cognate *System.* Furthermore, it can be observed that the usage of the German words *Versuch, Formation* and *Geräte* imply a slight semantic shift compared to the English–German cognate pair *system/ System.*

Summary and conclusions

We presented a comparative English–Slovene and English–German study of cognates from a translatological perspective. In summary, it can be said that the Slovene–English translations do not follow a unique translation strategy. But a great variety of native equivalents can be found when the cognate is considered 'too foreign' (e.g. Slovene *vidik* instead of Slovene *aspekt*). Moreover, fixed native translations exist for some common cognates (e.g. Slovene *merilo/ merila* for English *criterion/ criteria*). If cognates are used in Slovene, they often disregard semantic shifts (e.g. English *action,* Slovene *akcija* as well as English *modern,* Slovene *moderen*). Furthermore, it happens that some cognates translate with other cognates (e.g. English *structure,* Slovene *sistem*).

For English–German translations the observation is true that German seems to be less reluctant to using cognates. The use of cognates as well as native words often reflects the translator's uncertainty with the chosen translation. In cases in which the translator does not exactly know what the source language expression means both the cognate and the native word can be found in the translation (e.g. English *computer models,* German *Computermodelle, Computerberechnungen*). In other cases the use of native target-language words depends on the compounds which can be found in the source language (e.g. English *cloud systems,* German *Wolkenformationen*). Finally, the choice of native equivalents is frequently motivated through the style or the register of the source-language text which is to be translated adequately. In such cases, a translator tries, for example, to avoid repetitions by using the cognate as well as native words (e.g. English *volcanic activity,* German *vulkanische Aktivität, vulkanische Tätigkeit, vulkanische Ausbrüche, vulkanische Bewegung*).

In general, it can be said that the context of a word is very important for the choice between the cognate or the native word. Nevertheless it seems that German is more receptive to the use of cognates than Slovene. This observation can be confirmed for translated text as well as originals. An explanation could be that Slovene as a 'minor language' tries to avoid foreign language material by using native words only. In contrast to that, the frequent use of cognates in English–German translations could be interpreted as one source for the importation of anglicisms into German, which reflects the strong influence English has on the German language. The tendency towards cognates or against them is undoubtedly related also to the overall language – and translation – policy in the target society. Thus, in a new democracy such as Slovenia language issues are closely linked to issues of a still evolving national identity, which may result in a climate of linguistic purism and protectionism.

The present study also shows that the quality of a translation cannot be assessed through the frequent occurrences of cognates and/or native words, but that these choices are motivated through contextual factors within and beyond the text.

Notes

1 URL: http://cpan.valueclick.com/authors/id/JHI/
2 URL: http://copora.ids-mannheim.de/~cosmas
3 URL: http://www.fida.net/eng

References

Baker, Mona (1995) 'Corpora in translation studies: An overview and some suggestions for future research', *Target* 7(2): 223–43.

Baker, Mona (1996) 'Corpus-based translation studies: The challenges that lie ahead', in Somers, Harold (ed.) *Terminology, LSP and Translation: Studies in Language Engineering in Honour of Juan C. Sager.* Amsterdam: John Benjamins, pp. 175–86.

Laviosa-Braithwaite, Sara (1996) The English Comparable Corpus (ECC): A Resource and a Methodology for the Empirical Study of Translation. PhD thesis, UMIST, Manchester.

Sager, Juan C. (1984) 'Reflections on the didactic implications of an extended theory of translation' in Wilss, Wolfram and Thome, Gisela (eds) *Die Theorie des Übersetzens und ihr Aufschlußwert für die Übersetzungs- und Dolmetschdidaktik / Translation theory and its implementation in the teaching of translating and interpreting.* Tübingen: Gunter Narr, pp. 333–43.

Sager, Juan C. (1994) *Language engineering and translation: consequences of automation.* Amsterdam: John Benjamins.

Simard, Michel, Foster, George and Isabelle, Pierre (1992) 'Using Cognates to Align Sentences in Bilingual Corpora', in *Proceedings of the 4th Conference on Theoretical and Methodological Issues in Machine Translation (TMI).* Montréal, Québec.

Teich, Elke (2001) 'English–German contrast and commonality in system and text. A methodology for the investigation of parallel and multilingually comparable texts', Habilitationsschrift, Saarbrücken: Saarland University.

Toury, Gideon (1995) *Descriptive Translation Studies and Beyond.* Amsterdam: John Benjamins.

21 Trilingual corpus and its use for the teaching of reading comprehension in French

Xu Xunfeng and Régis Kawecki

Introduction

This paper reports on a research project undertaken within the English Department of the Hong Kong Polytechnic University. It tries to explore and examine the effectiveness of integration of the new technologies into the curriculum by creating an online multilingual corpus and using it in the teaching of reading comprehension to the students of French.

Thanks to a grant from the Departmental Learning and Teaching Committee, the project was started in 1998, as an answer to the new trends within the tertiary education sector in Hong Kong. First of all, universities are encouraging independent learning from students and therefore the emphasis is on creating self-access materials. The second factor was an increase in the number of students doing French in Hong Kong universities either as an elective or as a core subject of a degree course. The Hong Kong Polytechnic University is teaching French as part of its BA (Honours) in Language Studies with Business. In a three-year period, students are taught all four skills (speaking, listening, reading and writing) from *ab initio* up to an advanced level. The emphasis is both on General French and on French for Business. After graduating, students work as trilingual business communicators in either a French company or in a Hong Kong/international company which is doing business with French-speaking countries. The third reason was the high profile of the new technologies in Hong Kong. Lecturers are given laptop computers so that they can use them during lectures and seminars. Students are offered personal computers at very competitive prices and are provided with broadband access to the Internet from numerous desktop computers on campus. In addition, the majority of their families have a PC at home with access to the Internet.

This online corpus was a response to all the above developments. It was meant as a self-access tool for improving the reading comprehension skills of our students and also of the increasing pool of Hong Kong students learning French in all the other tertiary institutions.

The project was carried out in two stages: an English/Chinese/French trilingual texts corpus was first built and put online and experiments were then conducted in order to test the usefulness of this new tool to help students learn French.

The online trilingual corpus

The emphasis is very much on up-to-date articles on various aspects of French society, i.e. on business matters, on the place of women, on French movies, on tourism, etc. They were taken from a high-quality magazine, *Label France*, published in many different languages by the French Ministry of Foreign Affairs, which is readily available on the Internet and is free of copyright.

In addition, we also selected a literary piece, *Le petit prince*, because of its notoriety for and appeal to Chinese students. The screenshot below shows the index page of the website hosting this trilingual corpus.

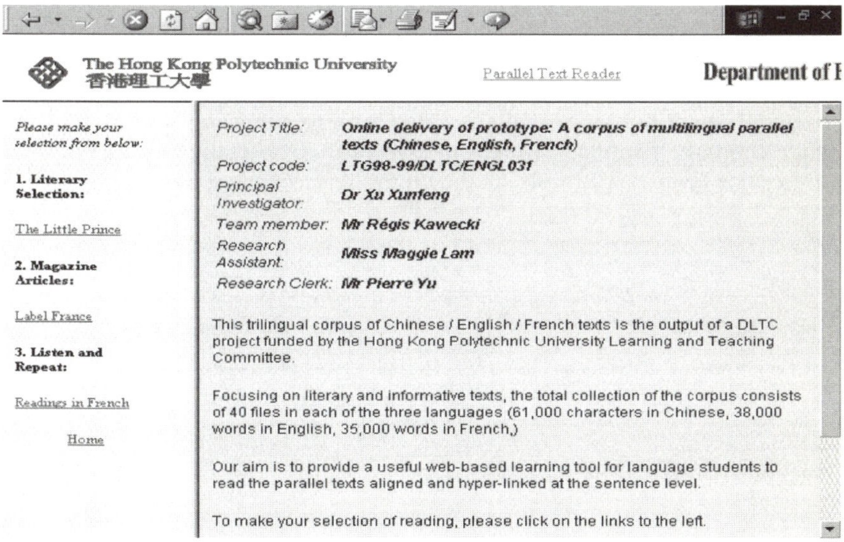

Figure 21.1 The front page of the trilingual corpus website

The total collection of the corpus consists of 40 files in each of the three languages (61,000 characters in Chinese, 38,000 words in English, 35,000 words in French). These well-matched texts are presented in pairs and hyperlinks in HTML format have been inserted at the sentence level to link up the two corresponding texts. This allows the user to scroll through one text and jump to a corresponding sentence in the other language by a single click on the hyperlink.

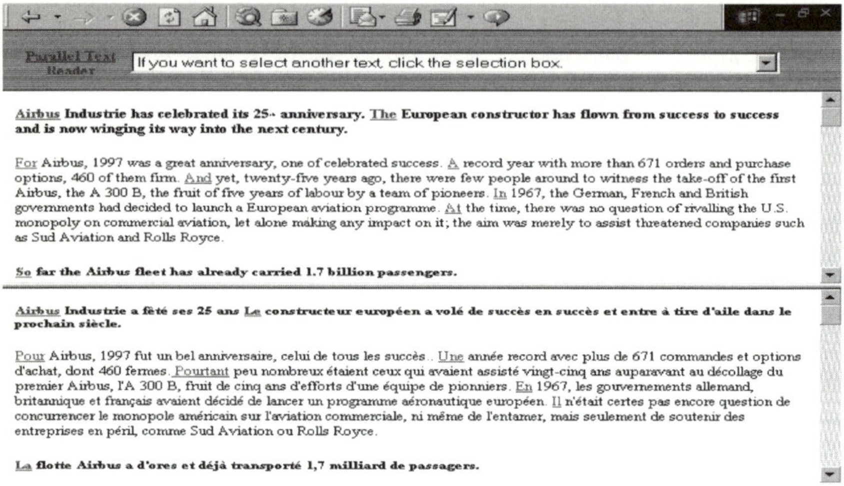

Figure 21.2 The English/French parallel text

As shown in the screenshot above, the parallel texts are displayed in pairs through frames. The upper frame shows the English version while the lower frame displays the French text. Each sentence starts with a hyperlink that contains a bookmark and an html link to the same sentence in the other language. Similarly, users can assess the texts in the pair of English/Chinese or French/Chinese (as shown in the screenshot below).

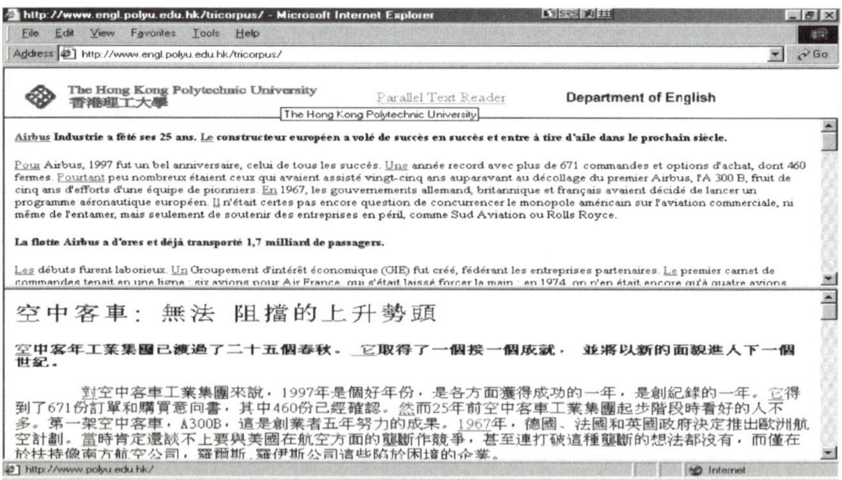

Figure 21.3 The French/Chinese parallel text

The experiments

In order to test the effectiveness of such an online parallel corpus for the purpose of helping our students improve their reading comprehension skill, an experiment was carried out and three groups of students were invited to participate: the Hong Kong Polytechnic University Year 3 students learning French, a group of final-year students from the Hong Kong Baptist University and Form 7 pupils from Li Po Chun United World College, an elite international secondary school in Hong Kong. The Hong Kong Polytechnic University group was the experiment group and the other two groups were control groups. Two reading comprehension tests of equal lengths were administered to the students, one as pre-test and one as post-test with a time gap of six weeks.

For the tests, two texts from *Label France*, not yet online, were selected and two corresponding reading comprehension questionnaires were designed accordingly. In between the two tests, students of the experimental group were introduced to the parallel corpus and each week they read one of the articles online followed by an in-class discussion with the tutor, these sessions being the only time when reading comprehension was the focus of the teaching. Students of the control groups carried out their routine learning activities as their programme required, but without the benefit of using the online parallel corpus to enhance their reading comprehension ability.

The statistics in the following table describe the results of the pre-test:

Table 21.1 Pre-test – Descriptive statistics

	N	Mean	Standard deviation	Min.	Max.
HK PolyU	12	6.5833	2.4664	3.00	10.00
HK BU	12	9.3333	1.3707	7.00	11.00
LPC UWC	9	10.0000	1.8708	7.00	12.00
TOTAL	33	8.5152	2.4254	3.00	12.00

It is obvious that students of French at the Hong Kong Polytechnic University are much weaker than both those at the Hong Kong Baptist University and those at the Li Po Chun United World College. The mean score for the HKPolyU group is less than 7 with a standard deviation of 2.4664 while both of the other two groups are higher than 9 or 10 and with a much smaller standard deviation (1.3707 and 1.8708). This in fact was not a surprise since the Hong Kong Baptist University students were actually Year 4 students, having all spent at least a whole year in France while only 4 of the 12 PolyU students had such an experience abroad. In the case of the students at the Li Po Chun United World College, they had been learning

French since the beginning of their secondary studies and they had all been making preparations for their IB French test.

Such a difference is further evidenced by a one-way ANOVA test on the pre-test scores as it has yielded quite a large value for the F ratio (F=9.429, df=2 and 30, p=0.01).

Table 21.2 ANOVA test on the pre-test scores of the three groups

	Sum of squares	***df***	**Mean square**	***F***	**Sig.**
Between groups	72.659	2	36.330	9.429	.001
Within groups	115.583	30	3.853		
TOTAL	188.242	32			

The F ratio of 9.429 in the ANOVA test as listed in the above table confirms that the difference in the test results among the three groups of students is statistically significant. Obviously, at the start of our experiment, students of French at the Hong Kong Polytechnic University were far from being on a par with students at the Hong Kong Baptist University and the students from Li Po Chun United World College in terms of their ability in reading comprehension in French. They belong to different populations.

Thanks to the treatment the students at the Hong Kong Polytechnic University received within the six weeks, their reading comprehension ability has been improved and therefore the gap between them and the other two groups of students has been narrowed.

Such an improvement is testified by results in the post-test by the Hong Kong Polytechnic University students in comparison with those for the other two groups. The table below summarizes the descriptive statistics for the post-test.

Table 21.3 Post-test – Descriptive statistics

N	**Mean**	**Standard deviation**	**Min.**	**Max.**	
HK PolyU	12	5.4167	1.9287	2.00	8.00
HK BU	12	5.7500	1.8647	3.00	9.00
LPC UWC	9	8.0000	2.5981	4.00	11.00
TOTAL	33	6.2424	2.3188	2.00	11.00

Although the mean score for the HK PolyU group still remains the lowest among the three, it is much closer to the mean score for all the three groups (5.4167 with a standard deviation of 1.9287). The difference is less than 1, and it is a big reduction from that of close to 2 for the pre-test (see Table 21.1).

Such an improvement can be further testified by a one-way ANOVA test for the post-test scores for the three groups as shown in Table 21.4 below: it yields a much smaller F ratio which is no longer statistically significant (F=4.381, df=2 and 30, p=0.01).

Table 21.4 ANOVA test on the post-test scores of the three groups

	Sum of squares	***df***	**Mean square**	***F***	**Sig.**
Between groups	38.894	2	19.447	4.381	.021
Within groups	133.167	30	4.439		
TOTAL	172.061	32			

After six weeks of training and practice in online reading of the trilingual texts, the experimental group is more on par with the other two groups. It confirms our hypothesis that such a web-based learning tool could be very helpful to the students in their endeavour to improve their reading comprehension ability in French.

Conclusions

Follow-up discussions with students revealed that students liked this new self-access learning tool. They only sometimes complained about the quality of the Chinese version, which they thought did not sound very Chinese. They found this corpus very useful not only for improving their reading comprehension skill, but also for increasing their ability to translate from English into French and vice versa, something which is required from them as well.

Hong Kong Chinese students being very much 'new information technology' orientated, with most of them using computers and browsing the web several times each day, they see no problem in using such a device. As our contact hours with students are actually on the decrease, we are compelled to develop self-access materials and encourage language learners' autonomy in order to achieve the same results as before. The World Wide Web seems to be the best practical place to store a big amount of data with the possibility of immediate retrieval and printing for further use.

Recently, the project has attracted more funding and more trilingual texts are being made available to students with reading comprehension tests being added to some of them (with an online automatic correction device). Furthermore, an online concordancer will also be added to the site together with three sizable corpora in the three languages to allow the user to search for and analyse language patterns in all the three languages.

References

Ashworth, David E. (1996) 'Hypermedia and CALL', in Pennington, M. C. (ed.) *The power of CALL.* Houston, TX: Athelstan.

Brown, James D. (1997) 'Computers in Language Testing: Present Research and Some Future Directions', *Language Learning & Technology* 1(1). http://polyglot.cal.msu.edu/llt/vol1num1/brown/default.html

Finnemann, Michael (1996) 'The World Wide Web and Foreign Language Teaching', *ERIC/CLL News Bulletin* 20 (1). http://www.cal.org/ericcll/News/Sep96.html

Flowerdew, Lynne (1995) 'Designing CALL courseware for an ESP situation: A report on a case study', *English for Specific Purposes* 14: 19–35.

Gillespie, John and McKee, Jane (1999) 'Does it Fit and Does it Make Any Difference? Integrating CALL into the Curriculum', *Computer Assisted Language Learning* 12(5): 441–55.

Hatch, Evelyn and Lazaraton, Anne (1991) *The Research Manual: Design and Statistics for Applied Linguistics.* Boston: Heinle & Heinle.

Johns, Tim and Davies, Flo (1983) 'Text as a vehicle for information: The classroom use of written texts in teaching reading in a foreign language', *Reading in a Foreign Language* 1(1): 1–20.

LeLoup, Jean W. and Ponterio, Robert (1999) 'Interactive Language Exercises on the Web: An Exemplar', *Language Learning & Technology* 3(1). http://polyglot.cal.msu.edu/llt/vol3num1/onthenet/index.html

Levy, Mike (1997) *Computer-Assisted Language Learning – Context and Conceptualization.* Oxford: Oxford University Press.

Opp-Beckman, Leslie (1999) 'Classroom practice: Authentic audience on the Internet' in Egbert, J. and Hanson-Smith, E. (eds) *CALL Environments: Research, practice, and critical issues.* TESOL.

Ushi, Felix (1999) 'Exploiting the Web for language teaching: selected approaches', *ReCALL* 11(1): 30–7.

Index